THE HOPEFUL

The Hopeful Year

A COLLECTION OF READINGS
GATHERED AROUND SWEDENBORGIAN THEMES

G. ROLAND SMITH

SEMINAR BOOKS
LONDON

THE HOPEFUL YEAR
This collection first published in 2002
by Seminar Books, 20-21 Bloomsbury Way, London. WC1A 2TH

First Edition 2002

ISBN 0-907295-31-2 (paperback)
ISBN 0-907295-32-0 (cased)

Distributed by New Church House
34 John Dalton Street, Manchester. M2 6LE

A CIP catalogue record for this book
is available from the British Library.

Seminar Books are published by The Missionary Society
of the New Church (Registered Charity No.231408)
c/o Swedenborg House, 20-21 Bloomsbury Way, London. WC!A 2TH

Printed in England by Cantate Bishops, Orpington, Kent. BR5 2HB

ACKNOWLEDGEMENTS

Our warmest thanks are due to the Ian P.Johnson for his meticulous and sympathetic editorial work in connection with this collection, and especially for all his patience and tenacity in the pursuit of copyright.

The publishers gratefully acknowledge permissions granted as follows:-

Johnny Appleseed & Co - for 6d

Blakemore, Professor Colin - for 13e

Gwen Bowen (Knight) - for 13c

Chrysalis Books plc - for 8e and 48d

James Clarke & Co Ltd - for 15g

Constable & Robinson Publishing Ltd - for 41d

Curtis Brown Group Ltd., London - for
9c - extract from '*English Country Houses*' Copyright © Vita Sackville-West 1941, reproduced by permission of Curtis Brown Ltd., London
19d - reproduced with permission of Curtis Brown Group Ltd, London on behalf of the Estate of James Hilton, Copyright James Hilton 1934

Darton, Longman & Todd Ltd - for
17g - taken from *The Jerusalem Bible*, published and copyright 1966, 1967 and 1968 by Darton, Longman and Todd Ltd and Doubleday & Co Inc, and used by permission of the publishers.

Deseret Books - for 44d

Everyman Publishers plc - for
42e *Emile* by Jean Jacques Rousseau, translated by Barbara Foxley, published by J.M.Dent & Sons Ltd 1955, copyright Everyman Publishers plc, Gloucester Mansions, 140A Shaftesbury Avenue, London.
Reprinted with permission of Everyman Publishers plc

Faber & Faber Ltd - for 2d, 21f, and 31c

Harcourt, Inc for 45d
Excerpt from *THE CONDITION OF MAN*
Copyright 1944 and renewed 1972
by Lewis Mumford.
Reprinted by permission of Harcourt, Inc.

HarperCollins Publishers Ltd - for 8f, 24e, 27f, 38g, and 50g

Harvill Press - for 32c - Extracts from *Doctor Zhivago* by Boris Pasternak
© Giangiacomo Feltrinelli Editore, 1958. English translation © Harvill 1958.
Reproduced by permission of the Harvill Press.

David Higham Associates - for 5f, 7e, 16f, 26c, 26e, 27e, 30f, and 31d.

Hodder & Stoughton Ltd - for
Scripture quotations (2e, 3f, 5c, 8c, 14c, 18d, 21e) taken from the *HOLY BIBLE,
NEW INTERNATIONAL VERSION.* Copyright c 1973 1978, 1984 by International
Bible Society. Used by permission of Hodder & Stoughton Limited. All rights
reserved. "NIV" is a registered trademark of International Bible Society. UK
trademark number 1448790
28g - reproduced by permission of Hodder & Stoughton Limited

Beth Johns - for 22f

Linda Landers - for 38e

The C S Lewis Company Ltd - for
2g and 40f Extracts from *"The Problem of Pain"* and *"The Last Battle"*
© C S Lewis Pte. Ltd.1940 & 1956, reprinted by permission.

MENSA - for 36f and 42g

Methodist Publishing House - for
21g & 33d - from *Fireside Papers* by S L Bensusan © 1946 Epworth Press. Used
by permission of Methodist Publishing House

John Murray (Publishers) Ltd - for 32g

New Church College - for 27c

The Orion Publishing Group Ltd - for 1e, 33e, and 36c

Oxford University Press - for 24g
26f &43f - from *The Notebooks of Leonardo da Vinci*, selected and edited by Irma
A. Richter, 1952, by permission of the Oxford University Press

Pan Macmillan Ltd - for 10c

Pearson Education - for 14g and 28f

The Random House Group Limited - for
8d - Extract from *The Doors of Perception* by Aldous Huxley originally published by Chatto & Windus.
Reprinted by permission of The Random House Group Ltd
© the Estate of Mrs Laura Huxley
46c - Extract from *An Angel at my Shoulder* by Glennyce Eckersley published by Rider/Ebury. Used by permission of The Random House Group Ltd
50e - Extract from *The Orion Mystery* by Robert G.Bauval
published by Heinemann.
Used by permission of The Random House Group Ltd
51d - Extract from *Tarka the Otter* by Henry Williamson
published by Bodley Head.
Used by permission of The Random House Group Ltd
52d - Extract from *The Justification of Johann Gutenberg* by Blake Morrison
published by Chatto & Windus.
Used by permission of The Random House Group Ltd

Routledge - for 45f

SCM Press - for 1c, 2c, 5e, 20e, 29e, and 35e

SPCK Publishing - for 48f

Stainer & Bell Ltd - for
45e - reproduced by permission of Stainer & Bell Ltd

Abner Stein - for 8g and 30e

Swedenborg Foundation Publishers - for 30g, 31g, 36d, and 49d

Swedenborg Society - for 4d

Thames & Hudson - for 4g, 6e, 10f, and 27d

Virgin Publishing - for 22d and 42d

A P Watt Ltd on behalf of the Council of Trinity College, Cambridge - for 51g

Yale University Press - for 9f

Dedicated to the memory of
Phillip Smale
Artist, Sceptic & Good Friend

P R E F A C E

Devotional books are for devotional people, but this anthology is not like that at all. The pieces gathered here were drawn together by no divine thread, so far as I am aware - but who knows? Religious thinking, it seems to me, concerns itself for the most part with all those things we mortals do *not* know, about which our deepest uncertainties revolve. So, although a spirit of optimism links this odd assortment, it springs not from conviction, but from aspiration.

One who *did* claim insight into the eternal mysteries, and who spoke from *utter* conviction, was the eighteenth-century seer, Emanuel Swedenborg (1688-1772). Few have reported from actual observation, as he apparently did, and surely no-one has ever written about spiritual things so voluminously nor, indeed, so laboriously. I choose, therefore, to examine a little of what he wrote, and I use him to spark-off each weekly selection.

I have condensed and rephrased these extracts in a style such as Swedenborg just *might* have used, had he been writing today for the 'ordinary reader'. Scholars will say that I have taken such liberties as to alter him beyond all recognition. Perhaps we had better say, then, that these are adaptations rather than quotations. Even so, I do not put new words into his mouth unless they enlighten what he is evidently trying to tell me.

On day two there follows a commentary in which I attend to some of the problems, and to the many comforts, that may be found in Swedenborg's uncompromising and often dogmatic pronouncements. These are my own reflections.

The remaining five days of each week are each given to some quotation chosen for its relevance to the theme in hand - not always because I find it true, but simply because it interests me in some strange way.

The week concludes with a short supplication - I hesitate to call it a prayer - in which I seek to encapsulate a personal hope for the future.

What is it all for? An assortment such as this may help us to refine our ideas about God, about heaven, about the world in which we find ourselves, about our own hidden ambitions, and other profound matters. Perhaps this is what people mean these days when they use woolly terms like 'self-awareness', but, at all events, I hope these pages will entertain. A daily dose could maybe strengthen the reader in the search for meaning and purpose in this perilous world.

G. Roland Smith. Hadlow. 2001

C O N T E N T S

1   THE BENEFIT OF THE DOUBT
- The Charitable View

1a   **Some think that loving your neighbour means giving money to charitable causes, and going around doing good to everybody, but charity actually involves using your wits to bring about some lasting improvement. Helping out a poor or needy villain could easily backfire.**

Charity belongs to everything we do - not just relieving poverty. A judge exercises charity when he seeks to uphold justice: a priest exercises charity when he goes on about what is good and true for its own sake.

Anyone who acts sincerely and justly, in business and in daily life, exercises charity because he loves those in whom sincerity and justice may be found. Charity, for such people, is life's chief delight: it enters into their every thought and action, whether they get paid for what they do or not. Goodness itself is their neighbour.

Those who work only for the sake of personal gain haven't a clue about what true charity is. They think that the loss of worldly profits would leave them desolate, whereas in fact it is in true charity that heavenly joys begin.

Heavenly Doctrine 100-105

1b   A heavenly society would, I suppose, have to be a non-profit-making society, unless, of course, *everyone* profited. Not being an economist, I have this nasty feeling that, in this life at any rate, one person's profit is another's loss. Somewhere along the line someone misses out.

Registered charities must be 'non-profit-making', it is the law. They are not allowed to share out the proceeds among themselves. They exist for the good of others. We may take some comfort in this, especially if we count ourselves among the 'others' - the needy. But hang on! Commerce is not always the work of the devil: it also has

7

its place. Job-satisfaction may be a marvellous thing, but there's little satisfaction in starving for want of a working wage. Altruism at all costs may be an expensive luxury.

Inevitably enmeshed in an intricate network of goods and services, we have little option but to profit from each other. The battle in the market place between the winners and the losers has gone on long enough. Count me among the conscientious objectors.

1c   Let us consider two men, both fighting for a generous ideal - for example, for liberty of conscience and tolerance. They may put forward identical arguments with equal ardour, and yet both are not actuated by the same force. In the same way a radio station may draw its power from the grid or from its own generators, and yet broadcast the same programme. Without realising it, one of these men in crusading for tolerance is really seeking vengeance on his father, who in the past has exercised an improper moral constraint upon him. The other has a genuine vocation. The strength of each is derived from a different source: the one is psychological, the other spiritual.

Paul Tournier, *The Strong and the Weak*

1d   When you reap your harvest in your field, and you forget a sheaf in the field, you shall not go back to fetch it; it shall be for the settler, the fatherless, and the widow, so that the Lord your God may bless you in all the work of your hands. When you beat your olive tree, you shall not go over the branches again; it shall be for the settler, the fatherless, and the widow. When you gather from your vineyard, you shall not glean behind you; it shall be for the settler, the fatherless, and the widow. And you shall remember that you were slaves in the land of Egypt; therefore I command you to do this thing.

Deuteronomy 24, 19-22

1e   Charity makes no distinctions; it excludes no-one. The recipient of the act of charity need only be suffering or be somehow in jeopardy.

With charity, there is no danger of its being turned to the advantage of any particular group. It is incontestably a moral act. Charity differs from caring, then, precisely in its being directed toward everyone rather than toward particular individuals; the typical beneficiary of the charitable act is the nameless beggar lying in the street, not the person lying on top of me in the cattle car or under me in the infirmary. Pascal, in fact, expressly recommends that one avoid knowing personally those to whom one would extend charity so as not to risk diminishing the virtue of the act by becoming attached to the recipient and acting out of love for the person rather than out of love for God.

Tzvetan Todorov, *Facing the Extreme*

1f   White is consistently helpful to other people, with some ulterior motive. He may be doing penance for past wickedness, covering up for present wickedness, making friends in order to exploit them later or seeking prestige. But whoever questions his motives must also give him credit for his actions. After all, people can cover up for past wickedness by becoming more wicked, exploit people by fear rather than generosity and seek prestige for evil ways instead of good ones. Some philanthropists are more interested in competition than in benevolence: 'I gave more money (works of art, acres of land) than you did.' Again, if their motives are questioned, they must nevertheless be given credit for competing in a constructive way, since there are so many people who compete destructively. Most people (or peoples) who play 'Happy to Help' have both friends and enemies, both perhaps justified in their feelings. Their enemies attack their motives and minimise their actions, while their friends are grateful for their actions and minimise their motives. Therefore so-called 'objective' discussions of this game are practically non-existent. People who claim to be neutral soon show which side they are neutral on.

Eric Berne, *Games People Play*

1g   I have said it often enough, but I must say it once again, since it is so much part of my case for handicraft, that so long as a man allows his daily work to be mere unrelieved drudgery he will seek happiness in vain. I say further that the worst tyrants of the days of violence were but feeble tormentors compared with those Captains of Industry who have taken the pleasure of work away from the workmen. Furthermore, I feel absolutely certain that handicraft joined to certain other conditions, would produce the beauty and the pleasure above mentioned, and if that be so, and this double pleasure of lovely surroundings and happy work could take the place of the double torment of squalid surroundings and wretched drudgery, have we not good reason for wishing, if it might be, that handicraft should once more step into the place of machine-production?

William Morris (as quoted in *Country Life in England* - Martin)

Everyone has something to offer in the market place of life. May I always make my own goods widely available at a fair price and acknowledge the debt I owe to other people.

---

2   THE SEEDS OF HOPE
- Remnants

2a   **There are simple God-given notions of goodness and truth learned from early childhood and stored in the memory. They are responsible for some of the innocence of childhood and tend to produce loving attitudes towards parents and siblings, teachers and neighbours. Young children are often capable of deep sympathy for the poor and needy.**

     God stores away these ideas in the sub-conscious, in a compartment of their own, so to speak, where they are all preserved safely, untainted by any of the horrors people dream up for themselves as they go through life. I know this for a fact because I have seen how all these states of mind re-appear in the next world. They can all be re-enacted, and when this happens God is able to call up innocent and charitable thoughts to counterbalance the evil ones. If it were not for these residual delights from childhood, there would not be much hope for us.

Arcana Caelestia 561

2b   Translators of Swedenborg do their best, but Latin does have a nasty way of producing stilted English. In an attempt to render his *reliquae* they have sometimes used dreadful words like 'remains' or 'remnants' conjuring up all sorts of ghastly pictures. I find myself thinking of corpses - 'human remains' - something decayed and rotten, or left-overs - odd bits, 'bargain remnants' up for grabs after the January sales, or the bones left on the side of the plate. Maybe it's just my wicked imagination, but such images are quite the reverse of Swedenborg's intention. You do need to be careful with words. I think what he meant were those precious little gems of kindness and concern that snuggle comfortably forgotten in the richest, deepest, most inaccessible boreholes of the mind. They lie quiescent until the Prince of Peace awakens them - just when they are needed most.

2c The weak man bears powerful witness to the faith when after a religious experience he shows himself all at once freed from fear, from despair, and from inhibitions of various kinds. I once heard of a nice remark made by a child. One evening as he was telling his mother that he was afraid of ghosts, she suggested that he should say his prayers. A few moments later the child said: 'I'm not frightened any more now. Jesus has told me that he'll see to the ghosts.' And one of my patients once expressed her experience of the Christian life as being like flying in a glider - you have to find the rising currents.

Paul Tournier, *The Strong and the Weak*

2d Free-will cannot be debated but only experienced, like a colour or the taste of potatoes. I remember one such experience. I was very small and I was sitting on the stone surround of the pool and fountain in the centre of the park. There was bright sunlight, banks of red and blue flowers, green lawn. There was no guilt but only the plash and splatter of the fountain at the centre. I had bathed and drunk and now I was sitting on the warm stone edge placidly considering what I should do next. The gravelled paths of the park radiated from me: and all at once I was overcome by a new knowledge. I could take whichever I would of these paths. There was nothing to draw me down one more than the other. I danced down one for joy in the taste of potatoes. I was free. I had chosen.

William Golding, *Free Fall*

2e Then little children were brought to Jesus for him to place his hands on them and pray for them. But the disciples rebuked those who brought them. Jesus said, "Let the little children come to me, and do not hinder them, for the kingdom of heaven belongs to such as these." When he had placed his hands on them, he went on from there.

Matthew 19, 13

2f   I learned very early on in my life that nothing was for ever; so I should have been aware of disillusion in early middle age: but, somehow, we try to obliterate early warnings and go cantering along hopefully, idiotically...

No matter that the tide will turn once again and destroy all that you build (and in the depths of your soul you know that this will happen), you thrust the spade in the hard-packed rippled sand, outline the beginning of a moat. Soon the fort will arise, decorated all about, once again, with shells and weed, with towers and turrets, arches and a drawbridge, each turret capped with a conical limpet shell. As glorious as the first one ever was, probably even better from the experience gained by its destruction, and every bit as impermanent...

How odd it is that one is not prepared for the 'dissolving of the fort' one has constructed with such care in later life. But we do not learn. We always believe that it'll be all right for us. That our fort will stand, the tide will never turn. But, of course, it does.

Dirk Bogarde, *A Short Walk from Harrods*

2g   Are not all lifelong friendships born at the moment when at last you meet another human being who has some inkling (but faint and uncertain even in the best) of that something which you were born desiring, and which, beneath the flux of other desires and in all the momentary silences between the louder passions, night and day, year by year, from childhood to old age, you are looking for, watching for, listening for? You have never *had* it. All the things that have ever deeply possessed your soul have been but hints of it - tantalising glimpses, promises never quite fulfilled, echoes that died away just as they caught your ear. But if it should really become manifest - if there ever came an echo that did not die away but swelled into the sound itself - you would know it. Beyond all possibility of doubt you would say "Here at last is the thing I was made for".

C.S.Lewis, *The Problem of Pain*

It is hard enough to keep one's balance in this precarious world. When the time for decisions is come, let me not forget my hidden resources.

3   FAIR PROGRESS
- Freedom and Regeneration

3a   No-one is really free until he is spiritually reawakened: before that, he is in a moral straitjacket. So long as evil passions rule, that's bondage; when goodness and truth are in charge, that's freedom. The libertine may *think* he is free because he seems to be doing just what he pleases - after all, everyone thinks himself free when he actually *loves* what is only leading him by the nose. All the time, however, he is blissfully unaware that he is just a slave to his baser appetites. Without them, so he thinks, life wouldn't be worth living: he finds the idea of the next world unconvincing, and in any case someone has probably told him that you can't get to heaven unless you first pay dearly with a hard and miserable life. What a load of nonsense !

Nobody knows what freedom is until God introduces him to the love of goodness and truth. Only then can he see, for the first time, what life is all about - only then does the fun really start - only then does the real distinction between good and evil become apparent. This is freedom, an escape from the Devils' Island of hell.

Arcana Caelestia 892

The freedom of the angels of heaven originates in God. Since they love goodness and truth and are in mutual affection one with another, their happy state permeates the entire heavenly community. Communication knows no barriers, so the heavenly life is open, free and uninhibited.

That other sort of 'freedom', derived from selfish pursuits and worldly ambitions, is so alien to the angels that if they give it any thought at all they get dreadful bellyache. Likewise if the evil ones in hell think for a moment about the unselfish freedom of the angels, their guts feel knotted too. Hell for one is heaven for another, and vice-versa. All are distinguished by the delight of their lives, whatever that may be.

To delight in evil may seem like freedom, but it is not: to delight in love really is freedom because it is from God.

Arcana Caelestia 2872-3

3b   Here is Swedenborg the schoolmaster, telling us again that we have much to learn. He identifies two kinds of freedom - the youthful I-know-what-I-want variety and the now-I-see-what-matters sort which some people surprisingly achieve in their dotage. All becomes crystal clear in the afterlife. Fine if you can go along with the idea, but not much help for the worldly wary for whom eternity is a closed book, and all that beckons is a blank wall. Not for them the final graduation day when the scales fall from their eyes. They can but explore the perimeter of this life for signs that there may be something beyond.

I do sometimes get a curious feeling in my bones that maybe we are all being put through some kind of psychological assault course - that we have been rudely catapulted into a training ground, which, if it is true, raises the intriguing question - training for what? The reception camp - it that's what life is - makes no sense on its own. Logic or justice demands some follow-up - an afterlife. So if life is a learning process it presumably has direction, it leads somewhere. There are signs that the world may be a vast comprehensive crammer. And education, after all, is for life, not life for education.

3c   But far short of 'behaviourism', we are bound to recognise important elements of determination, of cause and effect, in education. This presupposition, legitimate up to a certain point, can, however, be very dangerous if it discounts in its practice the possibility, the important possibility, of *freedom*. The consideration of freedom presents a different picture. The person has a history, true. The present has been shaped by the past, and the future will be shaped by what happens now. But an idea of 'shaping' and 'moulding' in education, which assumes that the living child is simply an object to be moulded and shaped according to our or society's desires, is an idea which leaves out what *may* be the most important fact about a human person. Is there not, it may be asked,

another aspect of every personality which is in some sense
independent of its history, which can in some measure at least stand
off from its own states, its own history, judge it, criticise it, choose,
and, perhaps, move off in a *new* direction ?

Louis Arnaud Reid, *Philosophy and Education*

3d   Freedom is complete obedience to the element for which we were
designed...Complete obedience to the pursuit of truth. Not the truth
of facts or of science, but the truth that is wholeness and integrity.
And complete obedience to the calls and demands of love. For there
is in each of us a potential nurturer and healer and tender lover and
faithful friend. Freedom is complete obedience to the *special*
elements for which we were designed. For some, the element of
listening. For others, of being a bridge-builder, or bone-grafter, or a
community-catalyst. Of fashioning meaning out of words or musical
sounds, or out of movement. Of gardening or teaching or translating
or pastoring. Just as discovering our element is the focus of our
search and the key to our vocations, so is obedience to our element
the entrance into freedom.

Joan Puls, *Every Bush is Burning*

3e   Those servants who take their wages in advance are continually in
need, and the man who eats before he has earned his food seldom
dies out of debt. He should first do his duty, and complete his day's
work; for until a workman has finished his job, no-one can see what
he deserves for it. If he takes money in advance, how can he be sure
that his work will not be rejected? - And so I say to you rich men: it
is wrong to expect heaven in your present life, and another heaven
hereafter, like a servant who first takes his payment in advance, and
then claims it again afterwards as though he had never received it
before. Such a thing cannot be - witness these words of St.Matthew:
"It is difficult to pass from one delight to another."

But if you rich folk have pity on the poor and reward them well,
and live by the law of God and act justly to all men, then Christ in
his courtesy will comfort you in the end, rewarding with double

riches all who have pitying hearts. And just as a servant who has received his wages beforehand is sometimes given a further reward, a coat or a jerkin, for doing his duty well, so Christ gives heaven both to rich and to poor, if they lead lives of mercy. And all who do their duty well shall have double pay for their labours, the forgiveness of their sins and the bliss of heaven.

William Langland, *Piers the Ploughman*

3f To the Jews who had believed him, Jesus said, "If you hold to my teaching, you are really my disciples. Then you will know the truth, and the truth will set you free." They answered him, "We are Abraham's descendants and have never been slaves to anyone. How can you say that we shall be set free?" Jesus replied, "I tell you the truth, everyone who sins is a slave to sin. Now a slave has no permanent place in the family, but a son belongs to it for ever. So if the Son sets you free, you will be free indeed. I know you are Abraham's descendants. Yet you are ready to kill me, because you have no room for my word. I am telling you what I have seen in the Father's presence, and you do what you have heard from your father." "Abraham is our father," they answered. "If you were Abraham's children," said Jesus, "then you would do the things Abraham did. As it is, you are determined to kill me, a man who has told you the truth that I heard from God. Abraham did not do such things. You are doing the things your own father does." "We are not illegitimate children," they protested. "The only Father we have is God himself."

John 8, 31-41

3g Domestic happiness can never be a complete happiness; on either view of man's nature he cannot expect complete happiness in this life. On the materialist view he is a finite being with a mind capable of framing concepts of infinity, a being confined between two nothings before birth and after death. If he considers his situation, which is nothing less than that of impending annihilation, it robs his achievements of all but a trace of their lasting significance. On the religious view he is, in a crude phrase, a square peg in a round hole, an eternal soul in a mortal body, a creature made to know and love God, in a world in which God's presence is never allowed to be complete. Death to him is not the concern it may be to the atheist; it is the way to a better place. But the contrast between his own failures and his immortal duties is infinitely more painful.

William Rees-Mogg, *An Humbler Heaven*

Freedom without purpose is no better than chaos, so may I seek those sign-posts that give direction to my life.

4   HOLY ECHOES
- Correspondences

4a   **Every single thing in nature, and every anatomical detail of the human body, corresponds to something spiritual. Nobody seems to have known this, but the ancients knew all about it: they regarded this universal code as the greatest wonder of the world, and it coloured all their writing. Now since divine mysteries appear in the world as correspondences, the Bible, being God's 'Word', uses the same language. These linguistic terms are not merely stylistic tricks or figures of speech but they actually embody spiritual realities - they *correspond*. Jesus himself spoke from divine inspiration using the same consistent system.**

I am told that before the flood the enlightened ones were so heavenly they could talk with the angels, using correspondences. This improved their education enormously, so that whatever took their eye here spoke to them not only of this world but of the next.

True Christian Religion 201-2

4b   The prospect of an afterlife has pretty serious implications. What would it be like? How should I fit in? After all, it would have to be *different* from this life - otherwise there would be little point in going there, we might as well stay put. But not *too* different. My eternal home would have some familiar landmarks, I hope. My fellow survivors would be recognisably human, like me, and the general habitat would be welcoming and congenial. I derive no comfort from reports of bejewelled cities and shining glories: bright lights bother me, and regal splendours are only all right at a safe distance - I have no wish to be part of the show.

Swedenborg's 'correspondences' fill the bill marvellously. The idea that heaven is a realm of human qualities - love, wisdom, truth, goodness, intelligence and so on, and that these somehow give rise to all the tangible props and patterns of everyday life - this might account for the human situation - even though we are told nothing much about how God does it. It also brings heaven and earth together, because it suggests that our work-a-day world *already* performs against a heavenly backdrop. I'm all for that. So trees and rivers, mountains and rocks, tiddlers and tadpoles all have spiritual meanings, if only we can work them out.

4c   All kinds of animals have their peculiar correspondences, in agreement with their forms, characteristics and uses; for they all derive their existence from spiritual causes, and, by virtue of their instinct, are in momentary connection with the spiritual world.

In the Word of God the beasts of the earth - the tame and useful as well as the wild and ferocious, the clean and the unclean, correspond in general to various good or evil affections, according to their orders and qualities, and the subject of which they are predicated.

The birds, or winged tribes of animals, distinguished by their astonishing quickness of sight - both clean and unclean - agreeably to their respective genera and characters, and the subject treated of, correspond to the various kinds and degrees of thought, reason, intelligence, and the power of understanding, and are predicated both of what is holy and what is profane. For these faculties and their attainments impart to man intellectual acuteness and penetration, enabling him to fly, as it were, with wings, and disport himself in the atmosphere of knowledge.

The fishes and the reptiles, according to their respective forms and habitudes, correspond to those low external principles of man's earthly nature, which, before the mind is regenerated, flit and grovel among sensual objects and selfish pursuits.

Edward Madeley, *The Science of Correspondences Elucidated*

4d   These things - the being and nature of God, the spiritual world, the soul, and all co-related subjects - are the subject matter of revelation: not history, not science, not anything which lies within the province of the senses. Moreover, and because all our knowledge in this present world is derived through the senses of our bodies, the subject-matter of revelation must perforce be revealed to us through symbols, the symbols being for the most part the objects and ideas of this natural world. It would not be untrue to say that all revelation is made through symbols...

The symbols employed by the 'divine revealer' to disclose divine and spiritual realities, are actual correspondences... The natural universe comes forth from the spiritual world and both are creations by God. Between the natural and the spiritual world there is a cause and effect relationship and this relationship is denominated "correspondence". Between the spiritual universe and the infinite love and thoughts of God a like relationship exists, so that between it and the infinite things which are in the creator, there is likewise correspondence; and correspondence is the language of revelation.Correspondences, however, since they are true cause and effect relationships and not mere sequences of events in time, are themselves revealed knowledges, since genuine causes are spiritual and divine and these, in themselves, transcend our sense-experience.

Clifford Harley, *Spirit and Life within the Genesis Story*

4e   Quite young children seem to enjoy counting. Once they have learned the names of the numbers to twelve, then the numbers thirteen, fourteen, fifteen, as far as nineteen, trip happily off the tongue with a light trochaic rhythm, ending with "twenty", spoken with the finality of an "amen". After a delay of some months, the system for numbers from twenty to a hundred is rehearsed privately until one night, long after bedtime, a little voice calls out "Daddy", and in reply to the inevitable "I thought you were asleep", a pleased and contented child announces "I've counted all the way up to a hundred". The interest in counting shown by these young children seems to lie in the numbers themselves, in repetition and in the patterns of the numbers, rather than in actually counting things. It is a preliminary enjoyment of pure rather than of applied mathematics.

Frank Land, *The Language of Mathematics*

4f   Supposing we say: "John very much wanted to do so-and-so, but hesitated for fear of the consequences"; that is a plain statement. If we say: "In John's mind desire and fear contended for the mastery" we are already beginning to speak allegorically: John's mind has become a field of battle in which two personified emotions are carrying on a conflict. From this we can easily proceed to build up a full-blown allegory. We can represent the object of John's ambition as a lady imprisoned in a castle, which is attacked by a knight called Desire and defended by a giant called Fear, and we can put in as much description of the place and people as will serve to make the story exciting. We can show Desire so badly battered by Fear that he is discouraged and ready to give up, until rebuked by his squire, called Shame, who takes him to have his wounds dressed by a cheerful lady named Hope. Later, he is accosted by a plausible stranger called Suspicion, who says that the lady is much less virtuous and good-looking than she is made out to be... And so forth, introducing as many personifications of this kind as may be needed to express John's successive changes of mind. In this way we can work out quite a complicated psychological pattern, and at the same time entertain the reader with an exciting and colourful tale of adventure. In this purest kind of allegory, John himself never appears: his psyche is merely the landscape in which his personified feelings carry out their manoeuvres. But there is also a form in which John himself - or what we may perhaps call John's conscious self, or super-self - figures among the personages of the allegory, as a pilgrim or knight-errant, exploring the wildernesses of his own soul and fighting against opposition both from within and without.

Dorothy L.Sayers, *Introduction to Dante's Divine Comedy*

4g In a second, the faintest perfume may send us plummeting to the roots of our being, our whole life verticalised by a fleeting sensation: we have been connected by a mere smell to another place and another time. The amount we have changed in the recognition of this moment - this is the spiral: the path we have followed to reach the same point on another winding.

All our experiences are like that haunting scent: situations recur with almost boring familiarity until we have mastered them in the light of the previous time round. The more we do this, the steeper the gradient, which is the measure of our growth. The spiral we travel round life is the means we have to compare ourselves with ourselves, and discover how much we have changed since we were last in the city, met our brother, or celebrated Christmas. Time itself is cyclic, and by the spiral of its returning seasons we review the progress and growth of our own understanding.

Ours is the spiral house we build to keep us from life's continuous outpouring, from an otherwise unchecked flow into the unknown. Since what is unknown has power over us, we should otherwise be as vulnerable as the snail would be if his shell grew long and straight. The familiarity of life's experiences curls round and protects us, creating those mysterious mountain views of half-concealed windings which keep us bright with speculation and anticipation

The steepness of the straight path is prohibitive for most of us. The mystic calls this the 'shortcut', the path of illumination; but that which lights the mystic's way blinds the ordinary man, unprepared for the light of full knowledge. For him, unveiled truth is death; instead he must make his gradual ascent, allowing himself the protecting reassurance of its gentle windings.

Jill Purce, *The Mystic Spiral*

Life is not just a merry-go-round: there is a steam organ at its very heart. Show me how to understand what the music is playing.

5   INSIDE / OUTSIDE
- The Internal and the External Person

5a   **No-one these days really knows what to make of the terms 'Internal person' and 'External person'. The distinction seems meaningless because people suppose that the good they do, and the truth they think, are of their own making. But the 'internal' and the 'external' are, in fact, poles apart - as different as heaven and earth. Most thinkers, whether brainy or not, hold the view that the 'internal' consists of thought because it is out of sight, and the 'external' is the body, with all its sensations, because it shows. But this is a mistake: brain power is not the prerogative of the 'internal' at all. The 'internal' is deeper than that, consisting of notions of goodness and truth implanted there by God. After all, even the most depraved have brainwaves: so mental faculties are not that special - they are part of our everyday 'external' apparatus. 'External', however, doesn't refer simply to the material body and its sensations either. Spirits, whose bodies are spiritual, also have an 'external' as we do.**

The 'internal person' relates to what is heavenly, and the 'external person' to what is sensual - not necessarily tied to an earthly body, but originating in bodily desire.

Arcana Caelestia 978

5b   Swedenborg seems to be struggling here, seeking to identify the unseen bright interior of the human soul - that part of us which is beyond thought. No wonder he finds the right words hard to come by. But the notion that there are levels beyond conscious thought is no longer a new idea. The 'subconscious' and the 'unconscious' are terms we have now learned to live with.

So we each have a secret self which we take with us to the grave. Since, then, we don't really know who we are while we're here, it's odd to think we may be destined never to find out. Another powerful reason for life after death is the unthinkability of eternal ignorance. To suppose that death is the end is like leaving the theatre during the interval and never seeing the dénouement of the play.

5c   Once, having been asked by the Pharisees when the kingdom of God
      would come, Jesus replied, "The kingdom of God does not come
      visibly, nor will people say, 'Here it is,' or 'There it is,' because the
      kingdom of God is within you."

Luke 17, 20-21

5d   We can, therefore, speak of an inner personality with as much
      justification as, on the grounds of daily experience, we speak of an
      outer personality. The inner personality is the way one behaves in
      relation to one's inner psychic processes; it is the inner attitude, the
      characteristic face, that is turned towards the unconscious. I call the
      outer attitude, the outward face, the *persona*; the inner attitude, the
      inner face, I call the *anima*. To the degree that an attitude is habitual,
      it is a well-knit functional complex with which the ego can identify
      itself more or less. Common speech expresses this very graphically:
      when a man has an habitual attitude to certain situations, an habitual
      way of doing things, we say he is quite *another man* when doing
      this or that... it is as though another personality had taken possession
      of the individual, as though "another spirit had got into him." The
      same autonomy that very often characterises the outer attitude is
      also claimed by the inner attitude, the anima. It is one of the most
      difficult educational feats to change the persona, the outer attitude,
      and it is just as difficult to change the anima, since its structure is
      usually quite as well-knit as the persona's. Just as the persona is an
      entity that often seems to constitute the whole character of a man,
      and may even accompany him throughout his entire life, the anima
      is a clearly defined entity with a character that, very often, is
      autonomous and immutable.

Carl Gustav Jung, *"Definitions" Psychological Types*

5e   If God exists, he is self-existent, necessary Being. If we are to regard
      his existence as probable, we would not merely expect him to leave
      his footmarks, by the act of creation and by pointers to design in the
      evolution of the cosmos and in the development of life. If he intends

human beings to emerge from the evolutionary process who are capable of freely entering into communion and fellowship with himself, then we would expect such beings to be aware of him, and to experience the moral and aesthetic and spiritual values of which he is the source. And this is just what we do find. It seems to me far more probable that the experience of moral, aesthetic and spiritual values is explained by God who is their source, rather than that they are the product of the human mind. It seems to me much more probable that the experience of conscience is due to the existence of God rather than it is merely the result of psychological mechanisms of the brain. It seems to me even more probable that religious experience which is very widely diffused is due to the existence of God rather than that it is totally based on illusion.

Hugh Montefiore, *The Probability of God*

5f   'But, Beneditx, on the face of it, the intellect depends on the senses for the origin of knowledge, and knowledge gathered from sensible things cannot lead the human intellect to the point of seeing the divine substance... A babe hasn't the means...'

'You speak of evening knowledge - knowledge of things as they are and have been in the visible world. I speak of morning knowledge - knowledge of things as they were created, things as they are meant to be. The knowledge of angels is of both these kinds at once, but in mankind there is a difference. Inborn knowledge of God is morning knowledge.'

Jill Paton Walsh, *Knowledge of Angels*

5g   Viktor Frankl spent much of the Second World War in Nazi concentration camps, and he observed that the prisoners without any sense of purpose or hope succumbed most readily to the appalling conditions. Abraham Maslow had made a similar observation.

Man is the only animal whose basic instinct seems to be to *evolve*. His mind is intended to flow forward, like a stream. If forced to stand still, it becomes stagnant, and various illnesses develop. One could use another simile and say that man is like an automobile whose battery becomes flat if he is left in storage for too long. It is the use of his *will* that keeps his vital batteries recharged.

Colin Wilson, *Mysteries*

Since I have to live, not just in the world, but inside my own head, may my spiritual batteries never die, and may a loving purpose guide my every move.

6 A SPIRITUAL WORLD MAP
- 'Maximus Homo'

6a **In the next world everyone is perfectly well aware that everything in the human body, every little bit, corresponds to something in heaven. There are heavenly communities of every conceivable turn of mind, both spiritual and celestial, internal and external. They are so systematically arranged, like the organs of the body, that the whole heavenly set-up represents one man -** *Maximus Homo*. **Thus we may say that any specific community belongs to this or that bodily part. The underlying reason for this is that God is the only veritable 'Man' and heaven is a reflection of him.**

Arcana Caelestia 2996

Altogether heaven is a divine organism of the most immense proportions; in the sight of God like one man. There is not a single heavenly community which does not correspond to some aspect of human anatomy, so there is a working relationship between heaven and mankind. In heaven they say that such-and-such a community is in the region of the liver, the pancreas, the spleen, the stomach, the eye, the ear, the tongue, and so forth. The angels know precisely where they live.

True Christian Religion 65

6b In this world, when ideas get too big for us, we give up trying to make pictures, and make do with diagrams instead. Swedenborg's 'Grand Man' is, however, more than a mere diagram or metaphor: he assures us that it is so, this is how things *are*. If we want a working model of heavenly society we need look no further than our own bodies - provided, of course, that they are in good shape. We know that the human form - at least the female version - may look heavenly on the outside: we have Rodin and Botticelli to thank for pointing that out; but the idea that it is heavenly on the *inside* is by no means so obvious.

So long as we think only geographically the whole thing seems slightly ridiculous. Imagine my celestial address: Cell No.12, The Vertebrae, Thoracic Lane, Upper Chest. It sounds phoney. But as a means of containing a vast kingdom of uses the human body is sublime. Every microscopic unit has a part to play; every organ its specific function; all plugged into a miracle of wiring and pipework that only the Almighty could ever unravel. If we think in terms of dynamics then Swedenborg offers us a heaven of interaction and movement. He might also shed some light on the theory of evolution - but we'd better not go into that.

6c   Nothing in nature stands still. There is constant movement in everything, but often the movement is so slow that we do not notice it. Patterns are changing all the time and the patterns we see around us are the outcome of a long process of change. Consider the nautilus: its pattern shows how it grows. Each time it adds another chamber to its house, it makes it a bit larger than the previous one, and in the end all the chambers link up into a pattern. As in the case of the leaf, there are many different ways of applying this principle...The tree pattern occurs frequently in nature. In the human body, it is repeated over and over again. An electrical discharge can be shown to have the same pattern. Even a chart of the evolution of life takes the shape of a tree. Much of the living world appears to be organised in this pattern. Remembering that nature's purposes are always practical, to understand nature's patterns we must first try and understand what caused them, Only then will they make sense to us. We do not fully understand the leaf until we have realised how it stretches itself out, thrusting its cells towards the light. The nautilus shell will mean much more to us when we understand that it grows in a spiral, getting larger all the time. Artists of all periods have tried to understand the patterns of nature and have not been content merely to copy their appearance...As well as being practical, all natural patterns have something else in common. They are all based on mathematical principles. You would expect a master builder to have definite ideas about the way he builds, and to use the same ideas in many different ways when it suited him.

Kurt Rowland, *Pattern and Shape*

6d   The lungs work with blood, which works with all the tissues; particular uses fitting together that there may be an overall use, that the person may live and act. And the person takes care of his body and its organs. This is also the image of society. The farmers work with packers, who work with grocery stores that we might eat and live. This is also an image of heaven, where individuals make their unique contribution to societies (which are like organs of the body) which contribute to the One Man, the Grand Man. Every time Swedenborg's Grand Man puzzles you, look at your own form, which is an image of all there is. *The reason that all these patterns of uses working together tend toward heaven is that in uses we look across from the part toward the whole.* What use are my hands unless they do something, and in this doing I have reached beyond myself toward creation. The carpenter's uses extend into the family and through them into their friends and contacts. The great wonder of use as a method is that it enables us to go beyond ourselves, to reach through creation.

Wilson van Dusen, *The Country of Spirit*

6e   In the symbolism of all religions a geometric construction representing the heavenly city or map of paradise has a central place. It occurs in sacred art as a mandala, a concentric arrangement of circles, squares and polygons, depicting in essence the entire universe. Related images include the labyrinth, the paradisial garden, the walled enclosure or temple precinct, the world tree, the enchanted castle on a rock, the sacred mountain, stone, well or spring and all other symbols of the universal axis which remains fixed and constant amid the ever-changing world of phenomena. The effect of these symbols is to exert an orderly influence on society and the individual mind...The ancient philosophers venerated the established image of the celestial city and based all their studies on it, regarding it as the true, revealed image of God's creation and thus the appointed standard for all human affairs.

John Michell, *The Dimensions of Paradise*

6f   The Hereford map (The *Mappa Mundi*) is the largest and perhaps the best surviving example of medieval cartography. It has many of the attributes of Isidore's encyclopedia, the *Etymologiae*, another outstanding product of medieval scholarship. Both are eclectic, uncritical, illogical, unoriginal in that they depended entirely on outside sources, and consistent only in their unswerving loyalty to Christian principles. Taken together, these attributes of medieval times reflected a manner of thought which contrasts with that of both preceding and following times. A basic difference appears to be in medieval other-worldliness taken to the point of indifference to the realities of the physical world. That was viewed, not from first hand, but as it was described in ancient sources, without thought of their possible errors or widely varying quality and without attempts to evaluate their validity or to improve on them. The attitudes of the Greeks and Romans which prevailed before the Middle Ages were dissimilar, but neither were so sharply divorced from reality, and the contrast of medieval with modern attitudes is equally clear. But the Hereford map has one positive attribute which merits our consideration. Much attention was given to make it beautiful, both in its overall organisation and in the quality of its individual illustrations. Medieval drawings have an undeniable charm. They may seem naïve, but they somehow catch the essence of what they are intended to portray in a way that a photograph or modern drawing does not always do. Perhaps we can learn something from the Hereford map that may be applicable to our own view of the World.

Jonathan T.Lanman, *Glimpses of History from Old Maps*

6g   The different organs in the body have specialised in order to meet different demands. While the function of individual cells differs, and they are constructed to meet different demands, their basic structure is similar. Cells organise into organs and groups of organs, and here the main characteristic is specialisation for the different tasks required. Finally the organs form an organism, a whole, where the most important feature is not specialisation but co-ordination. While their versatility is obvious, the collaboration among organs for the benefit of the whole is much more important. The various parts of the body must be strongly united to assure survival.

The nervous system is mainly responsible for the co-ordination of activities in the body. Hormones, which circulate in the bloodstream, also play an important rôle by adjusting the body to the various demands of the environment. Hormones are chiefly produced in the endocrine glands - that is, glands that secrete directly into the blood. Some hormones exert specific effects on particular organs - their 'target' organs - while others have more generalised effects...

These extremely complex reactions and interactions strive to bring about a state of balance among the billions of cells that make up a human being - an individual who has the ability to act freely and independently, and to influence the world about him.

Lennart Nilsson, *Behold Man*

As it appears there is no-one quite like me, help me to find that special purpose that might earn me a place of my own in the anatomy of heaven.

7   MUSIC OF THE INNER EAR
- Spiritual Hearing

7a   **If someone hears an angel or spirit, the voice sounds as clear to them as that of another person, but no-one else can hear it. This is because angelic speech communicates directly with the mind, and only then addresses the ear, so to speak, from the '*inside*'. Ordinary human speech, however, causes air-waves that are then picked up by the ear from '*outside*'. Since both affect the ear they are both audible. Inner speech also causes the tongue to vibrate slightly, but not enough to give utterance...**

Those who live alone sometimes hear harmless spirits. Likewise, those who brood on religious matters may begin to hear spirit voices, because when someone dwells on such things by himself, without reference to the practicalities of the real world, they tend to take over his thinking.

The most heavenly of all the angels don't tuck truths away in their memories: they immediately put them into action. Their wisdom results from what they *hear*, not from what they *see*. Visual experience is stored in the memory so it can be chewed-over in debate. But *hearing* the truth implies obedience to it - and that is not just a matter of understanding: it is a matter of living.

Heaven & Hell 248, 249, 271.

7b   People who hear voices inside their heads seem pretty weird to the rest of us who don't. I'm not sure that listening to spirits is really to be recommended. Swedenborg certainly didn't recommend it, and anyway, judging from the dubious reports of mystics and mediums, I get the impression that spirits seldom have anything very worthwhile to say.

There are many people, however, who can vouch for the fact that head-noises are very real, even though others cannot hear them. Sound waves can come from within as well as from without. Some musicians can even read a musical score and 'hear' the music mentally.

Just as the healthy body has its inner tempo, so too, I sometimes sense, an undiminished mind hears a heartbeat of its own. Despite disaster, the world with its seasons and tides, its clocks and calendars, suggests an ideal rhythm. Maybe our thoughts and feelings likewise embrace an inner pulse of which we are seldom aware. Every human spirit plays its own tune if we are not too busy to hear it.

7c [Mr Byrd] halted in his lesson again, driving strange thoughts along the thoroughfare of his mind such as these that follow. At the moment of my death will I comprehend the musique of the spheres at last, which all my life I have strained to hear? Will I be taken up into the empyrean, of which I have sought the traces within the muddy vesture of this earth? If so I sit upon thorns until I be gone, gone into that region of harmony whence all our musique derives. I may lose these humane faces and these humane voices, but I shall look upon another Face and hear another Voice; and all my airs will be at last completed. Yet perhaps I earnestly aspire to such things since I am come to my end: these young scholars are at their beginning and eagerly seek their own music. How much of that will be my own in imitation (as I did imitate the great masters), how much sweetly set forth as the natural air of their own country, and how much the spark of some divine original? They know not now, but in time they will learn that all true music springs from origins much greater than themselves. That is the meaning of my death, as I suppose, to return to that source from which all my music flows.

Peter Ackroyd, *English Music*

7d Though working-class adults do not as a rule attend any place of worship regularly, they are not consciously anti-clerical. Towards the parson their attitude is likely to be faintly cynical; he is in with the bosses. But it is usually a cheerful cynicism with no active hostility behind it. 'It's a good racket if you can get in on it,' they will say, 'good luck to 'em.' We're all rogues under the skin is the assumption, and opportunity's a fine thing: I'd probably do the same if I had the chance...

They believe, first, in the purposiveness of life. Life has a meaning, must have a meaning. One does not bother much about defining it, or pursue abstract questions as to its nature or the implications which follow from such a conclusion; but clearly it is so. 'We're 'ere for a purpose,' they say, or, 'There must be some purpose or we wouldn't be 'ere'. And that there is a purpose presupposes that there must be a God. They hold to what G.K.Chesterton called 'the dumb certainties of existence', and Reinhold Niebuhr called 'those things [like free-will and the existence of the individual] which we know to be so, though all the arguments are against them'.

Richard Hoggart, *The Uses of Literacy*

7e   We now know for certain that the brain in a complex organism functions as an integrating whole, delegating responsibility for particular sensations to specific areas. There is a visual area in the posterior part of the cortex, there are auditory areas in the temporal lobes, and even a language centre in the first and second convolutions on the left side of right-handed people. Every week our anatomical maps and our physiological knowledge become more detailed, but there is also an ever increasing awareness that these mechanistic explorations are not enough. There is something else there that just can't be reached by scalpels or electrodes. Total blindness, deafness or loss of speech can occur as a result of hysteria, or of direct suggestion under hypnosis. And for these phenomena there seems to be no simple physical explanation...

We grow and change, but remain recognisably ourselves. Which means, very simply, that a sense of identity, an individual personality, cannot depend only on the substance of the body. It must be integrated somehow, somewhere else. Something has been added to make us more than machines.

Lyall Watson, *Lifetide*

7f   Gödel's Theorem was once explained to me by a patient, gentle mathematician, and just as I was taking it all in, nodding appreciatively at the beauty of the whole idea, I suddenly felt something like the silent flicking of a mercury wall switch and it all turned to nonsense inside my head. I have had similar experiences listening to electronic music, and even worse ones reading poetry criticism. It is not like blanking out or losing interest or drifting off, not at all. My mind is, if anything, more alert, grasping avidly at every phrase, but then the switch is thrown and what comes in is transformed into an unfathomable code.

This brings me to my theory about the brain, my brain anyway. I believe there is a centre someplace, maybe in the right hemisphere, which has a scrambling function similar to those electronic devices attached to the telephones of important statesmen which instantly convert all confidential sentences to gibberish...

A scrambler in the brain would be a protective device, preserving the delicate centre of the mechanism of language against tinkering and meddling, shielding the mind against information with which it has no intention of getting involved.

Lewis Thomas, *The Medusa and the Snail*

7g   As I wander through the dark, encountering difficulties, I am aware of encouraging voices that murmur from the spirit realm. I sense a holy passion pouring down from the springs of Infinity. I thrill to music that beats with the pulses of God. Bound to suns and planets by invisible cords, I feel the flame of eternity in my soul. Here, in the midst of the every-day air, I sense the rush of ethereal rains. I am conscious of the splendour that binds all things of earth to all things of heaven - immured by silence and darkness, I possess the light which shall give me vision a thousandfold when death sets me free.

Helen Keller, *My Religion*

In a noisy world, let me listen for the melody.

8   NEW SPECTACLES
- Spiritual Vision - Seeing

8a   **Scarcely anyone, these days, can define the word 'spiritual' or grasp the idea that spirits might actually have human features. So new arrivals in the hereafter are quite bowled over to find themselves still in one piece, with their bodies apparently intact, and with all their senses still functioning normally. When they have pulled themselves together, they start to wonder why the church never told them about all this before**
- why, since everyone ends up there, was nothing ever explained about heaven and hell - why were there no visions to clinch the matter?

This could, in fact, have been easily arranged, had God so intended, but it would have done no good. People who have made up their minds that the soul is blown to the four winds at death are not likely to be convinced by visions - at least, not for long. Moreover, they would be in mortal danger because those who recognise the truth and then violate it are in extreme peril...

Earthly sight and spiritual sight are as different as evening and high-noon. The light of heaven is nothing less than divine truth, so angelic eyesight picks up every tiny detail. The angels enjoy keenness of understanding, and thus keenness of vision.

Heaven and Hell 456, 462a

8b   As with so much of his writing about the next world, Swedenborg here doesn't really tell us how it works: he simply tells us that it is so - take it or leave it. This is dogmatism. In deciding whether or not to take these ideas on board, we have to use our own wits, we have to look for logical patterns - to see whether it all adds up. I know he said he'd been there, but we only have his word for that.

However, I do take comfort from the obvious fact that we are also in the dark concerning all the psychological cogs and cogitations that nevertheless enable us to blunder about in *this* life. The most sophisticated brain scan cannot exhibit *precisely* what I am feeling or what I am thinking. It may pin-point *where* something is going on: it is unlikely to show exactly *what*. Consciousness - our spiritual eyesight - remains a mystery, and yet we use it all the time, here and now: we don't know how it works, but it is so.

As children we may have made magic spectacles with tinted cellophane: you put them on, or you take them off, and the world changes colour. Likewise, when we die, maybe it is not so much a matter of place, but of perception - a dimensional shift enabling us to take in our surroundings in a new light.

8c They brought to the Pharisees the man who had been blind. Now the day on which Jesus had made the mud and opened the man's eyes was a Sabbath. Therefore the Pharisees also asked him how he had received his sight. "He put mud on my eyes," the man replied, "and I washed, and now I see." Some of the Pharisees said, "This man is not from God, for he does not keep the Sabbath." But others asked, "How can a sinner do such miraculous signs?" So they were divided. Finally they turned again to the blind man, "What have you to say about him? It was your eyes he opened."

The man replied, "He is a prophet." The Jews still did not believe that he had been blind and had received his sight until they sent for the man's parents. "Is this your son?" they asked. "Is this the one you say was born blind? How is it that now he can see?" "We know he is our son," the parents answered, "and we know he was born blind. But how he can see now, or who opened his eyes, we don't know. Ask him. He is of age; he will speak for himself." His parents said this because they were afraid of the Jews, for already the Jews had decided that anyone who acknowledged that Jesus was the Christ would be put out of the synagogue. That was why his parents said, "He is of age; ask him."

A second time they summoned the man who had been blind. "Give glory to God," they said, "We know this man is a sinner." He replied, "Whether he is a sinner or not, I don't know. One thing I do know: I was blind but now I see!"

John 9, 13-25

8d   To see ourselves as others see us is a most salutary gift. Hardly less important is the capacity to see others as they see themselves. But what if these others belong to a different species and inhabit a radically alien universe? For example, how can the sane get to know what it actually feels like to be mad? Or, short of being born again as a visionary, a medium or a musical genius, how can we ever visit the worlds which, to Blake, to Swedenborg, to Johann Sebastian Bach, were home?...

For those who theoretically believe what in practice they know to be true - namely, that there is an inside to experience as well as an outside - the problems posed are real problems, all the more grave for being, some completely insoluble, some soluble only in exceptional circumstances and by methods not available to everyone. Thus it seems virtually certain that I shall never know what it feels like to be Sir John Falstaff or Joe Louis. On the other hand, it had always seemed to me possible that, through hypnosis, for example, or auto-hypnosis, by means of systematic meditation, or else by taking the appropriate drug, I might so change my ordinary mode of consciousness as to be able to know, from the inside, what the visionary, the medium, even the mystic were talking about.

Aldous Huxley, *The Doors of Perception*

8e   The forms of art are symbols of grace and bear witness to deeper revelations of being than do the unconscious forms of nature, such as the stars of crystals, the zebra's stripes, the whorls of the shell. Lovers of nature, in the ordinary sense, are seldom good judges of art... In art there is always something that is strange, alien to self-complacency, so many reject or misunderstand it.

'Although the world is fair to see
the artist will not let it be.
He fiddles with the works of God,
and makes them look uncommon odd.'

Margaret Bulley, *Art and Understanding*

8f   A nation needs a common vision, a shared dream. A dream which is
no-one's nightmare because it promises hope and life in a new way
for all. The message of Pentecost is that all people, young and old,
Jew and Gentile, black and white, rich and poor, are brought within
the scope of God's action through the Spirit. All people may be
transformed and so transcend the barriers of race and class which
divide nations and turn the dreams of some into the nightmares of
others. This is the promise of the gospel in our land, a vision of
righteousness and justice. Without such a shared vision the people
will perish, and all our dreams will become a nightmare.

John de Gruchy, *Cry Justice*

8g   There are many forms of visions and many ways of facilitating
them, yet visions remain among the most extraordinary phenomena
of the human mind. Perhaps an odder phenomenon still is that they
are seldom studied by psychologists.

Many of us have grown up in an atmosphere charged with tales
of biblical visions. Who among us familiar with the Bible has not
marvelled at Ezekiel's wheel within a wheel, or at Jacob's ladder, or
the entire book of Revelation? No wonder many of us consider these
ancient visionaries to be uncommon individuals with rare and
mysterious powers to commune with the divine.

These days many tend to pathologise visions. They assume that
people who say they have visions are schizophrenic, or delirious, or
even sociopathic. This perception is changing now, since a growing
number of demographic studies show that the visionary experience
is a common one in the *normal* population. Legions of people have
been having visions all along. They were simply reluctant to
mention them for fear of being labelled insane.

Raymond Moody, *Reunions*

**However satisfactory things may appear, give me the courage to
grant that there may be a new and better way of looking.**

---

9 PENTHOUSES AND PALACES
- Spiritual Architecture

9a There are houses in heaven, more or less prestigious according to the status of the occupants. The angels, after all, are real people living in organised social groups. I have chatted with them about their homes, and told them that people here can't imagine angelic properties, either because they just have never seen them, or because they confuse heaven with empty sky, and think of angels as ethereal forms flitting about in space.

But, speaking from experience, having myself set foot in their houses, I assure you that angels do have spacious well-designed apartments, better than ours, but still with rooms and surrounding gardens. Where there are close social links the town-planning is wonderful with streets, courtyards, walkways and open spaces as we have. I have strolled around and taken it all in with all my wits about me.

I have also seen palaces beyond description, glowing like gold above, and sparkling beneath like gemstones. Similarly inside, there were ornamental features which no words can describe. Outside were formal gardens with silvery leaves and golden fruit, and flower-beds like rainbows. More palaces could be seen in the distance. Heavenly buildings are the very epitome of architectural achievement. Angels have told me that God shows them many such marvels which are a delight to their minds rather than their eyes, because everything there has a divine meaning.

Heaven and Hell 183

9b Although Swedenborg moved among the aristocracy, and was no doubt perfectly at ease in a palace, his own pad in Stockholm was a modest little place with a timber-built house and a trim garden. His lodgings, when abroad, were simple, and his life-style frugal.

I can still detect a faint aroma of 18th.century wood-smoke wafting around his heavenly townscapes, too. There are plenty of stately mansions, not many hovels, and, of course, no multi-storey car-parks. His heavenly palaces, like those on earth, seem built to impress the populace by their outward appearance instead of offering comfort within. Bejewelled buildings are not really my scene.

I don't wish to imply, however, that Swedenborg imagined it all: I merely suggest that the actual building blocks of heaven are perhaps nothing less than the hopes and expectations - the aspirations of the people - 'angels' if you will. Their tastes maybe give automatic substance and reality to their surroundings. They literally see what suits them: so what? This is heaven, don't forget, and the reassuring thing is that we should feel *at home*.

9c   If these English houses of ours were all to be turned into institutional buildings, schools, asylums, hotels and the like, something of our national heritage of pride and beauty would be gone. Museums? A museum is a dead thing; a house which is still the home of men and women is a living thing which has not lost its soul. The soul of a house, the atmosphere of a house, are as much part of the house as the architecture of that house or as the furnishings within it. Divorced from its life, it dies. But if it keeps its life it means that the kitchen still provides food for the inhabitants: makes jam, puts fruit into bottles, stores the honey, dries the herbs, and carries on in the same tradition as has always obtained in the country. Useful things, practical things, keeping a number of people going throughout the year. So much for the house itself, but there is the outside life too; the life in which the landlord is a good landlord, assisting his farmers, keeping his cottages in good repair, adding modern labour-saving improvements, remitting the rent in a case of hardship, employing woodmen to cut trees for his own hearth and theirs.

V. Sackville-West, *English Country Houses*

9d   There is a queer stillness and a curious peaceful repose about the Etruscan places I have been to, quite different from the weirdness of Celtic places, the slightly repellent feeling of Rome and the old

Campagna, and the rather horrible feeling of the great pyramid places in Mexico, Teotihuacan and Cholula, and Mitla in the south; or the amiably idolatrous Buddha places in Ceylon. There is a stillness and a softness in these great grassy mounds with their ancient stone girdles, and down the central walk there lingers still a kind of homeliness and happiness. True, it was a still and sunny afternoon in April, and larks rose from the soft grass of the tombs. But there was a stillness and a soothingness in all the air, in that sunken place, and a feeling that it was good for one's soul to be there.

The same when we went down the few steps, and into the chambers of rock, within the tumulus. There is nothing left. It is like a house that has been swept bare: the inmates have left: now it waits for the next comer. But whoever it is that has departed, they have left a pleasant feeling behind them, warm to the heart, and kindly to the bowels.

They are surprisingly big and handsome, these homes of the dead. Cut out of the living rock, they are just like houses. The roof has a beam cut to imitate the roof-beam of the house. It is a house, a home.

D. H. Lawrence, *Etruscan Places*

9e   'Mid pleasures and palaces though we may roam,
Be it ever so humble, there's no place like home;
A charm from the sky seems to hallow us there,
Which, seek through the world, is ne'er met with elsewhere.
Home, Home, sweet, sweet Home!
There's no place like Home! there's no place like Home!

An exile from home, splendour dazzles in vain;
O, give me my lowly thatched cottage again!
The birds singing gaily, that came at my call,-
Give me them,- and the peace of mind, dearer than all!
Home, Home, sweet, sweet Home!
There's no place like Home! there's no place like Home!

How sweet 't is to sit 'neath a fond father's smile,
And the cares of a mother to soothe and beguile!
Let others delight 'mid new pleasuress to roam,
But give me, oh, give me, the pleasures of home!
Home, Home, sweet, sweet Home!
There's no place like Home! there's no place like Home!

To thee I'll return, overburdened with care;
The heart's dearest solace will smile on me there;
No more from that cottage again will I roam;
Be it ever so humble, there's no place like home.
Home, Home, sweet, sweet Home!
There's no place like Home! there's no place like Home!

John Howard Payne

9f   'The first thing we have to realise is that heaven is not something
      spiritual as some suppose, but something corporeal, made of some
      kind of matter and having form and substance... What joys could the
      saints' five senses have, if in heaven nothing could be seen except
      for a huge, immense space?' Consequently, God fills heaven with 'a
      real river, real trees, real fruit, and real flowers that please our
      vision, taste, smell, and touch in unsurpassable ways.' The blessed
      thus spend their days strolling 'about the heavenly flower-gardens
      and the heavenly meadows and fields, beholding and plucking those
      pleasant little flowers and all kinds of noble little plants.' The
      mansions of heaven are also real. The palace of Christ dominates the
      heavenly city, followed in diminishing splendour by the palace of
      the Virgin Mary, the twelve palaces of the apostles, and finally the
      palaces and mansions of the other saints.

                Friar Martin of Cochem (1634-1712), *Das grosse Leben Christi*
        (As quoted by Colleen McDannell and Bernhard Lang in *Heaven – a History*)

9g   Architecture is, like music, a metaphysical art; it deals with the
      abstract qualities of proportion, balance of form, and direction of
      line, but without any imitation of the concrete facts of nature. The
      comparison between architecture and music is an exercise of the

fancy which may indeed be pushed too far, but there is really a definite similarity between them which it is useful to notice. For instance, the regular rhythm, or succession of accentuated points in equal times, which plays so important a part in musical form, is discernible in architecture as a rhythm in space.

H. Heathcote Statham, *Architecture for General Readers*

May the tree-house of the mind, which I build for myself, be supported by living timbers, that I might make all the right connections.

10   VOICES OF ANGELS
- Spiritual Speech - Language and Communication

10a   **Angels chat about this and that, just as we do: they talk about their homes, civic and moral affairs, as well as spiritual matters. There's no difference, except that they are generally brighter than we are, and think more deeply. I have often enjoyed their company as a friend, sometimes as a stranger, but, being on the same wave-length it felt just like any ordinary earthly conversation.**

    Angels have mouths, tongues and ears, so they make sounds and form words. There is a spiritual atmosphere which suits them perfectly for breathing and speaking. There are no language barriers in heaven: thoughts and feelings spontaneously find a common tongue. The tone of the voice expresses feelings, whilst the ideas that arise are conveyed by its articulation into words.

    It's clear enough, if you think about it, that every thought has an intention, and every bright idea can be traced to some underlying motive. So angels can size-up someone just by the way he speaks: the sound quality lays bare what he loves, and the words betray his state of mind... Human language can scarcely compare with heavenly language, though I have heard that once, long ago, men did speak in similar fashion. Hebrew still bears traces of such an ancient tongue. Since angelic speech is an expression of love to God and to the neighbour, you see how eloquent it is, not only to the ear, but to the innermost mind.

Heaven and Hell 234-238

10b   Communication technology has come on a bit since Old Testament times, so I reckon we shall soon be in a position to have a shot at another Tower of Babel. This chattering globe, however, might do better to aim at some semblance of heaven at ground level. Our faith in sophisticated communication networks could be a driftnet that ensnares us into thinking that words and symbols are ends unto themselves. It's odd that electronic language should enable us to say so much, whilst we still cannot believe a half of what we are told. Every computer, I suggest, should, by law, be fitted with a divine lie detector, rather like a spell-checker, to filter out all the hogwash at the press of a button.

Swedenborg's heavenly observations are given as revealed fact - on that point he would never yield an inch. But, even if we cannot accept them on that level - even if he were simply using a literary device, like *Gulliver's Travels,* we should still have a lovely description of an ideal state of total honesty. Such a prospect of shared emotional transparency is surely something to be cherished. It may be unlikely yet to have much impact on international politics, but in this life where we are all so easily misunderstood, it is perhaps something to look forward to.

10c   Writing, too, must reflect the changes that happen to words in meaning and use. In the continual traffic of language words are lifted up or cast down; they come into fashion and then go out again; they graduate from the colloquial to the literary language; they lose or gain a figurative significance; they take on a new relationship with other words in the sentence. They are, in fact, living things, with all that that implies for those who use them, whether in writing or in speech.

G. H. Vallins, *Better English*

10d   And he came thither unto a cave, and lodged there; and, behold, the word of the Lord came to him, and he said unto him, What doest thou here, Elijah? And he said, I have been very jealous for the Lord God of hosts: for the children of Israel have forsaken thy covenant, thrown down thine altars, and slain thy prophets with the sword; and I, even I only, am left; and they seek my life, to take it away.

And he said, Go forth, and stand upon the mount before the Lord. And, behold, the Lord passed by, and a great and strong wind rent the mountains, and brake in pieces the rocks before the Lord; but the

Lord was not in the wind: and after the wind an earthquake; but the Lord was not in the earthquake: And after the earthquake a fire; but the Lord was not in the fire: and after the fire a still small voice.

And it was so, when Elijah heard it, that he wrapped his face in his mantle, and went out, and stood in the entering in of the cave. And, behold, there came a voice unto him, and said, What doest thou here, Elijah? And he said, I have been very jealous for the Lord God of hosts: because the children of Israel have forsaken thy covenant, thrown down thine altars, and slain thy prophets with the sword; and I, even I only, am left; and they seek my life, to take it away.

1 Kings 19, 9-14

10e Children beginning to talk frequently apply old names to new uses - sometimes with quaint and happy results. Whether this is due to what is too readily called imagination (not the same thing as invention) or to a poverty of their linguistic resources may not be so easily settled. In the writer's opinion there is no necessity for a romantic explanation in the majority of instances. Occasionally, however, the novel effect produced is obviously due to accident rather than to design: as, for example, in the following cases where different children were heard to speak of shoes on the wrong feet as making the feet look *cross-eyed*, of a pen making thick lines by opening its *beak*, of the penguin who *stood up* sitting down, of the parrot with a lump of sugar in his claw as having a *hand* on one leg and a foot on the other, and so on. But the child who asked his nurse after a bath not to rub him but *blot* him and the child who spoke of an echo as the *shadow* of the sound were doing something more than just using words incompetently but still with unforeseen novelty of effect.

A.F.Watts, *The Language and Mental Development of Children*

10f Socrates pinpointed our ambivalence towards writing in his story of the Egyptian God Thoth, the inventor of writing, who came to see the king seeking royal blessing on his enlightened invention. The king told Thoth: 'You, who are the father of letters, have been led by your affection to ascribe to them a power the opposite of that which they really possess... You have invented an elixir not of memory, but of reminding; and you offer your pupils the appearance of wisdom, not true wisdom, for they will read many things without instruction and will therefore seem to know many things, when they are for the most part ignorant.' In a late 20th-century world drenched with written information and surrounded by information technologies of astonishing speed, convenience and power, these words spoken in antiquity have a distinctly contemporary ring.

Andrew Robinson, *The Story of Writing*

10g   Yes, there's a powerful, dreaming holiness around Lindisfarne. It drifts through the great sea winds, through those wide stretches of sand dotted by pools and the curling mounds of the lugworm. You can hear it even in the fluting calls of the sandpipers, in the flapping wings of the stork pinning a beautiful arc of flight against the clear sky and the low distant roar of the incoming tide.

But, most of all, holiness is not suggested by a great edifice which had taken hundreds of years and thousands of lives to build. Here, on Lindisfarne, it is etched across our minds by the line of old, broken sticks stretching across the sands to mark out Pilgrim's Way. Holiness is always best expressed by the simple, the humble and the poor. And here those sticks sing a song of holiness to the sea winds; they surround the journeying pilgrim with the very music of the Cross as he makes his way across the softly sinking sand to Holy Island itself.

Tom Davies, *Stained Glass Hours*

With so many words at my disposal, teach me to use them wisely, with honesty and compassion.

11   A HOMELY LANDSCAPE
- Spiritual Topography

11a   Whatever turns you on here has its exact counterpart in the
hereafter, as I have seen for myself. Those who have deliberately
rejected the Bible and the Church, and have revelled in evil,
shun the light of heaven and hide away in caves and crevices,
seeking the dark. They become quite agoraphobic. Those who
harbour crafty machinations do the same, muttering dark
schemes to one another: they like it that way.

Those who have steeped themselves in worldly studies, piling
up information simply to impress other people, likewise take no
pleasure in the open fields, but much prefer arid deserts.
Doctrinal experts who have made no attempt to practise what
they preach have no patience with gardening but grovel among
the rocks and surround themselves with heaps of stones, and
those who have become famous by stealth devote themselves to
magic.

Those, however, who have lived and loved in the light of
heaven find themselves bathed in heavenly sunlight, and in that
light they enjoy inward perception, whilst outwardly they see
living forms which embody truth from God, and which reflect
their hearts' desire.

Those who have loved truth itself, from no devious motive,
dwell in sunny uplands enjoying a vernal climate, and looking
out over cornfields and vineyards. The view from their windows
is crystal clear, and inside their houses there is a gem-like
luminosity about everything. All these things - fields, vineyards,
gems and crystals - are biblical expressions of heavenly qualities,
so those who have loved biblical verities immediately recognise
them in their new angelic environment. Everything is alive with
laughter and meaning.

Those of an intellectual turn of mind, who have not turned
their backs on God, but delight in goodness and truth, occupy
formal gardens all neatly set out with ever-changing rows of

trees and plants. By subtle variations of heavenly meaning, they are a constant source of inspiration. Those for whom nature is merely God's toolbox, so to speak, see everything suffused with light and colour, wherein they perceive an aurora of interior delights.

Heaven and Hell 488, 489

11b   If we are being told that the bad guys always end up living like cavemen, and the virtuous inescapably inherit lush tracts of sunlit parkland, then Swedenborg's descriptions are no more convincing than Dante's - and rather less imaginative.

Swedenborg's own travels and personal tastes inevitably colour his view of the next world. The lifestyles of future generations could scarcely be taken into account. *Star Trek* had not yet expanded our expectations of new dimensions.

But this is beside the point. We can forget the old idea that everyone gets what's coming to them, whether they like it or not: the notion that we each create our own spiritual landscape is infinitely more plausible. We are not being offered a fixed agenda, however it may seem, but an on-going atonement with our own personal surroundings - an environment that inevitably reflects our innermost desires. So, although in my case I don't count myself among the cave dwellers, I do hope to be spared the bright lights also.

11c   I lie here and feel Earth rustling through space, its rotundity between me and the sun, the shadow above me acting as a searchlight to reveal the stars whose light left them long before there were eyes on this planet to receive it. Now the two little globes of my eyes, unlit in the darkness, look up at their shining globes, and who shall say that we do not gaze at one another, affect one another?

Jacquetta Hawkes, *A Land*

11d   Landscape has two faces, the open and the secret. The immediate impact of a skyline fringed with elms, stark and fragile in winter, dense and stooping in summer; skies ridged with cloud, scattered with rooks and lapwings; the blaze of a church spire among summer-heavy chestnuts; spare, stripped winter fields edged with rusty docks and skeletal heads of cow-parsley. And, behind and beyond this, the hidden clues about why, and who, and when. Why a field is shaped like this, or a green road runs between hedges and abruptly stops, and who first farmed this land, and when this village began to die, and this one to prosper. Begin to ask these questions, and you never cease. Places are never quite the same again. You see them on two different levels. You watch the shifting light that changes the mood of a piece of country from season to season and from hour to hour, from the dark greens and bright golds of high summer to the misty receding greys of winter, and at the same time you see a hedge or a twist in a road that you never noticed before, and are sent back to the maps and the books to try to find out when, and how...

Penelope Lively, *An Ancient Place*

11e   Home! That was what they meant, those caressing appeals, those soft touches wafted through the air, those invisible little hands pulling and tugging, all one way! Why, it must be quite close by him at that moment, his old home that he had hurriedly forsaken and never sought again, that day when he first found the river! And now it was sending out its scouts and its messengers to capture him and bring him in. Since his escape on that bright morning he had hardly given it a thought, so absorbed had he been in his new life, in all its pleasures, its surprises, its fresh and captivating experiences. Now, with a rush of old memories, how clearly it stood up before him, in the darkness! Shabby indeed, and small and poorly furnished, and yet his, the home he had made for himself, the home he had been so happy to get back to after his day's work. And the home had been happy with him, too, evidently, and was missing him, and wanted him back, and was telling him so, through his nose, sorrowfully, reproachfully, but with no bitterness or anger; only with a plaintive reminder that it was there, and wanted him.

     The call was clear, the summons was plain. He must obey it instantly, and go. 'Ratty!' he called, full of joyful excitement, 'hold on! Come back! I want you, quick!'

Kenneth Graham, *The Wind in the Willows*

11f A brilliant November morning with a sky of diamond blue above the
     bay and the red flowers of a long summer still glowing darkly on the
     Rock. The intense blackness of the lampless night had rolled away
     to reveal, incandescent on the northern horizon, the country we had
     come to seek. It crouched before us in a great ring of lion-coloured
     mountains, raw, sleeping and savage. There were the scarred and
     crumpled valleys, the sharp peaks wreathed in their dusty fires, and
     below them the white towns piled high on their little hills and the
     empty roads running crimson along the faces of the cliffs. Already,
     across the water, one heard, or fancied one heard, the sobbing of
     asses, the cries and salty voices cutting through the thin gold air.
     And from a steep hillside rose a column of smoke, cool as marble,
     pungent as pine, which hung like a signal over the landscape,
     obscure, imperative and motionless.

                                                 Laurie Lee, *A Rose for Winter*

11g The July sun shone over Egdon and fired its crimson heather to
     scarlet. It was the one season of the year, and the one weather of the
     season, in which the heath was gorgeous. This flowering period
     represented the second or noontide division in the cycle of those
     superficial changes which alone were possible here; it followed the
     green or young-fern period, representing the morn, and preceded the
     brown period, when the heath-bells and ferns would wear the russet
     tinges of evening; to be in turn displaced by the dark hue of the
     winter period, representing night.

                                    Thomas Hardy, *The Return of the Native*

**Long may the ever-changing contours of the mind give shape
and variety to my life. Let me never be groundless, nor let me
forget the promise of a place of my own.**

12 THE ETERNAL JOB CENTRE
- Spiritual Employment - Uses

12a Everyone in heaven has some occupation: no-one is useless. Any layabout who prefers to remain idle is not tolerated. Newcomers are given a job and a house to go with it, the more prestigious nearer to the town centre. Job satisfaction is no problem: everyone enjoys his work. They shun idleness like the plague because they love being useful in their various ways, contributing to the common good and inspired by a general spirit of community. Heavenly society has any number of spiritual pursuits which defy earthly description.

As in a living body, the bloodstream serves every part, and every part contributes to the whole - so with society: it is an excellent arrangement.

A person is truly 'charitable' when he asks for nothing better than to get on with his daily work from the sheer love of being useful. (Even in hell, they work, but not because they want to.) When professional integrity is a person's chief delight, however, that is a hallmark of real charity, but he must first approach God and avoid evil.

Now what about priests, governors, civil servants, judges, army commanders, officers, common soldiers, businessmen, workmen, farmers, ships'captains, sailors and servants? *[Swedenborg then sets down the priorities in each of these occupations.]*

Charity 137, 138, 142, 146, 158

12b Swedenborg's sociology may be a bit primitive, but it is none the worse for that. It does no harm to be brought back to basics, or to be reminded that human happiness hangs on a need to feel useful. His job list mentions no actors, dentists, journalists or computer programmers, but I think we can probably work out for ourselves what their responsibilities might be.

What we cannot always work out is what spiritual counterparts there may be in a heavenly society. Angels don't suffer from corns and bunions, surely, so what, for example, will the chiropodists do, I wonder. Maybe their function in the celestial economy is to regulate the zeal of those who too easily lose touch with the practicalities of life - whose feet seldom touch the ground. We can only speculate, but the notion that we each have a niche in the heavenly job market is a comfort indeed.

In this technological new world of ours, we need more than ever to be told that the individual still counts - that there are eternal uses on offer, even for the so-called 'unemployed'.

2c   It is convenient for a husband to have sheep of his own, for many causes, and then may his wife have part of the wool, to make her husband and herself some clothes. And at the least way, she may have the locks of the sheep, either to make clothes or blankets and coverlets, or both. And if she have no wool of her own, she may take wool to spin of cloth-makers, and by that means she may have a convenient living, and many times do other works. It is a wife's occupation, to winnow all manner of corns, to make malt, to wash and wring, to make hay, shear corn, and in time of need to help her husband to fill the muck-wain or dung-cart, drive the plough, to load hay, corn and such other. And to go or ride to the market, to sell butter, cheese, milk, eggs, chickens, capons, hens, pigs, geese, and all manner of corns. And also to buy all manner of necessary things belonging to household, and to make a true reckoning and account to her husband, what she hath paid. And if the husband go to the market, to buy or sell, as they oft do, he then to show his wife in like manner. For if one of them should use to deceive the other, he deceiveth himself, and he is not likely to thrive. And therefore they must be true either to other.

John Fitzherbert *Wife and Husband, (1523)*

2d   Man goeth forth unto his work and to his labour until the evening. O Lord, how manifold are thy works! in wisdom hast thou made them all: the earth is full of thy riches. So is this great and wide sea, wherein are things creeping innunerable, both small and great beasts. There go the ships: there is that leviathan, whom thou hast made to play therein. These wait all upon thee; that thou mayest give them their meat in due season. That thou givest them they gather: thou openest thine hand, they are filled with good. Thou hidest thy face, they are troubled: thou takest away their breath, they die, and return to their dust. Thou sendest forth thy spirit, they are created: and thou renewest the face of the earth.

Psalm 104, 23-30

12e   We pray thee for those who bear authority in our towns and cities: that they may devote themselves to the common good, and that the skill and beauty of art and craft may be drawn into the service of our common life, for thy glory and the delight of man. Give them inspiration and courage, O God, to sweep away all mean streets and unworthy dwellings, and in all ways to forward the health and strength of thy people.

Anon. *New Every Morning*

12f   From our point of view, the most relevant parts of the Rule are those concerned with the running of the monastery: the arrangement of the dormitories, hours of sleep, numbers of lights to be kept burning; the times of meals, what is to be eaten and how much, cooking, serving; caring for the sick; the entertainment of guests; distribution of charity; amount and type of clothing, laundry and extra clothes for journeys; rules for novices and new members; punishments; delegation of authority (the abbot was elected by the monks and although sovereign was expected to consult them before taking any important decision); the upkeep of the church and buildings; security against attack and so on. St.Benedict omits nothing...

Ian Richards, *Abbeys of Europe*

12g   He walked through the warm sun westward into those tracts of Egdon with which he was best acquainted, being those lying nearer to his old home. He saw before him in one of the valleys the gleaming of whetted iron, and advancing, dimly perceived that the shine came from the tool of a man who was cutting furze. The worker recognised Clym, and Yeobright learnt from the voice that the speaker was Humphrey

Humphrey expressed his sorrow at Clym's condition; and added, 'Now, if yours was low-class work like mine, you could go on with it just the same.'

'Yes; I could,' said Yeobright musingly. 'How much do you get for cutting these faggots?'

'Half-a-crown a hundred, and in these long days I can live very well on the wages.'

During the whole of Yeobright's walk home to Alderworth he was lost in reflections which were not of an unpleasant kind. On his coming up to the house Eustacia spoke to him from the open window, and he went across to her.

'Darling,' he said, 'I am much happier. And if my mother were reconciled to me and to you I should, I think, be happy quite.'

'I fear that will never be,' she said, looking afar with her beautiful stormy eyes. 'How *can* you say "I am happier," and nothing changed?'

'It arises from my having at last discovered something I can do, and get a living at, in this time of misfortune.'

'Yes?'

'I am going to be a furze and turf cutter.'

Thomas Hardy, *The Return of the Native*

Whether or not we follow any trade, calling or profession, may we hold to the prospect of an eternal dynamic, wherein we each have a part to play.

---

13 ESCAPE FROM TIME AND SPACE
- The Unknown Dimension

13a **To live in this world you need two things - time and space. In the next life, however, they no longer apply. New arrivals, in the world of spirits, bring natural ideas with them so, at first, there is a kind of space/time feeling, but eventually they catch on to the fact that time and space don't exist any more - only 'states'.**

This is utterly incomprehensible to us, of course, but the angels of heaven are different - they don't think in terms of space and time at all - they have left all that behind. When people on earth are asleep they may experience a kind of dream-time which is more to do with 'state' than with ordinary everyday time.

There are two main states - one to do with 'being' or 'goodness', and one to do with 'demonstration' or 'truth'. The first feels a bit like space, and the second rather like time. But the angels discern deeper meanings that would simply never occur to us.

Arcana Caelestia 2625, 4814

13b Swedenborg and his translators seem to get themselves into more of a tangle with this space/time thing than with any other issue. Hardly surprising, I suppose, since they are trying to use sequential words to talk about non-sequential states.

We all know perfectly well that everything that happens here takes time - even if only a split second. Without time, nothing would happen. Space is not quite such a problem because big thoughts and little thoughts obviously don't take up any room. Even so, thinking in a spatial vacuum is far from comfortable.

But surely this is something we should neither *expect* nor want to understand: it would be a disappointment if we could. For what we are being told is that there is another dimension that we, here, cannot begin to grasp. So when I am terrified alike by the prospects of mortality *and* immortality, I can at least take refuge in the suggestion of a new kind of existence altogether. If the limitations of time and space are a mental treadmill from which, at death, we actually escape, I could settle for that.

13c   The first pale brush strokes of the coming day
Stretched across the night
Stretched and spread, until the world
Stirred from its sleep.
And in the greyness of that time
Between the oblivion of the night and wide-eyed day,
A thrush threw, into the stillness,
Its summons to the light.
Echoing its song
As if it might forget that first careless phrase.
And to that summons
Your spirit rose, and soared into its dawn
Beyond the place, where once you strode
Strong and tall,
Your step firm and purposeful,
Knowing its direction.
Greeting fellow travellers along the way
With open-hearted warmth and twinkling eye.
And, pied-piper like, your music called
And drew its hearers into your world,
Until they were lifted
Beyond the levelled dullness of the day,
And for a while, paused
In a place where all was harmony

Now has that music stopped.
Nothing but silence remains
Where once the air was full of sound.
But in that silence
The thrush sings on.

Gwen Bowen (Knight), *Journey into Dawn*
(On the death of Bernard Knight)

13d Sitting somewhere in this huge mathematical space are humans and hyenas, amoebas and aardvarks, flatworms and squids, dodos and dinosaurs. In theory, if we were skilled enough at genetic engineering, we could move from any point in animal space to any other point. From any starting point we could move through the maze in such a way as to recreate the dodo, the tyrannosaur and trilobites. If only we knew which genes to tinker with, which bits of chromosome to duplicate, invert or delete. I doubt if we shall ever know enough to do it, but these dear dead creatures are lurking there forever in their private corners of that huge genetic hypervolume, waiting to be *found* if we but had the knowledge to navigate the right course through the maze. We might even be able to *evolve* an exact reconstruction of a dodo by selectively breeding pigeons, though we'd have to live a million years in order to complete the experiment. But when we are prevented from making a journey in reality, the imagination is not a bad substitute.

Richard Dawkins, *The Blind Watchmaker*

13e For most of us, it is impossible to relate the recondite problems of mathematics or quantum mechanics to any kind of everyday experience. If the first requirement for explaining something is that you should *understand* it, no wonder that most of us have difficulty in thinking of things that we cannot imagine. Perhaps the skill that distinguishes an Einstein or a Newton from the rest of us is a very rare ability to translate the most abstract of concepts - gravity, time, infinity - into models that can be manipulated in the mind. An important point here is that the models that we make are enriched by our general knowledge of the world around us: the more that we already know, the more that we are able to know how to know. And the operations that we perform on the models that we make in our mind can be far from the cold rules of logic and statistics. Tolstoy once wrote that if human beings controlled their lives on the basis of pure reason, all chance of spontaneity would be lost.

Colin Blakemore, *The Mind Machine*

13f Now, one intriguing aspect of Big Bang and Kabbalah is that Kabbalah conceives of such a thing - a God who inheres in the universe - precisely in a structure that resembles the cosmological model. In Kabbalah, as in Hartle and Hawking's conception, the whole of space and time is imagined (though in a different sense, of course), but one does not look someplace else for the deity. The deity is *here*. Hawking speaks of God's creation as a thing that is somehow *apart* from God. But what Big Bang and Kabbalah suggest is that it may rather be *a part* of God. If the Kabbalistic view of creation really is, in some way, in tune with what we have learned through cosmology, that fact is fascinating, momentous, and worth pursuing. But even if it is just a coincidental overlap of images, we learn from it that, in the model that we now have from science, the deity need not be looked for *outside* of the universe. In the Kabbalistic conception, God is *in* the universe (and the universe is in God).

Richard Elliott Friedman, *The Disappearance of God*

13g So life's sad at times, but it is not a tragedy. If it were that, it would be absurd; and as a wise priest once said to me: 'We give ourselves away all the time - even atheists - we do not act as if life were absurd.' And surely one cannot whistle in the dark continuously for three score years and ten. Most of us sense, I think, that we have a purpose, even if we are not quite sure what it is. Seeing it is God's purpose, having to do with some further existence, it is unlikely that we should be sure. I think it involves developing our faculties of love, which we shall need wherever we're going... To be unable to love is close to being in Hell.

Gerald Priestland, *The Tragedy of Life*

While space probes can only explore time and space, may we never stop probing for another way out of those things that ensnare us.

14   MAYBE THE DICE ARE LOADED
- Planning and Providence - Chaos/Order

14a **God's overseeing providence is universal, covering every microscopic particular. God misses nothing, however minute. Since order itself proceeds from the Almighty and pervades the entire universe, that must include every sub-atomic particle, not forgetting 'the very hairs of your head,' which, as it says in the Bible, 'are all numbered.'**

Providence has its sights on what is infinite and everlasting, its main preoccupation and purpose being the formation of a heaven peopled by human beings. This requires their 'regeneration' - the achievement of a God-like combination of goodness and truth.

However, anyone who looks to God only when things go badly wrong, is unlikely to be regenerated, because the man's freedom is then impaired. When things take a turn for the better, he may revert to a state in which he could scarcely care less. A genuinely 'God-fearing' character will always be afraid of offending against God.

So when things get desperate, as in battles, duels, shipwrecks, falls, fires, financial collapse, redundancy and so on, then any thoughts of God are usually just a matter of self-preservation, which is a kind of mental straitjacket. But people are only reformed when they are in their right mind.

Arcana Caelestia 1919, 2694
Divine Providence 56-59, 148

14b The idea that God is doing his best to protect me from falling rocks, slippery road surfaces or dodgy brakes seems slightly ridiculous to me, because, however successful he may have been in my case, he has clearly failed concerning countless others, less fortunate. Such a naïve view of providence is incompatible with all the ghastly suffering that is plainly rife in this hazardous world: in any case, it is inconsistent with free-will. Could anyone be free with God constantly holding him by the hand?

Providence simply doesn't work like that. God may *take account* of the minutiae of everyday life, but he won't interfere: his providence doesn't apparently *operate* at that level: its concern is with higher things. Our little corner of the universe might have been all nice and tidy until man got his hands on it, I don't know, but God's first priority now, I suggest, is to preserve spiritual order *despite* natural chaos. Should we all be blown to bits tomorrow, our spiritual prospects would remain intact - if that's any comfort!

Swedenborg seems to be saying that providence is *super*natural - that the evils of this life are somehow noted and circumscribed or contained. So, if the dice are loaded, then in the long run they are loaded in our favour.

14c   I lift up my eyes to the hills - where does my help come from? My help comes from the Lord, the maker of heaven and earth. He will not let your foot slip - he who watches over you will not slumber; indeed, he who watches over Israel will neither slumber nor sleep. The Lord watches over you - the Lord is your shade at your right hand; the sun will not harm you by day, nor the moon by night. The Lord will keep you from all harm - he will watch over your life; the Lord will watch over your coming and going both now and for evermore.

Psalm 121

14d   From a long way off I heard the sound of an express train - racing towards where I was standing. My brain could only register surprise that the sound of a train, all that way beneath me in Folkestone, should carry so far, and so loudly - when, with a roar, the huge cross-Channel shell burst in the sloping field just below me. I remember the light, even brighter than the hazy sun, and then the blast wave threw me backwards, and I landed on my back in the long grass at the edge of the airfield. The rise of the ground had sheltered me, just as the thick foliage of the orchard's trees had diverted the explosion of the buzzbomb at White Gates.

The stink of picric acid and high-explosive predominated as I slowly sat up, feeling myself for injuries. Only then did I realise that I was stone deaf. Even that minor inconvenience passed in a couple of hours, but I did feel shaky for a few days.

I only mention these odd scuffles with the 'Fates' because they more than ever convinced me that there was something, or someone, keeping an eye on me. Had I walked over the rise, instead of just standing below it, trying to remember why it was that I could see the panoramic view which before the war had been hidden, I would have been much nearer the blast and undoubtedly would have been blown to pieces.

Michael Bentine, *The Door Marked Summer*

14e   Pangloss taught metaphysico-theologo-cosmolo-nigology. He proved incontestably that there is no effect without a cause, and that in this best of all possible worlds, his lordship's country seat was the most beautiful of mansions and her ladyship the best of all possible ladyships.

'It is proved,' he used to say, 'that things cannot be other than they are, for since everything was made for a purpose, it follows that everything is made for the best purpose. Observe: our noses were made to carry spectacles, so we have spectacles. Legs were clearly intended for breeches, and we wear them. Stones were meant for carving and for building houses, and that is why my lord has a most beautiful house; for the greatest baron in Westphalia ought to have the noblest residence. And since pigs were made to be eaten, we eat pork all the year round. It follows that those who maintain that all is right talk nonsense; they ought to say that all is for the best.'

Voltaire, *Candide*

14f   One night a man had a dream. He dreamt he was walking along the beach with his Lord. Across the sky flashed scenes from his life. For each scene he noticed two sets of footprints in the sand, one belonging to him, the other to the Lord. When the last scene in his life flashed before him he looked back at the footprints on the sand. He noticed that many times along the path of his life there was only one set of footprints. He also noticed that it happened at the very lowest and saddest times of his life. This really bothered him, and he questioned the Lord about it. 'Lord, you said that, once I decided to follow you, you would walk with me all the way. But I've noticed that during the most difficult times in my life there is only one set of footprints. I don't understand why, in times when I needed you most, you would leave me.' The Lord replied, 'My precious child, I love you and would never leave you during your trials and sufferings; when you see only one set of footprints, it was then that I carried you.'

Margaret Fishback Powers, *Footprints*

14g There is a story of a man who prayed earnestly one morning for grace to overcome his besetting sin of impatience. A little later he missed a train by half a minute and spent an hour stamping up and down the station platform in furious vexation. Five minutes before the next train came in he suddenly realised that here had been the answer to his prayer. He had been given an hour to practise the virtue of patience; he had missed the opportunity and wasted the hour. There are also many stories of men who have similarly missed trains which have been wrecked, and who ascribe their escape to providence. If they are combining the thought of God as the celestial chess-player with the thought of God as pre-eminently concerned in their enjoyment of earthly life at the expense of others, there is not much to be said for their point of view. But if they are humbly acknowledging a call to further service on earth before they pass beyond, they are rightly interpreting their escape. In all probability all the events which led up to all these men missing their various trains could be adequately accounted for in terms of the interaction of natural law, human freedom, and divine grace. But at the very point within the interaction God sees what are its possibilities for good, and the man who shares his enlightenment and his power and gives himself to make that good come true, has found the meaning of that moment and his 'special providence'. The gates of the future are indeed open, the universe is in the making. But only if made aright can the making stand.... The end is sure, for he who at every moment in the process sees its possibilities for good is God omnipotent - omnipotent to turn all circumstances to good account, to turn today's defeat into tomorrow's victory. But this omnipotence will never be so exercised as to substitute the external compulsion of men for the internal eliciting of their freedom.

Leonard Hodgson, *Essays in Christian Philosophy*

We seem to have made the world a dangerous place in which to live. May we find strength to repair the damage wherever we can, but when that is beyond us, grant us to know that all is not lost.

15   'MALE AND FEMALE CREATED HE THEM'
- Marriage - Heavenly Nuptials

15a   **Everything in creation, from an angel to a worm, is an embodiment of goodness and truth in one form or another. These two components are united in one universal 'conjugial sphere' proceeding from God. The marriage of goodness and truth is the source of all fruitfulness, and of the reproductive impulse. The male and female forms each partake differently of this universal sphere - the male in his understanding, he being the more intellectual; and the female in her will, she being the more affectional. Sexual love can be traced to the same source.**

To see this difference between the sexes I have only to look at the children in the street outside. The boys make a great racket, setting about one another with fists and stones: the girls sit peacefully on doorsteps, with their dolls, or doing needlework. Oddly enough, they watch all the rumpus with obvious satisfaction. This is where it all starts. It's easy to see where an aggressive intellect could lead without a woman's love.

Conjugial Love 92, 218[2]

15b   Swedenborg's rather domesticated view of women's rôle in society would definitely *not* go down well with today's feminists. His 18th.century children are a bit quaint, too. His 'conjugial' principle, however, still makes sense, and after all, he does identify women as the motivators: men, to put it very simply, are the investigators. We can all think of exceptions, but the plain fact that human beings come in two sorts does make life infinitely more entertaining. Men and women don't just look different - they *are* different, as recent brain research tends to confirm.

By tracing sex back to the divine attributes of goodness and truth, Swedenborg points to an essential duality in practically everything. Marriage, then, is a gradual coming together - a unique combination or fusion, formed as each partner develops qualities which are distinctly their own. Maybe life's jigsaw is a gradual coming together in more senses than one.

15c   Let me not to the marriage of true minds
Admit impediments. Love is not love
Which alters when it alteration finds,
Or bends with the remover to remove:
O, no! It is an ever fixed mark,
That looks on tempests and is never shaken,
It is the star to every wandering bark,
Whose worth's unknown, although his height be taken
Love's not Time's fool, though rosy lips and cheeks
Within his bending sickle's compass come;
Love alters not, with his brief hours and weeks,
But bears it out even to the edge of doom.
If this be error and upon me proved,
I never writ, nor no man ever loved.

William Shakespeare, Sonnet 116

15d   Marriage love is the gift of the Lord. It comes to us with our very life. Jesus said, 'He who made them from the beginning made them male and female, and said, For this reason shall a man leave his father and mother and be joined to his wife, and the two shall become one flesh.' The Lord has created us men and women so that we may know the joy of marriage and see our happiness in the life of another. In true marriage, a wife comes to love her husband's wisdom and true purpose, while the husband comes to love his wife's affection and unselfish ideals. Each is then drawn away from self into a truer relationship of loving service. Neither seeks to dominate or control the other, but to love what the other thinks and wills. Such a union cannot be based on the personal ambition or selfish desires of either of them. It can only grow from a mutual heavenly desire to help and care for others. This is why children are born as the Lord's gift to the love of a husband and wife, because a helpless baby can be cared for and helped to grow into life. Thus marriage love becomes the centre of a home.

From the Marriage Service, Book of Worship

5e   Then Almitra spoke again and said, And what of Marriage, master?
And he answered saying:
You were born together, and together you shall be for evermore.
You shall be together when the white wings of death scatter your
days.
Aye, you shall be together even in the silent memory of God.
But let there be spaces in your togetherness.
And let the winds of the heavens dance between you.

Love one another, but make not a bond of love:
Let it rather be a moving sea between the shores of your souls.
Fill each other's cup but drink not from one cup.
Give one another of your bread but eat not from the same loaf.
Sing and dance together and be joyous, but let each one of you be
alone,
Even as the strings of a lute are alone though they quiver with
the same music.
Give your hearts, but not into each other's keeping.
For only the hand of Life can contain your hearts.
And stand together yet not too near together:
For the pillars of the temple stand apart,
And the oak tree and the cypress grow not in each other's shadow.

Kahlil Gibran, The Prophet

5f   Only modern psychology rediscovered the wisdom that life is so
much bigger than the narrow scope of Reason, and that the real
problems of Life cannot be thought out by pure reason but must be
solved by the immanent logic of Life and by its intrinsic laws of
growth. For women all this is self-evident, and it is an alluring
speculation that to women has been assigned the task of taking
Life's revenge on Reason: women tell the 'Truth', they know what
really 'is'. Men tell the 'correct' thing, that can be proved, and when
practically applied furnishes useful results. Men approach reality
only through the medium of reason, and only that section of reality
is accessible to them that can be grasped by reasoning...

With women knowing and being coincide, both are the same
function, whereas it is given to men only to 'know', for which

reason they can never, unaided, get down to reality, to the being, to the 'thing as such'. This aid they get from women.

Oswald Schwarz, *The Psychology of Sex*

15g I sit high, high up in the mountains. The most incredible snowy peaks panoramically displayed before my eyes. So many, many times in the past I felt your large body beside me as we gazed in wonder at this magnificence before us.

Oh, Job, Job. Where are you now? Do you also see this from another dimension? I cannot conceive of you not being here in some form or other. You, who so delighted in the majesty of these pristine peaks. You would not, could not miss the opportunity of once more feasting your eyes on this splendour, of sharing this moment with me. If only I could be sure that it is possible to drift through the spheres, that this comforting presence I so often feel is really you.

Kay van Dijk, *Can I Let You Go, My Love ?*
(Originally set as verse)

There is magnetism in this revolving earth : may we always be aware of an enduring magnetism between people.

16   ZOOLOGICAL GARDENS
- Animals and Birdsong

16a   **Everything on earth has a spiritual meaning - trees, animals, birds, fish - everything. Long long ago those who had more than an inkling of all this liked to surround themselves with carvings and models of such things to remind them of heaven. They displayed these in their temples and in their homes, not as idols, but simply to represent religious ideas. So in ancient Egypt they made calves, oxen, snakes, children, old men, young women and suchlike. Calves and oxen stood for natural affections and abilities, snakes represented the shrewdly sensual, children meant innocence and charity, old men wisdom, young women affections for truth and so on.**

Then the meanings were forgotten, and people got it into their heads that the statues erected by their ancestors must be somehow holy in themselves, so they began to make gods of them.

Holy places were also chosen for their meanings - hills and mountains because they represented the heavens, gardens and orchards because of the wisdom they stood for, and the trees they contained. The olive meant the goodness of love, the vine truth thus derived, and the cedar rationality in respect of goodness and truth.

Animal species all refer to varieties of human affection and thought, or, if you like, to love and faith. In the next life all manner of animals appear according to the affections and thoughts of angels and spirits.

True Christian Religion 205 [1] *Arcana Caelestia 10,042*

16b   To the casual observer, the natural world appears to have serious design faults - volcanoes, icebergs, disease, ferocious and poisonous animals, not to mention all the additional hazards introduced by man. The creator, we may feel, could perhaps have made a better job of it.

I am particularly upset when I see how so many animal species prevail only by slaughtering and eating one another. I ask myself could not the Almighty have devised some better system? Where is the peaceable kingdom?

Swedenborg's momentous claim that the animal realm originates in the pitiful menagerie of *human* notions and emotions does put the whole situation on a rather different footing. Our own thoughts and feelings clearly prey on one another as we go through life. If the animals are inevitably acting out a whole range of carnal passions, they may be powerless to resolve their differences until we resolve ours.

16c   In the six hundredth year of Noah's life, in the second month, the seventeenth day of the month, the same day were all the fountains of the great deep broken up, and the windows of heaven were opened. And the rain was upon the earth forty days and forty nights. In the selfsame day entered Noah, and Shem, and Ham, and Japheth, the sons of Noah, and Noah's wife, and the three wives of his sons with them, into the ark; they, and every beast after his kind, and all the cattle after their kind, and every creeping thing that creepeth upon the earth after his kind, and every fowl after his kind, every bird of every sort. And they went in unto Noah into the ark, two and two of all flesh, wherein is the breath of life. And they that went in, went in male and female of all flesh, as God had commanded him: and the Lord shut him in. And the flood was forty days upon the earth; and the waters increased, and bare up the ark, and it was lift up above the earth. And the waters prevailed, and were increased greatly upon the earth; and the ark went upon the face of the waters.

Genesis 7, 11-18

16d   An enraged elephant broke loose one dark night, at an encampment near Cawnpore, and ran wild among the tents, roaring and trumpeting with his trunk, and driving before him men, women, children, camels, cows, and horses. He was followed in his flight by swordsmen and spearmen, who shouted and vociferated; but regardless of the clamour he still ran on, pushing down the tents, upsetting everything that impeded his progress, wounding and injuring many, and at last killing his keeper with a blow of his enormous trunk. The moment the poor man fell, and the elephant saw that he did not rise, he suddenly stopped, seemed concerned, looked at him with an eye of pity, and stood riveted to the spot. He paused for a few seconds, then ran towards the place from whence he had broken loose, and went quietly to his station, in front of which lay a little girl, about two years old, the daughter of his unfortunate keeper. In a moment he took the child gently round the waist, lifted it from the ground, and caressed and fondled it for some time. Every beholder trembled for its safety, and expected that it would share the fate of its poor father. But no; the harassed creature, having turned the child round three times, quietly laid it down, and drew some clothing on it, that had fallen off. After this, he stood over the child, with his eyes fixed upon it, 'and if,' said the narrator, 'I did not see the penitential tear steal from his eye, I have never seen it in my life.' He then submitted to be chained by some other keepers, and stood motionless and dejected, as if sensible that he had done a wrong he could not repair. His dejection became more and more visible, as he stood and gazed on the fatherless babe, who, from constant familiarity with the elephant, appeared unalarmed, and played with its trunk. From this time the animal was quiet, and he always seemed delighted when the little orphan was in sight. Many persons went to see the noble creature fondling his adopted; but there was a visible alteration in his health; he fell away, and died at Cawnpore six months after.

Anon, *Domesticated Animals considered with reference to Civilisation and the Arts*

16e   Brother Tebaldo once told us something that he himself had seen. When St. Francis was preaching one day to the people of Trevi, a noisy and ungovernable ass went careering about the square, frightening people out of their wits. And when it became clear that no-one could catch it or restrain it, St. Francis said to it, 'Brother ass, please be quiet and allow me to preach to the people.' When the donkey heard this it immediately bowed its head and, to everyone's astonishment, stood perfectly quiet. And the Blessed Francis, fearing that the people might take too much notice of this astonishing miracle, began saying funny things to make them laugh.

John R.H.Moorman, *The New Fioretti*

16f The cat by himself was a swift and efficient traveller. He had no difficulty at all in picking up the trail of the dogs from the point where they had turned off in a westward direction from the river, and the only thing that held him back was rain, which he detested. He would huddle miserably under shelter during a shower, his ears laid flat, his eyes baleful and more crossed than ever, waiting until the last drop had fallen before venturing out again. Then he would pick his way with extreme distaste through the wet grass and undergrowth, taking a long time, and stopping often to shake his paws.

He left no trace of his progress; branches parted slightly here and there, sometimes there was a momentary rustling of dried leaves, but never a twig cracked, and not a stone was dislodged from under his soft, sure feet. Without his noisier companions he saw everything and was seen by none, many an animal remaining unaware of the cold, silent scrutiny in the undergrowth, or from up a tree.

He came within touching distance of the soft-eyed deer drinking at the lake's edge at dawn; he watched the sharp, inquisitive nose and bright eyes of a fox peer from the bushes; he saw the sinuous twisting bodies and mean vicious faces of mink and marten; once he looked up and saw the otterlike head of a fisher high above him, framed in the leafless branches of a birch, and watched the beautiful tail stream out behind when the animal leaped a clear fifteen feet through the air into the swaying green obscurity of a pine; and he watched with disdain the lean grey timber wolf loping quietly along the trail beneath him as he rested on the limb of a tree above. Those that he encountered face to face would not meet his eyes and turned away. Only the beaver went about his business and paid him no heed.

Sheila Burnford, *The Incredible Journey*

16g   In nature, one creature devours another, and this is an essential part
       of all existence and of all being. It is not something to lament over,
       nor something to try to reform. The Buddhist who refuses to take
       life is really ridiculous, since if he eats only two grains of rice per
       day, it is two grains of life. We did not make creation, we are not the
       authors of the universe. And if we see that the whole of creation is
       established upon the fact that one life devours another life, one cycle
       of existence can only come into existence through the subjugating of
       another cycle of existence, then what is the good of trying to pretend
       that it is not so? The only thing to do is to realise what is higher, and
       what is lower, in the cycles of existence.

       It is nonsense to declare that there *is* no higher and lower. We
       know full well that the dandelion belongs to a higher cycle of
       existence than the hartstongue fern, that the ant's is a higher form of
       existence than the dandelion's, that the thrush is higher than the ant,
       that Timsy the cat is higher than the thrush, and that I, a man, am
       higher than Timsy.

                              D.H.Lawrence, *Reflections on the Death of a Porcupine*

**When we see ourselves reflected in the behaviour of the animals,
may we be warned by their ferocity, but warmed by their
constancy.**

17   SCIENTIFIC SATISFACTIONS
- Belief, Knowledge and Intelligence

17a   What you know is one thing; what you are reasonably convinced of is another; and what you grasp instinctively is yet another.

So long as someone, by learning and language in this world, manages to become balanced and fair-minded, then they stay that way in the next world, but by no means in proportion to their erudition. I met plenty of brainy widely-read people there who, despite all their Greek and Latin, had absorbed precious little by way of real understanding. They still clung to a jumped-up opinion of themselves although, in fact, they seemed to me to be pretty stupid.

Some had filled their heads with all sorts of knowledge, thinking that being well-informed amounted to wisdom, so when they spoke they simply spouted potted information. Trusting in memory knowledge alone, some of these simpletons would latch on to anything that paraded itself as high culture, even though they didn't follow a word of it. Some, by their lofty writing about everything under the sun, had earned quite a reputation. Some, shrewd enough to recognise the truth when it was presented to them on a plate, when left to themselves, were quite unmoved by it, so they lapsed into ignorance and denial: others simply hadn't a clue what it was all about. So they varied according to the sense they could make of all their second-hand information. Others, with an irrational phobia about religion had trained themselves instead in cooking up clever arguments, but truth can never be deduced from falsity.

Genuine rationality is like a freshly ploughed field; the memory is the ground; discernment and knowledge are the seeds; the light and heat from heaven cause them to spring forth.

Arcana Caelestia 1496 Heaven & Hell 464

7b   Swedenborg confirms my suspicion that education is an over-rated
      pastime. It's not what you know that matters, nor is it *whom* you
      know, but what you *do* with what you know. That's what unlocks the
      doors of heaven - or of hell.

      There is certainly no shortage of information these days: the
      planet is awash with it. We have to decide what we can use, and
      what we can safely ignore - an impossible task! I notice that
      Swedenborg doesn't suggest that we can do without it altogether.
      Language and learning are the scientific bedrock on which whole
      philosophies may be built. The important thing seems to be the
      decision-making once we are in possession of a few facts - the
      choosing between one course of action and another. Thus does our
      true identity gradually get filtered out.

      The idea that life is a progressive mental selection process
      implies some long-term purpose. We leave behind the dross, and end
      up with a fully-fledged personality well-adapted for life in the great
      beyond - a refinement of some sort. The notion that Earth is a huge
      psychological distillery rather appeals to me.

7c   Our mind has more thoughts than our memory can store; it delivers
      many judgements of which it could not give the reasons; it sees
      further than it can reach, it knows more truths than it can explain. A
      large part of itself could be very usefully employed in searching out
      the arguments which have determined it, in defining the perceptions
      which have touched and then escaped it. There is for the soul many
      a lightning-flash with which she has little to do; they pass over and
      illuminate her so rapidly that she loses the recollection of them. We
      should be astonished at the number of things she would be found to
      have seen if, in returning upon all that has passed within her, record
      could be made of it, if only from memory, and by a careful
      searching out of all the circumstances. We do not *hunt* enough in
      ourselves; and like children we neglect what we have in our pockets,
      and think only of what is in our hands, or before our eyes.

                                              Joseph Joubert, *Pensées*

17d   The one thing to be careful about in approaching nature is that we really come to be taught; and the same attitude is honourably due to its interpreter, science. Religion is probably only learning for the first time how to approach science. Their former intercourse, from faults on both sides, and these mainly due to juvenility, is not a thing to remember. After their first quarrel - for they began the centuries hand in hand - the question of religion to science was simply, 'How dare you speak at all?' Then, as science held to its right to speak just a little, the question became, 'What new menace to our creed does your latest discovery portend?' By and by both became wiser and the coarser conflict ceased. Then we find religion suggesting a compromise, and asking simply what particular adjustment to its last hypothesis science would demand. But we do not speak now of the right to be heard, or of menace to our faith, or even of compromises. Our question is a much maturer one - we ask what contribution science has to bestow, what good gift the wise men are bringing now to lay at the feet of Christ. This question marks an immense advance in the relation between science and Christianity, and we should be careful to sustain it. Nothing is more easily thrown out of working order than the balance between different spheres of thought.

The result of the modern systematic study of nature has been to raise up in our midst a body of truth with almost unique claims to acceptance. The grounds of this acceptance are laid bare to all the world. There is nothing esoteric about science. It has no secrets....The mere presence of this body of truth, so solid, so transparent, so verifiable, immediately affects all else that lies in the field of knowledge. Some things it scatters to the winds at once. They have been the birthright of man for ages, it may be; their venerableness matters not, they must go. And the power of the newcomer is so self-evident that they require no telling, but disappear of themselves. In this way the modern world has been rid of a hundred superstitions.

Henry Drummond, *Lecture in Free Church College, Glasgow.*

17e   From these primary qualities, Reasonableness and a Sense of Values, may spring a host of secondaries: a taste for truth and beauty, tolerance, intellectual honesty, fastidiousness, a sense of humour, good manners, curiosity, a dislike of vulgarity, brutality, and over-emphasis, freedom from superstition and prudery, a fearless acceptance of the good things of life, a desire for complete self-expression and for a liberal education, a contempt for utilitarianism and philistinism, in two words - sweetness and light. Not all societies that struggle out of barbarism grasp all or even most of these, and fewer still grasp any of them firmly. That is why we find a considerable number of civilised societies and very few highly civilised, for only by grasping a good handful of civilised qualities and holding them tight does a society become that....

[Societies] less surely tell us something about themselves through the literature, science and art, which they may or may not have appreciated, but which was created by artists and thinkers whom they produced. All these taken together may be reckoned - none too confidently - to compose a legible symbol of a prevailing attitude to life. And it is this attitude, made manifest in these more or less public and permanent forms, which we call civilization.

Clive Bell, *Civilization*

17f   Science and Art are the consciously determined pursuit of Truth and of Beauty. In them the finite consciousness of mankind is appropriating as its own the infinite fecundity of nature. In this movement of the human spirit types of institutions and types of professions are evolved. Churches and Rituals, Monasteries with their dedicated lives, Universities with their search for knowledge, Medicine, Law, methods of Trade - they all represent that aim at civilisation whereby the conscious experience of mankind preserves for its use the sources of Harmony.

A.N.Whitehead, *Adventures of Ideas*

17g   I, Qoheleth, have reigned in Jerusalem over Israel. With the help of wisdom I have been at pains to study all that is done under heaven; oh, what a weary task God has given mankind to labour at! I have seen everything that is done under the sun, and what vanity it all is, what chasing of the wind! What is twisted cannot be straightened, what is not there cannot be counted.

I thought to myself, 'I have acquired a greater stock of wisdom than any of my predecessors in Jerusalem. I have great experience of wisdom and learning.' Wisdom has been my careful study; stupidity, too, and folly. And now I have come to recognise that even this is chasing the wind. Much wisdom, much grief, the more knowledge, the more sorrow.

Ecclesiastes 1, 12-18

May we pursue science, not for superiority, but to serve and inspire. Let me not waste my time learning a whole lot of stuff that is no use to anybody.

---

18   ENTRANCES AND EXITS
- Birth and Death

18a   Movements, in the next world, denote changes of state. So the Biblical phrase 'going in and coming out' springs from this other-worldly condition, and means a complete state of mind from beginning to end. People in the next world walk in and out of places just as we do, but, although they are not aware of it, their movements are reflections of their thoughts and feelings. 'Going in and coming out' thus means an entire state of life. When the ancients used this expression they were well aware of what it meant in spiritual terms.

When the natural body finally cracks up and can no longer translate spirit into action, then the lungs stop breathing and the heart stops beating and the person dies. The important part, however, the thinking, feeling part, the real person lives on, not in this world but another.

Arcana Caelestia 9927 Heaven & Hell 445

18b   Swedenborg does sometimes indulge himself rather laboriously stating the obvious. The suggestion that 'going in and coming out' signifies a *complete* episode is not really very surprising: we could probably have worked out that one for ourselves.

His claim, however, that death is merely the end of a chapter - not the end of the book, is maybe more likely to command our interest, despite the fact that the supporting arguments are often missing. Each person, we are assured elsewhere, is a unique one-off creation - that's the entrance, and everyone dies, as we are all too well aware - that's the exit.

Many appear to be prematurely cut off, seemingly extinguished before they have properly begun. But the elderly, I notice, often display a curious readiness to die - a sort of awareness that the interval between birth and death is somehow *complete* - a 'going in' *and* a 'coming out'. In a throw-away society, I suppose a life that has run its full course could be simply scrapped or recycled. But for those who are content with their life's span, completeness can also be the prerequisite, the springboard for a new departure, like leaving school when the exams are over.

18c   All the world's a stage,
       And all the men and women merely players:
       They have their exits and their entrances;
       And one man in his time plays many parts,
       His acts being seven ages. At first the infant,
       Mewling and puking in the nurse's arms.
       And then the whining schoolboy, with his satchel,
       And shining morning face, creeping like snail
       Unwillingly to school. And then the lover,
       Sighing like furnace, with a woful ballad
       Made to his mistress' eyebrow. Then a soldier,
       Full of strange oaths, and bearded like the pard,
       Jealous in honour, sudden and quick in quarrel,
       Seeking the bubble reputation
       Even in the cannon's mouth. And then the justice,
       In fair round belly with good capon lin'd,
       With eyes severe, and beard of formal cut,
       Full of wise saws and modern instances;
       And so he plays his part. The sixth age shifts
       Into the lean and slipper'd pantaloon,
       With spectacles on nose and pouch on side,
       His youthful hose well sav'd a world too wide
       For his shrunk shank; and his big manly voice,
       Turning again towards childish treble, pipes
       And whistles in his sound. Last scene of all,
       That ends this strange eventful history,
       Is second childishness, and mere oblivion,
       Sans teeth, sans eyes, sans taste, sans everything.

                    William Shakespeare, *As You Like It* Act II, Scene vii. 139

18d   Then the man brought me to the gate facing east, and I saw the glory
       of the God of Israel coming from the east. His voice was like the
       roar of rushing waters, and the land was radiant with his glory. The
       vision I saw was like the vision I had seen when he came to destroy

the city and like the visions I had seen by the Kebar River, and I fell
face down. The glory of the Lord entered the temple through the
gate facing east. Then the Spirit lifted me up and brought me into
the inner court, and the glory of the Lord filled the temple.

While the man was standing beside me, I heard someone
speaking to me from inside the temple. He said: "Son of man, this is
the place of my throne and the place for the soles of my feet. This is
where I will live among the Israelites for ever. The house of Israel
will never again defile my holy name - neither they nor their kings -
by their prostitution and the lifeless idols of their kings at their high
places. When they placed their threshold next to my threshold and
their doorposts beside my doorposts, with only a wall between me
and them, they defiled my holy name by their detestable practices.
So I destroyed them in my anger. Now let them put away from me
their prostitution and the lifeless idols of their kings, and I will live
among them for ever.

"Son of man, describe the temple to the people of Israel, that
they may be ashamed of their sins. Let them consider the plan, and
if they are ashamed of all they have done, make known to them the
design of the temple - its arrangement, its exits and entrances - its
whole design and all its regulations and laws. Write these down
before them so that they may be faithful to its design and follow all
its regulations.

This is the law of the temple: All the surrounding area on top of
the mountain will be most holy. Such is the law of the temple.

Ezekiel 43, 1-12

8e   The shipwright who made the Ark left empty a place for a nail in it,
      because he was sure that he himself would not be taken into it.
      When Noah went into the Ark with his children, as the angel had
      told him, Noah shut the windows of the Ark and raised his hand to
      bless it. Now the Devil had come into the Ark along with him as he
      went into it, and when Noah blessed the Ark the Devil found no
      other way but the empty hole which the shipwright had left
      unclosed, and he went into it in the form of a snake; and because of

the tightness of the hole he could not go out nor come back, and he was like this until the Flood ebbed; and that is the best and worst nail that was in the Ark.

Anonymous Irish fable [16th.century?]

18f What reason do atheists have to say that one cannot rise from the dead? Which is the more difficult, to be born or to be reborn? That that which has never existed should exist, or that that which has existed should exist again? Is it more difficult to come into being than to return to it? Custom makes the one seem easy, absence of custom makes the other seem impossible: a vulgar way of judging!

Blaise Pascal, *Pensées*

18g If death is the end of our individual and conscious being; if nothing remains but the ashes from the burnt taper, or a formless essence that soars away and mingles with the elements; if our glowing hopes, our lofty aspirations, our consciousness of capacities for knowledge and happiness which have just begun to expand, are all cut off by death, and buried in the grave, - then, indeed, man is the greatest enigma in the universe. But if death is only the completion of the first little round of life, the first short flight; if it marks the end only of his seed time; if his budding hopes, his lofty aspirations, and dawning consciousness of desires which no earthly good can fill, are but the swelling germs of faculties that are to blossom and bear immortal fruit; if he leaves in the grave only the swaddling-clothes of his spiritual infancy, and rises as from a deep sleep, in perfect human form, with all his memory, his consciousness of individual being, to enter upon an endless career, in which hope is changed to fruition and aspiration into attainment, then death is the grand step in life.

Chauncey Giles, *The Nature of Spirit and of Man as a Spiritual Being*

When the time inevitably comes, give me a key to death's doorway, and the presence of mind to look for the keyhole.

19   MEMORY AND THE BOOK OF LIFE
- Judgment

19a   Whatever anyone thinks or says or does on purpose stays with them; it may be good or bad. Everyone has a natural superficial memory, and an inner intrinsic memory. This inner memory contains everything the person has ever deliberately thought or said or done: it's all there in the 'book of life', ready for assessment after death.

There is good and evil in everyone. The good is from God, but the evil is the person's own. Evil alone would squeeze all the life out of them: likewise good alone if it were to smother the person in a divine stranglehold. So there is good *and* evil in everyone.

Everything hinges on which prevails - on whether the person is really hooked on evil and only outwardly concerned with the good - or vice-versa. Either way, God sees to it that the distinction doesn't become too blurred, and after death good and evil are finally sorted. All that remains is what the person has actually taken to heart, despite worldly appearances.

Those, however, who once lived in genuine goodness, and then changed their tune are really in a mess because good and evil then get hopelessly entangled. Such creatures belong neither in heaven nor in hell: they lose their wits, and look like bony sexless spectres.

Divine Providence 227

9b   Specialised memory banks in the brain enmesh our everyday lives, weaving together past and present so that we may plan our earthly futures. But brain cells die: they come and go. What we hold dear, however, finds its way into a separate cerebral strongroom where angels hold the keys, but even these cherished memories sometimes fly away into thin air.

But, Swedenborg informs us, in his usual take-it-or-leave-it fashion, that our long-term meaningful memories are never lost -

they remain available to some sort of mysterious 'spiritual' retrieval system. So the final cure for human amnesia lies in another world. There, we're told, in all but the most depraved, the good and the evil are easily distinguished. The matter is not, however, decided by some celestial supreme court convened for the purpose: it is rather a matter of a good memory and sound 'judgment' on the part of the deceased himself. It is a comforting thought.

19c *Memory*: in the abstract and most general sense, that characteristic of living organisms, in virtue of which what they experience leaves behind effects which modify future experience and behaviour, in virtue of which they have a history, and that history is recorded in themselves; that characteristic which underlies all *learning*, the essential feature of which is retention; in a narrow sense it covers *recall* and *recognition* - what we call remembering - but there may be *learning* without *remembering*.

James Drever, *A Dictionary of Psychology*

19d He sat in his front parlour at Mrs.Wickett's on a November afternoon in thirty-three. It was cold and foggy and he dare not go out. He had not felt too well since Armistice Day; he fancied he might have caught a slight chill during the chapel service. Merivale had been that morning for his usual fortnightly chat. "Everything all right? Feeling hearty? That's the style - keep indoors this weather - there's a lot of 'flu about. Wish I could have your life for a day or two."

His life... and what a life it had been! The whole pageant of it swung before him as he sat by the fire that afternoon. The things he had done and seen; Cambridge in the sixties, Great Gable on an August morning; Brookfield at all times and seasons throughout the years. And, for that matter, the things he had *not* done, and would never do now that he had left them too late - he had never travelled by air, for instance and he had never been to a talky show. So that he was both more and less experienced than the youngest boy at the School might well be; and that, that paradox of age and youth, was what the world called progress.

James Hilton, *Goodbye Mr.Chips*

9e   The commonly accepted idea is that these experiences have been 'stored up' in the mind, but nobody seriously believes that ideas can literally be stored up in this way - it is only a metaphor, as indeed is the phrase 'the storehouse of memory'; ideas are not 'things' that they can be stored. But if these psychic processes are not 'stored up' in the mind, and do not exist when they cease to be conscious, how are they retained? For experiences are certainly retained in some way and can be reproduced, or else we should not have memory of what we did yesterday, and why we should not have a hysterical pain arising from experiences years before. In what form, then, or in what way are these experiences - whether personal, according to Freud, or racial, according to Jung - retained?

     The truth appears to be that what persists are not ideas or emotions as such, but the *conditions for their revival* - just as a gramophone or pianola record makes the reproduction of a musical composition possible. When someone wants to play the pianola we say 'the music is in the cupboard' - but of course it is not the music that is in the cupboard but only a roll of paper with certain perforations. For music is only music when it is musing, that is, when it is actually functioning. What is in the cupboard is not the music but the physical conditions of its revival. Furthermore, the reproduction is not identically the same music; it is a new experience, similar to the original but never *it*. So with mental processes; they are only mental when they are actually conscious, whether thinking or feeling. But there must be certain basic conditions which retain the record of past events and which when activated produce ordinary memories, memories of yesterday, of childhood, and perhaps reproductions of archaic material. What then are these 'conditions of the revival' of memories, personal or racial?

J. A. Hadfield, *Dreams and Nightmares*

9f   I slept until my servant called me, rose wearily, dressed and shaved in silence. It was not till I reached the door that I asked the second-in-command, 'What's this place called?'

     He told me and, on the instant, it was as though someone had switched off the wireless, and a voice that had been bawling in my ears, incessantly, fatuously, for days beyond number, had been suddenly cut short; an immense silence followed, empty at first, but gradually, as my outraged sense regained authority, full of a multitude of sweet and natural and long forgotten sounds: for he had spoken a name which was so familiar to me, a conjuror's name of such ancient power, that, at its mere sound, the phantom of those haunted late years began to take flight.

Outside the hut I stood awed and bemused between two realities and two dreams. The rain had ceased but the clouds hung low and heavy overhead. It was a still morning and the smoke from the cookhouse rose straight to the leaden sky. A cart-track, once metalled, then overgrown, now rutted and churned to mud, followed the contour of the hillside and dipped out of sight below a knoll, and on either side of it lay the haphazard litter of corrugated iron, from which rose the rattle and chatter and whistling and catcalls, all the zoo-noises of the battalion beginning a new day. Beyond and about us, more familiar still, lay an exquisite man-made landscape. It was a sequestered place, enclosed and embraced in a single, winding valley. Our camp lay along one gentle slope; opposite us the ground led, still unravished, to the neighbourly horizon, and between us flowed a stream - it was named the Bride and rose not two miles away at a farm called Bridesprings, where we used sometimes to walk to tea; it became a considerable river lower down before it joined the Avon -, which had been dammed here to form three lakes, one no more than a wet slate among the reeds, but the others more spacious, reflecting the clouds and the mighty beeches at their margin. The woods were all of oak and beech, the oak grey and bare, the beech faintly dusted with green by the breaking buds; they made a simple, carefully-designed pattern with the green glades and the wide green spaces - Did the fallow deer graze here still? - and, lest the eye wander aimlessly, a Doric temple stood by the water's edge, and an ivy-grown arch spanned the lowest of the connecting weirs. All this had been planned and planted a century and a half ago so that, at about this date, it might be seen in its maturity. From where I stood the house was hidden by a green spur, but I knew well how and where it lay, couched among the lime trees like a hind in the bracken. Which was the mirage, which the palpable earth?

Evelyn Waugh, *Brideshead Revisited*

19g   Yes, I remember Adlestrop -
The name, because one afternoon
Of heat the express-train drew up there
Unwontedly. It was late June.

The steam hissed. Someone cleared his throat.
No one left and no one came
On the bare platform. What I saw
Was Adlestrop - only the name

And willows, willow-herb, and grass,
And meadowsweet, and haycocks dry,
Not whit less still and lonely fair
Than the high cloudlets in the sky.

And for that minute a blackbird sang
Close by, and round him, mistier,
Farther and farther, all the birds
Of Oxfordshire and Gloucestershire.

Edward Thomas, *Adlestrop*

Not all my life is memorable. Let me judge wisely what to keep, and what to throw away.

20 BOARD AND LODGING, ALL FOUND
- Daily Bread - The Taste of Life

20a   The ancient Israelites had 'manna' every morning, and any left-overs promptly went bad: this means that every day God will provide, and we have no need to worry about the future. If we try too hard to take matters into our own hands we are liable to end up with a can of worms. The same is meant by the *'daily bread'* in the Lord's Prayer, and by several New Testament references about taking 'thought for the morrow'.

    This seems to suggest that all necessities will arrive on the doorstep by a divine delivery service, but it's not quite that simple. We are not really talking here about food and clothing and shelter and suchlike: it's perfectly in order to take precautions against shortages of that sort. No, we are concerned here with people who trust only in themselves and are never satisfied - the perennial worryguts, always grasping, always bemoaning their lot - those who fret if they can't get what they want.

    It is quite different with those who trust God. They do prepare for the future as best they can, but they are not hung-up about it. They have peace of mind, whatever befalls. Remember that Divine Providence is universal, and in the long run, those who don't try to usurp the Almighty know that everything is working towards their eternal happiness, regardless of any worldly setback.

Arcana Caelestia 8478

20b   This text about 'manna in the wilderness' should be labelled with a health warning 'not for use when preaching to the destitute'. Swedenborg conveniently by-passes the terrible plight of the world's poverty-stricken millions. To tell *them* that even the starving can rejoice in the knowledge that their eternal happiness is secure, is really asking too much. There *are* limits.

Those of us who have the luxury to do so however, might reflect upon the curious fact that ours happens to be potentially a habitable, fertile planet, supportive of life, and it's high time we learned, as a species, to manage its resources more effectively.

But, as usual with Swedenborg, there is a deeper meaning for everyone, whether deprived or affluent. It's all about the human tendency to poison the present by being over-anxious about the future - the danger of 'wishing one's life away'. Some wines, it's true, mature slowly; they improve with age, they are for laying down. Others, however, if not drunk when young will go sour; they should not be left corked up. Likewise the human spirit, whilst it looks to the future, needs also to savour each passing moment to the full. If all our time is spent scheming for tomorrow, we could find that life itself loses its flavour.

20c   Out of evil, much good has come to me. By keeping quiet, repressing nothing, remaining attentive, and, hand in hand with that, by accepting reality - taking things as they are, and not as I wanted them to be - by doing all this, rare knowledge has come to me, and rare powers as well, such as I could never have imagined before. I always thought that, when we accept things, they overpower us in one way or another. Now this is not true at all, and it is only by accepting them that one can define an attitude toward them. So now I intend playing the game of life, being receptive to whatever comes to me, good and bad, sun and shadow that are for ever shifting, and, in this way, also accepting my own nature with its positive and negative sides. Thus everything becomes more alive to me. What a fool I was! How I tried to force everything to go according to my idea!

From a letter written to Carl Gustav Jung by one of his patients

20d   Since life itself is uncertain, nothing which has life for its basis can boast much stability. Yet this is but a small part of our perplexity. We set out on a tempestuous sea, in quest of some port, where we expect to find rest but where we are not sure of admission; we are not only in danger of sinking on the way, but of being misled by meteors mistaken for stars, of being driven from our course by the changes of the wind, and of losing it by unskilful steerage; yet it sometimes happens that cross winds blow us to a safer coast, that meteors draw us aside from whirlpools, and that negligence or error contributes to our escape from mischiefs to which a direct course would have exposed us. Of those that by precipitate conclusions involve themselves in calamities without guilt, very few, however they may reproach themselves, can be certain that other measures would have been more successful.

In this state of universal uncertainty, where a thousand dangers hover about us, and none can tell whether the good that he pursues is not evil in disguise, or whether the next step will lead him to safety or destruction, nothing can afford any rational tranquillity but the conviction that, however we amuse ourselves with unideal sounds, nothing in reality is governed by chance, but that the universe is under the perpetual superintendence of Him who created it; that our being is in the hands of omnipotent Goodness, by whom what appears casual to us is directed for ends ultimately kind and merciful; and that nothing can finally hurt him who debars not himself from the divine favour.

Samuel Johnson, *The Rambler, No.184. (1751)*

20e   [William] James thinks that we neither possess nor need to possess some one thing that by being one and unchanging secures our continuing identity for us. However, we do indeed have a complex image of ourselves as continuing persons. It is partly physical, depending on the continuity of our bodies, our looks, our clothing, our homes and our familiar surroundings; partly social, depending on the rôles we daily enact; and it is partly given us by the body of long and short-term projects on which we are at any time engaged. All these things, combining, give coherence and continuity to our lives, and therefore to our selves. But it is certainly possible for dissociation to occur within this complex whole, and in extreme cases it may produce a split personality. Less dramatically, the felt self may quite normally shift and change its location within the psyche just as the field of conscious attention may shift. James gives as an example the President who is a 'different man' when he is able to get away for a fishing holiday.

Against the background of this view of the self James has what is - again, by European standards - an amusing, original and very American conception of religion. Religion is simply a personal concern for one's own subjective well-being and goals. James makes his point by saying that science is to religion as menu to food. Science creates an objective diagram of the world from which individual subjectivity and its interests have been excluded, so that to someone trained in the scientific outlook religion cannot but appear as a relic of primitive animism and wishful thinking. Religion, however, is solider than science. It is 'the food', for religion is about the subjectively lived experience of life, its process, its self-affirmation and its destiny. So James declares roundly that religion is quite properly egoistical, or eudaemonistic. He disparages ascetics such as the Buddha and St John of the Cross, and at the end of the *Varieties* effectively identifies faith with the capacity to enjoy life.

Don Cupitt, *Only Human*

20f Children, if you dare to think
Of the greatness, rareness, muchness,
Fewness of this precious only
Endless world in which you say
You live, you think of things like this:
Blocks of slate enclosing dappled
Red and green, enclosing tawny
Yellow nets, enclosing white
And black acres of dominoes,
Where a neat brown paper parcel
Tempts you to untie the string.
In the parcel a small island,
On the island a large tree,
On the tree a husky fruit.
Strip the husk and cut the rind off:
In the centre you will see
Blocks of slate enclosed by dappled
Red and green, enclosed by tawny
Yellow nets, enclosed by white
And black acres of dominoes,

Where the same brown paper parcel -
Children, leave the string untied!
For who dares undo the parcel
Finds himself at once inside it,
On the island, in the fruit,
Blocks of slate about his head,
Finds himself enclosed by dappled
Green and red, enclosed by yellow
Tawny nets, enclosed by black
And white acres of dominoes,
But the same brown paper parcel
Still untied upon his knee.
And, if he then should dare to think
Of the fewness, muchness, rareness,
Greatness of this endless only
Precious world in which he says
He lives - he then unties the string.

Robert Graves, *Warning to Children*

From a missionary in China

20g   Our visitors were mainly townsfolk escorting relatives and friends
from the country, who had come to see the sights of town, amongst
which we, our cuckoo clock and the gramophone ranked high.

One old, white-haired lady, who came from a village six miles
away, was a Christian.

'My sons don't know I have come,' she said, as she beamed upon
us. 'They said I could not walk six miles, but I knew I could; and I
did want to hear those English songs, the one where the birds sing in
the trees ['*In a Monastery Garden*'], and I wanted to see the bird
come out of the clock, and say "Cuckoo".'

And she did, dear old lady, and hear!

A record they always appreciated was a most infectious laughing one. No-one could stand out against it for long and the company soon became hilarious.

'This is the sort of religion we need, a nice cheerful one,' one of them said one day as they wiped their eyes.

Cuckoo clocks and gramophone records were not all they heard in that room, and by and by many of them learned the true sources of Christian joy.

Edith Couche, *Lighting Chinese Lanterns*

Let not time be a tyrant unto me. Teach me to relish each new day, and not to fear the final deadline.

21 LANDS OF PROMISE
- A Forty Year Progress

21a The '*Most* Ancient Church' was a celestial religion that flourished in the land of Canaan before the Flood. *After* the Flood, the '*Ancient* Church' was also there, and elsewhere. So all the tribes, territories and landmarks there acquired heavenly meanings because these archaic people saw their world in symbolic celestial or spiritual terms. Rivers, mountains and boundaries each referred to some aspect of God's kingdom. Early Biblical place-names originated there. Abraham was directed there, the land being promised to his posterity - not because they were particularly virtuous, not by any means - but so that the ancient symbols should be preserved intact.

The old Israelites were a shallow, earthy lot, but their primitive sense of ritual nevertheless afforded some tenuous connection with heaven. The connection depended upon two conditions - (a) They should be quite unaware of any inner significance in their worship, and (b) They should regard the ritual itself as sacrosanct. [After all, if you're totally oblivious of any profound meaning you're in no position to accept or deny it: the mere performance then assumes a magic of its own.] This nation was simply not concerned with such things as divine love, or faith, or eternal life. When such things were eventually revealed to them they were sceptical and had to be expelled from Canaan lest they profane the ancient symbols.

Arcana Caelestia 3686, 10,500 Heavenly Doctrine 5

21b The devious and reluctant steps of the ancient Israelites were, I suppose, indicative of our own journey through life, and their 'promised land' turned out to be a bit of an anti-climax. Swedenborg seems to say that their unwitting function was to preserve the remains of an even more ancient culture about which they knew nothing. We, too, may sometimes suspect that we are being used for purposes we scarcely understand.

People are often drawn to religious movements, as, indeed, they are to other people, not so much on account of whatever they may have to say, but because of the way they say it. Some say it with anthems and architecture; others with vestments and incense. Such things acquire a fascination of their own. The irreligious, like as not, satisfy their need for ritual in their work, in the arts, in sports, or gardening, or in the faithful observance of an annual holiday abroad. In our search for the promised land we make do with outward forms and ceremonies, waiting for those rare moments when the mountain tops briefly emerge from the mist - fragments of a landscape that may one day come fully into focus.

1c   To be truly happy is a question of how we begin and not of how we end, of what we want and not of what we have. An aspiration is a joy for ever, a possession as solid as a landed estate, a fortune which we can never exhaust and which gives us year by year a revenue of pleasurable activity. To have many of these is to be spiritually rich. Life is only a very dull and ill-directed theatre unless we have some interests in the piece; and to those who have neither art nor science, the world is a mere arrangement of colours, or a rough footway where they may very well break their shins. It is in virtue of his own desires and curiosities that any man continues to exist with even patience, that he is charmed by the look of things and people, and that he wakens every morning with a renewed appetite for work and pleasure.

Robert Louis Stevenson, *El Dorado*

1d   With the utmost sincerity and single-mindedness we may spend our lives in defending a cause which we are profoundly convinced to be essential to our social well-being. But if God is convinced otherwise, he will accept merely the individual character built in the struggle; its life-work he will sweep ruthlessly away. Nowhere is this more evident than in the utter failure of the heroism, idealism and self-sacrifice of the millions who died in the last war,* to achieve any of the objects for which they gave life itself.

It is for this reason that it is so extremely important to have as clear an idea as possible of what it is that God is doing, and what his plans are. Otherwise we waste a lot of our own time and effort - as well as a lot of his.

In general lines, it is not difficult to trace the plan. He intends the individual to have the fullest possible opportunity to lead a happy, useful life, and both to develop his own character, and to make his contribution to the material and spiritual well-being of the community of which he is a member. In order to fulfil these purposes the individual needs adequate food, clothing and housing; adequate education to enable him to use his talents, and adequate liberty to discover how and where his particular talents can best be used.

So far as God is concerned, it is evident that he has provided all the requisite raw materials for this purpose for the individual to be carried out. That it is not carried out is due entirely to us. He is completely blameless in the matter. There is a famine in one part of the world while food is being destroyed in another part; there is a lack of money for proper education while the nations are spending millions on guns; there are innumerable tasks to be carried out and millions of unemployed. All these are our doing, not God's.

John Hadham, *Good God*

* Hadham is writing this during the Second World War

21e   When Moses sent them to explore Canaan, he said, "Go up through the Negev and on into the hill country. See what the land is like and whether the people who live there are strong or weak, few or many. What kind of land do they live in? Is it good or bad? What kind of towns do they live in? Are they unwalled or fortified? How is the soil? Is it fertile or poor? Are there trees on it or not? Do your best to bring back some of the fruit of the land." (It was the season for the first ripe grapes.)

So they went up and explored the land from the Desert of Zin as far as Rehob, towards Lebo Hamath. They went up through the Negev and came to Hebron where Ahiman, Sheshai and Talmai, the descendants of Anak, lived. (Hebron had been built seven years before Zoan in Egypt.) When they reached the Valley of Eshcol, they cut off a branch bearing a single cluster of grapes. Two of them carried it on a pole between them, along with some pomegranates and figs. That place was called the Valley of Eshcol because of the cluster of grapes the Israelites cut off there. At the end of forty days they returned from exploring the land.

Numbers 13, 17-25

1f   The Word of the Lord came unto me, saying:
O miserable cities of designing men,
O wretched generation of enlightened men,
Betrayed in the mazes of your ingenuities,
Sold by the proceeds of your proper inventions:
I have given you hands which you turn from worship,
I have given you speech, for endless palaver,
I have given you my Law, and you set up commissions,
I have given you lips, to express friendly sentiments,
I have given you hearts, for reciprocal distrust.
I have given you power of choice, and you only alternate
Between futile speculation and unconsidered action.
Many are engaged in writing books and printing them,
Many desire to see their names in print,
Many read nothing but the race reports.
Much is your reading, but not the Word of God,
Much is your building, but not the House of God.
Will you build me a house of plaster, with corrugated roofing,
To be filled with a litter of Sunday newspapers?

T. S. Eliot, *Choruses from 'The Rock' (Extract)*

1g   A curious part of the garden's life is that it expands as our own declines. A time comes when, instead of controlling the garden, we are controlled by it. Life shrinks; we leave all the circles we were accustomed to frequent, we turn from all the busy haunts of men and women, the theatres, and the restaurants, even the concert hall; we seek the peace and solitude of some garden which calls to us as never before. We ask not more than a fine day, and if it be possible to add a wood to the garden, happiness and contentment should be complete.

Our world has shrunk to small dimensions, but the limitations are not only acceptable but delightful. The garden is perhaps the last and most faithful of our friends, ever ready to give us of its best, accepting gratefully the service we tender, even if it be only for a few minutes, summoning all the songsters to our side, giving us a share in its own tranquillity. Active through spring, summer, and autumn, just as we were, it settles down to sleep when winter comes, but only for a very little while. From the last dahlia to the earliest winter jasmine is a brief span; winter aconite and Christmas rose pave the way for snowdrops, crocuses, and spring.

Those of us who know the countryside can bear witness to the number of very old folk, women as well as men, who contrive to potter about a garden long after they have been struck off the active list. If they can do no more than keep the garden company they feel that they have occupation, and it may be that in their hearts they give thanks for the gift that has given them some of their happiest hours. I have seen old men and women sitting in a porch or summer-house and looking over a flower-bed in perfect content; by reason of a little space of cultivated ground their lives have been cast in pleasant places. I know what they think, for I am of the company, spending more time in the garden today than I did in the years when I was of some real use to it...

I had an old friend, a labouring man, who cultivated his forty rod of garden ground in years when the farm could employ him no more. He was small, with a wisp of white hair and very blue eyes and a back bowed by nearly three-quarters of a century of toil.

'I like to muddle about me garden,' he would tell me; 'don't them plaguey weeds'd get the master o' me.'

He was a widower and lived alone - a woman from the village came in for a couple of hours a day 'to set the place to rights an' cook a mite o' vittles', as she phrased it.

The morning came, it was late spring, when she found him sitting in the porch, a basket of freshly picked rhubarb by his side. She called, but he did not answer.

'I lay he liked himself, gooin' off dead like that,' she said to me later, 'he 'ouldn't ha' wanted he should bin laid on his bed o' sickness an' see th' garden fallin' all to pieces.'

S. L. Bensusan, *Garden End*

When we think we have arrived, perhaps that is the time to plan the next stage of the journey. Let me recognise the clues that it is all leading somewhere.

22   TODDLERS FROM ETERNITY
- Childhood - Its Charms and its Challenge

22a   It is well known that the special love we have for infants tends to cool off a bit as they lose their innocence, and eventually go their own way. Some animals and birds even get chucked out of the nest when the appropriate time arrives, despite being 'family'. So it's innocence that sparks off this special love.

So long as infants are ignorant and helpless and dependent, their parents enjoy a unique kind of simple affection towards them - a state of *'rational* innocence' - but it fades as the children become more self-sufficient, and the need for protection and support recedes. This original love is actually an unconscious God-given innocence, revealed in the parents' thoughtful caring attitude. But as the practical conditions change, so too does the innocence. This is a human characteristic so that as the children grow up their needs may best be met by the free exercise of reason on the part of the parents. Animals, on the other hand, have only instincts.

Spiritual God-fearing partners and those of a more worldly disposition each apparently love their children in much the same way, but there is a difference. Spiritually-minded families tend to share a mutual innocence and a preoccupation with morals; if the children lack such virtues then the parents are inclined to distance themselves and care for their offspring simply from a sense of duty. Materialistic parents also, at first, experience a kind of innocence, and they too dote on their children, but from more self-centred motives. After the age of innocence they admire only those interests and natural attainments on which their own hearts are set.

Divine Providence 398, 399, 405

22b   Even the most macho of young ruffians has been known to turn into a buggy-bouncing softie when pitched into unsuspecting fatherhood. A baby's smile can melt the hardest heart. We call it 'love', but some neuro-scientists would have us believe that it is something to do with our genes - that when we drool over our offspring we are merely obeying a reproductive impulse - that parental affection is a species' survival mechanism, nothing more. I can see some evidence for this; I could even think it is true with regard to gorillas. I can't believe it is true when it comes to my own grandchildren.

Swedenborg plainly declares that the delights of parenthood are God-given, and that when we hold a baby in our arms, we are holding a miniature representative from the realms of heaven. I think he may be right. It doesn't last; the innocence fades, but although we grow out of our infancy, true innocence is maybe something we grow *into*.

2c   In her arms lay the delicate baby. Its deep blue eyes, always looking up at her unblinking, seemed to draw her innermost thoughts out of her. She no longer loved her husband; she had not wanted this child to come, and there it lay in her arms and pulled at her heart. She felt as if the navel string that had connected its frail little body with hers had not been broken. A wave of hot love went over her to the infant. She held it close to her face and breast. With all her force, with all her soul she would make up to it for having brought it into the world unloved. She would love it all the more now it was here; carry it in her love. Its clear, knowing eyes gave her pain and fear. Did it know all about her? When it lay under her heart, had it been listening then? Was there a reproach in the look? She felt the marrow melt in her bones, with fear and pain.

Once more she was aware of the sun lying red on the rim of the hill opposite. She suddenly held up the child in her hands.
'Look!' she said, 'Look, my pretty!'
She thrust the infant forward to the crimson, throbbing sun, almost with relief. She saw him lift his little fist. Then she put him to her bosom again, ashamed of her impulse to give him back again whence he came.
'If he lives,' she thought to herself, 'what will become of him - what will he be?'

D. H. Lawrence, *Sons and Lovers*

22d No child is born with a self-concept. He learns it from his mother and father, and, to a lesser extent, from brothers and sisters. He begins to learn as soon as he is born...in the stage of infancy. The infancy stage continues until your child is able to walk, at which time the next stage of development begins. The stage of infancy covers approximately the first year of life. What does a child learn during this stage? He learns his basic outlook on life.

He is forming, from a baby's point of view, his philosophy of life, his basic feelings about what it means to be alive. He is learning either a basic sense of trust and happiness or a basic sense of distrust and unhappiness.

You need to help your baby form a basic sense of trust in himself and his environment. This is determined by the atmosphere you and your wife provide for him. Early environment creates the first lenses of those self-concept spectacles through which he sees the world. If your baby's basic needs are fulfilled, then he will develop a sense of trust and optimism and attain the maximum development of his potentialities.

Fitzhugh Dodson, *How to Father*

22e A generation ago, the title of this book *[Children as Artists]* would have been considered facetious, not only by the general public but by the majority of the members of the teaching profession. For it was generally believed that although children could of course draw and even paint, their best attempts produced only bad drawings and bad paintings; that is, when these were compared with the work of adults and judged by academic standards - the only standards then generally accepted. Owing to the courage and tenacity of pioneer teachers, however, and the fuller understanding by the general public of modern developments in painting, all but a few will today accept the title of this book *[Children as Artists]* without question.

No claim is made by the author that children's drawings have the same art content as the work of adult artists, but he does contend that they have a similar appeal to the emotions. Much naturally depends on the sensibility of critics, and on their insight into the aesthetic mood and aims of the artist, however young or however mature he may be. Little is to be gained by consulting the dictionary for a definition of art; for art, being one of the fundamental things of human experience, can no more be defined than can life itself - or time, or love or any other basic principle or passion.

R. R. Tomlinson, *Children as Artists*

2f   To express wonder we have to be free of the need for perfect results. The *process* itself is always more important than the *product*, especially in the early years. As children grow up, the product begins to become more important to them. They need to feel some pride in their accomplishment or they will not appreciate its worth. If they have been sensitively led through the times when their critical awareness could have blocked their learning, they will be ready to try anything, just as they were back in the early primary years when their work showed so much promise. Their eyes and hands will be used to performing and their hearts will respond.

Perhaps what I'm trying to say boils down to the old advice, "Take time to smell the flowers." Walk through a meadow with a child - watching, listening, smelling, feeling. Sit for a time in a wood on a sunlit summer afternoon. Climb on the rocks by the sea and watch the crashing waves or poke in the tidal pools. Fly a kite and make up stories about the cloud pictures. Lie down in the cool grass and wait for the stars to come out.

Beth Johns, *Heads, Hearts, and Hands*

2g   Here is a mother with her baby girl. What does she do when she picks her up? Does she catch hold of her foot and drag her out of her pram and swing her up? Does she hold a cigarette with one hand and grab her with the other? No. She has quite a different way of going at it. I think she tends to give the infant warning of her approach, she puts her hands round her to gather her together before she moves her; in fact she gains the baby's co-operation before she lifts her; and then she lifts her from one place to another, from cot to shoulder. Does she not then put the baby up against her with her head snuggled in her neck, so that the baby may begin to feel her as a person?

Here is a mother with her baby boy. How does she bath him? Does she just put him in the electric washer and let the cleaning process happen mechanically? Not at all. She knows of bath-time as a special time both for her and for the baby. She prepares to enjoy it. She does all the mechanical part properly, testing the heat of the water with her elbow and not letting the baby slip through her fingers when he is soapy, but on top of this she allows the bathing to be an enjoyed experience which enriches the growing relationship, not only of herself to the baby, but of him to her.

Why does she take all this trouble? Can we not say quite simply, and without being sentimental, that it is because of love; that it is because maternal feelings have developed in her; because of the deep understanding of her baby's needs that comes from her devotion?

D. W. Winnicott, *The Child, the Family, and the Outside World*

Let me never lose sight of my childhood. May I always welcome the company of children, learn to respect their complexity, and to share in their simplicity.

---

23   ILLUMINATIONS
- Lamplight and Colour - Prisms and Promises

23a   In the natural world brain waves depend upon light waves. A person becomes aware of things by means of the senses. At first everything is new and exciting. Then, as a child, he finds that some things are more fun than others, and he becomes a bit more choosy. Eventually, by means of an inner heavenly light, it begins to occur to him that while some things are serviceable, others are fit neither for use nor ornament. Consequently he grasps what is meant by 'truth' - that it is somehow synonymous with 'use'. As the light from heaven glows ever brighter within he finds he can even discern truths within truths. Divine light dawns first on the interiors of the mind and thus into natural perception - not spiritual perception: that's something else.

The light of spiritual development is not so much about what you know, but how you *care*. Religious insights may be like beams of light, but the flame itself is love. The feeble glimmer of natural perception (*lumen*) is nothing compared with the radiance of heaven (*lux*).

All heavenly light comes from God. His truth - the shining forth of divine goodness - is seen by the angels, splintered into many colours reflecting their wisdom and intelligence in all its variety.

Arcana Caelestia 854, 9103, 9905

23b   Swedenborg offers us two kinds of light - spiritual illumination blazing away in heaven (Latin - *lux*) and a glow-worm version (Latin - *lumen*) which enables us to grope our way around on earth. I am more comfortable with the latter, deceptive though it may be.

I know we mortals like to bathe on sun-drenched beaches, but most of us can only take so much. We prefer our bright lights filtered. Let powerful rockets explode harmlessly in the night sky, but not in the back yard. Give me my own pool of lamplight in which to work, and the lambent comfort of candles on the supper table. You only have to *listen* to the word - *lumen* - to hear its gentle voice and to know that it speaks of a kindly nightlight adapted to our human condition. I can do without the glare of Swedenborg's spiritual headlamps: where is the dimmer switch?

But, of course, he is not talking about ophthalmics, but about extra-sensory perception. We see through dark glasses - or a 'glass darkly' - but the obscurity of the situation is itself a reason for hope. When death finally catches up with us and we are tempted to ask of life 'Is that *it*?' maybe we shall simply lay the shades aside.

23c   Though I speak with the tongues of men and of angels, and have not charity, I am become as sounding brass, or a tinkling cymbal. And though I have the gift of prophecy, and understand all mysteries, and all knowledge; and though I have all faith, so that I could remove mountains, and have not charity, I am nothing. And though I bestow all my goods to feed the poor, and though I give my body to be burned, and have not charity, it profiteth me nothing.

Charity suffereth long, and is kind; charity envieth not; charity vaunteth not itself, is not puffed up, doth not behave itself unseemly, seeketh not her own, is not easily provoked, thinketh no evil, rejoiceth not in iniquity, but rejoiceth in the truth, beareth all things, believeth all things, hopeth all things, endureth all things. Charity never faileth: but whether there be prophecies, they shall fail; whether there be tongues, they shall cease; whether there be knowledge, it shall vanish away. For we know in part, and we prophesy in part. But when that which is perfect is come, then that which is in part shall be done away.

When I was a child, I spake as a child, I understood as a child, I thought as a child: but when I became a man, I put away childish things. For now we see through a glass, darkly; but then face to face: now I know in part; but then shall I know even as also I am known. And now abideth faith, hope, charity, these three; but the greatest of these is charity.

1 Corinthians 13, 1-13

23d Entering the celestial city of Chartres cathedral, even on a bright sunny morning, one immediately feels the effect is of overwhelming darkness, even gloom. Only slowly, as our eyes adjust to the dark, do the luminous pools of blue and red from the stained-glass windows begin to emerge, suggesting a vision of that other world "garnished with all manner of precious stones" (Revelation 21,19). Though stained glass had been in use for centuries and some of the old cathedral's glass still survives at the west end of Chartres, the medium was given new emphasis in the thirteenth-century building. By removing the gallery, or tribune level, and, with the aid of flying buttresses, enlarging the windows of the clerestory level, the whole interior became a frame for its dazzling display.

The north transept rose window is another glowing vision of the Virgin, who is placed at its centre with the Christ-child on her knee. She is the window through which Christ, the light of the world, entered the terrestrial realm. But, as in all early stained glass, it is not so much the transparent qualities of the medium that are made manifest, but its dense, deeply-coloured materiality of ruby reds and sapphire blues, its jewel-like capacity to emit light rather than merely refract it. Glass was most often associated with the intense colours of gems, which Abbot Suger saw as possessing "sacred virtues". The purest form of light, that seen by mystics, was a manifestation of divine grace, but in its material form light was described by a rich Latin vocabulary. The word *lux* referred to the source of light such as that emitted from luminous bodies like the sun. Light which was multiplied in space was called *lumen* and light which was reflected off objects was called *splendor*. When Abbot Suger described the enlarged upper choir of St. Denis as "pervaded by the new light" (*lux nova*), he was imbuing the stained-glass windows there with the capacity to make light manifest. Whereas twentieth-century taste tends to associate the shiny with the gaudy glow of kitsch, nothing was more beautiful to a medieval beholder than this coloured brightness.

Michael Camille, *Gothic Art*

23e   O Light Invisible, we praise Thee!
Too bright for mortal vision.
O Greater Light, we praise Thee for the less;
The eastern light our spires touch at morning,
The light that slants upon our western doors at evening,
The twilight over stagnant pools at batflight,
Moon light and star light, owl and moth light,
Glow-worm glowlight on the grassblade.
O Light Invisible, we worship Thee!

We thank Thee for the lights that we have kindled,
The light of altar and of sanctuary;
Small lights of those who meditate at midnight
And lights directed through the coloured panes of windows
And light reflected from the polished stone,
The gilded carven wood, the coloured fresco.
Our gaze is submarine, our eyes look upward
And see the light that fractures through unquiet water.
We see the light but see not whence it comes.
O Light Invisible, we glorify Thee!

In our rhythm of earthly life we tire of light. We are glad when the
day ends, when the play ends; and ecstasy is too much pain.
We are children quickly tired; children who are up in the night and
fall asleep as the rocket is fired; and the day is long for work or play.
We tire of distraction or concentration, we sleep and are glad to
sleep,
Controlled by the rhythm of blood and the day and the night and the
seasons.
And we must extinguish the candle, put out the light and relight it;
Forever must quench, forever relight the flame.
Therefore we thank Thee for our little light, that is dappled with
shadow.
We thank Thee who hast moved us to building, to finding, to
forming at the ends of our fingers and beams of our eyes.
And when we have built an altar to the Invisible Light, we may set
thereon the little lights for which our bodily vision is made.
And we thank Thee that darkness reminds us of light.
O Light Invisible, we give Thee thanks for Thy great glory!

T. S. Eliot, The Rock

23f   Crystals with rainbows are particularly joyous and loving. I see
       rainbows, whether real or in a dream, as a blessing from God, a sign
       of angelic protection and love. Often the colour prisms which form
       the rainbows in crystals are there as the result of a hard knock or a
       flaw. For this reason too they are joyous companions reminding us
       that our own hard knocks and flaws may bring us beauty and joy. If
       you feel depressed or disillusioned by life try keeping a rainbow
       crystal in your pocket. You will soon feel better. The rainbow is a
       bridge between this and higher worlds - the rainbow crystal helps us
       to bridge the gap.

       During one of the most devastating periods of my life I went
       through months when I could not sleep or eat. I felt isolated, alone -
       betrayed by life and everything I believed in. It was as if thick, black
       smog hemmed me in on every side. I thought I would drown in it. A
       rainbow crystal came into my life Almost without thinking I put it
       under my pillow. That night I slept and had a dream. In the dream I
       faced a huge mountain made of granite steps. Each step was as tall
       as my body. By standing on tiptoe I could just reach the next step
       with the tips of my fingers and I dragged myself up. By the time I
       reached the top my body was raw and bleeding. I looked up and
       found myself confronting thick, black, evil-looking slime. It had no
       shape - it was just everywhere. It filled me with revulsion. It was the
       sum total of all that had happened and all I feared could and would
       happen. I moved to go back down the mountain but when I saw the
       height I was too afraid. Turning to the slime I smashed my fist into
       the middle of it. It burst into thousands of crystal rainbows which
       cascaded around me in an explosion of light and colour. I woke up
       electrified. I realised that by retreating from the blackness - because
       of the fear that it would engulf me - it expanded and grew. As soon
       as I faced it, touched it, it was instantly transformed and beautiful.
       This dream, combined with the rainbow crystal, changed my
       understanding and gave me the impetus to change my life.

                          Soozi Holbeche, *The Power of Gems and Crystals*

23g   He brought light out of darkness, not out of a lesser light; he can
       bring thy summer out of winter, though thou have no spring; though
       in the ways of fortune, or understanding, or conscience, thou have

been benighted till now, wintered and frozen, clouded and eclipsed, damped and benumbed, smothered and stupefied till now, now God comes to thee, not as in the dawning of the day, not as in the bud of the spring, but as the sun at noon.

John Donne, *From a Sermon at St.Paul's, (1624)*

Grant me always enough light to see where to put my feet, and, sometimes, when I am in the mood for it, a brighter vision of some sort of destination.

24   ORDER AND AUTHORITY
- The Decalogue

24a   Every nation on earth knows that it's not a good idea to kill, commit adultery, steal or tell lies, and any sensible society makes laws to protect itself accordingly. So why did the Israelites need to be reminded of them by the Almighty himself? His dramatic performance on Mount Sinai was, in fact, an attempt to impress upon them that these laws are not just for the sake of civil order, but are vital for *divine* order: thus, to break them is an offence against God. There are religious principles at stake. They are holy.

Although they don't say, in so many words, that you should love God and your neighbour, that is actually what the ten commandments are all about. What are expressly forbidden are offences *against* love. If anyone rejects evil, it goes without saying that they intend good. The first thing to do is to recognise evil, and oppose it: shove hell out of the way, and heaven then moves in.

The final two commandments refer back to the others, but now it's no longer sufficient to refrain from wickedness; nobody should even hanker after it.

The ten commandments encompass every religious principle to do with the relationship between God and man. The first three are laws of spiritual life, the next four are laws of civil life, and the last three are laws of moral life. Anyone who brushes aside any one of them, by implication denies the lot.

True Christian Religion 282, 326, 329, 523, 531

24b   Drawing up official guidelines has now become a thriving industry, so it is a little sobering to find that God was in on the act from the beginning, although by present-day standards his effort is of modest dimensions. In fact, his ten-clause document, inscribed in stone, is a model of brevity.

On the face of it, it looks like a straightforward set of rules about telling the truth, not swearing, going to church on Sundays, being polite to one's parents, and a few other rather more serious forms of anti-social behaviour. Swedenborg, however, goes to great lengths to show that the decalogue is, by no means, so simple. It refers, he says, to all levels of human life.

I am wary of irksome rules and regulations of any sort, and, if God is really so concerned about our freedom, surely he might show us how to outwit all the complex litigation with which we are now-a-days lumbered, even if it is our only protection against rampant selfishness on the part of our fellows: after all, it does make life very tedious. The stock answer, it appears, is that freedom only works when order prevails, and that's where the ten commandments come in. Their deeper levels describe the conditions for love to operate.

There may be, I imagine, somewhere on earth, one or two primitive societies where simple kindly souls still live in peace without legal systems, but the chances of global order seem pretty slender to me. Maybe, who knows, in another world things are different.

24c Now he came to think of it, to part with a soul, for someone in his situation, would be more comfortable than parting with a pound. 'It's just that it's difficult to describe it in a legal Contract. The Courts wouldn't like it, Mr Fishbane. They're sticklers for detail; and you can't be detailed about a soul. After all, what is it? How much does it weigh? Do you keep it on the public highway? Do you license it - or pay any tax on it? You see, Mr Fishbane, life is very complicated when you get down to brass tacks.'
'Where do you keep your soul, Dennis?'
The clerk stuck his pen behind his ear and tried to look serious and thoughtful.
'Somewhere inside, I suppose.'
'Then give me yourself - just a moment off the end of your life; no matter how short... just so long as I'll have you complete with your soul.'
'Fixtures and fittings, eh?'
'Put it how you like,'

'It's how the Courts like, sir. It's all for your protection, you understand.'

He frowned. A moment off the end of his life. What a crazy Contract! He shook his head; and then, from sheer force of habit, he began to examine the notion and see how it might be satisfactorily framed. He began to consider the words and see how they might be twisted and looped and knotted to his own advantage. He took the pen from behind his ear and began to write in an elegant but tiny script. The words danced off his pen nib like scurrying ants. He looked up. 'You said a moment, sir. I'm afraid one must be more exact than that. A moment might be anything. A Judge would laugh it out of Court, you know.'

'We mustn't have it laughed out of Court,' said Mr Fishbane anxiously.

'Never mind, sir. I'll put in an actual span from the end of my life. I'll tie it up legally. Now - as for the sum of money you had in mind -'

'The sum of money *you* had in mind,' said the old man; rather reproachfully, the clerk thought. 'I talked of the riches of the world. It was you who mentioned money, Dennis.'

'The riches of the world are generally expressed in terms of money,' said Mr Fast, a shade snappishly. 'It's only what the courts expect, sir,' he went on, relenting into a smile. 'There's nothing vague about money. One knows where one is. Whether it's a hundred or a thousand or a million, Mr Fishbane, it represents what you and I would call the riches of the world - heart's desire - happiness and all that sort of thing that simply can't be pinned down in any other way.'

Leon Garfield, *The Ghost Downstairs*

24d   I remember, on one occasion, - when the Browns, a family of Baptists who kept a large haberdashery shop in the neighbouring town, asked for the pleasure of my company 'to tea and games', and carried complacency so far as to offer to send that local vehicle, 'the midge', to fetch me and bring me back, - my Father's conscience was so painfully perplexed, that he desired me to come up with him to the now-deserted 'boudoir' of the departed Marks, that we might 'lay the matter before the Lord'. We did so, kneeling side by side, with our backs to the window and our foreheads pressed upon the horsehair cover of the small, coffin-like sofa. My Father prayed aloud, with great fervour, that it might be revealed to me, by the voice of God, whether it was or was not the Lord's will that I should attend the Browns' party. My Father's attitude seemed to me to be hardly fair, since he did not scruple to remind the Deity of various objections to a life of pleasure and of the snakes that lie hidden in the grass of evening parties. It would have been more scrupulous, I thought, to give no sort of hint of the kind of answer he desired and expected.

It will be justly said that my life was made up of very trifling things, since I have to confess that this incident of the Browns' invitation was one of its landmarks. As I knelt, feeling very small, by the immense bulk of my Father, there gushed through my veins like a wine the determination to rebel. Never before, in all these years of my vocation, had I felt my resistance take precisely this definite form. We rose presently from the sofa, my forehead and the backs of my hands still chafed by the texture of the horsehair, and we faced one another in the dreary light. My Father, perfectly confident in the success of what had really been a sort of incantation, asked me in a loud wheedling voice, 'Well, and what is the answer which our Lord vouchsafes?' I said nothing, and so my Father, more sharply, continued, 'We have asked Him to direct you to a true knowledge of His will. We have desired Him to let you know whether it is, or is not, in accordance with His wishes that you should accept this invitation from the Browns.' He positively beamed down at me; he had no doubt of the reply.

He was already, I believe, planning some little treat to make up to me for the material deprivation. But my answer came, in the high-piping accents of despair: 'The Lord says I may go to the Browns.' My Father gazed at me in speechless horror. He was caught in his own trap, and though he was certain that the Lord had said nothing of the kind, there was no road open for him but just sheer retreat. Yet surely it was an error in tactics to slam the door.

Edmund Gosse, *Father and Son*

24e   The power of words for good or ill is enormous. When we use words with insufficient thought, there is grave danger that we may blind ourselves into thinking we are that to which we verbally subscribe. Everyone would consent to St.Paul's statement that, 'The Harvest of the Spirit is love, joy, peace, patience, kindness, goodness, fidelity and self-control'. But we cannot have these things just by subscribing to them or praying for them. We cannot have fruits without roots or a harvest without growth, and it is the difficulty of growing these desirable qualities that receives insufficient attention. Some of the blackest pages in history have been written by men who failed to see the distinction between religious language and religious living. Men like Torquemada and Caiaphas are but two examples amongst the many who have used religious language as a cover for their disreputable emotions. Still more of us fail to see the dissociation that can so easily take place between our words and our lives. It was said of one preacher, 'He talked so much of heaven that he was of no earthly use'.

Margaret Isherwood, *Faith Without Dogma*

24f   Most people go through their lives without ever being arrested or involved in a court case; many never even have occasion to consult a solicitor. But no-one can live in a modern industrial society without meeting the law in many different ways each day.

Every time we go shopping, or travel by bus or train, we are involved in the law of contract. Every time we drive a car we must pay attention not only to the criminal law but also to the requirements of the civil law of negligence. Every time a visitor enters our homes we become legally responsible for his safety - we owe him what the lawyers call 'a duty of care', whether we know it or not.

Even the most private and natural parts of our lives - birth, marriage and death - have significant legal aspects; and the law regulates the everyday events of ordinary life, such as taking a job, drawing Social Security benefits, renting a flat or buying a house.

In all these ways the law is a framework for the actions of citizens. In its most familiar form it tells us not to do something. The criminal law supports these prohibitions by an elaborate system of threatened penalties; and civil law often has a similar purpose - it compensates the person injured by someone else's negligence, and so indirectly discourages negligent conduct.

But law is more than a network of rules saying 'Thou shalt not'. It also enables people to do the things they wish to do.....

The Law Our Safeguard

24g   Augustine sought to show, first of all, that God did not cause evil to exist. Accepting Plotinus's doctrine that evil was only the absence of good, Augustine argued that God was therefore not the cause of evil. Evil was not a created thing, but the lack of something else. Evil was akin to disorder, which is the absence of order, but not an existing entity. A room can become disordered, but not because "disorder" enters the room. "Disorder" is merely a term for order disrupted. Similarly, evil was the disruption of the order God created, not one of God's creations itself.

In creating the world, God had constructed human beings and all other creatures perfectly, giving them natures that were designed for pursuing their natural and (in the case of human beings) supernatural ends. According to Augustine, his Greek philosophical predecessors had described the natural purposes of human beings quite aptly, but they had been deluded or unclear about their supernatural destinies. They had not realised that God had provided human beings with a nature that was geared to their supernatural aim - mystical union with Him in a state of blessedness.

Robert C. Solomon & Kathleen M.Higgins
A Short History of Philosophy

In an untidy world, let us hope for tidy minds

25   CONSCIENCE & CONSCIOUSNESS
- Levels of Perception

25a   Obeying your conscience, if you have one, makes for peace of mind because spiritual life and the daily round are then in harmony. Spiritual life and a quiet conscience are quite inseparable. Denying your conscience means that you will be plagued with remorse.

There are two kinds of conscience - an inner conscience to do with what seems intrinsically good, and another work-a-day conscience simply to do with being law-abiding. Those who enjoy inward goodness have fair-mindedness as a bonus, but those who are interested merely in what is right and proper rarely grasp essential goodness until it is spelled out to them.

To put it another way - those of a charitable disposition have what might be called a 'knowing' conscience: those who act from a love of God have a 'loving' conscience, and enjoy a higher form of perception.

Human beings generally have pretty garbled notions about truth. What they perceive as true, like as not, is tainted with selfishness. Even so, God can work with our mistakes and imbue them with a conscience-forming measure of kindness and innocent concern. It doesn't necessarily matter that religious 'truths' tend to vary from one denomination to another: they are important to those who cling to them. Of course, the purer they are, the more perfect the conscience.

Heavenly Doctrine 133-135, Arcana Caelestia 2053

25b   Heaven-bent people who bother about their spiritual progress have their own inbuilt security alarm that tells them when their peace of mind is under threat. Swedenborg identifies two sorts of conscience - the off-the-peg model for the ordinary law-abiding citizen with a rule-book mentality, and another for those of us motivated by higher priorities. The first is fine so far as it goes, but the second is infinitely more sensitive to celestial influences. Animals, guided by appetite and instinct, are not much worried about such subtle distinctions.

The interesting thing, it seems to me, is that human beings alone should have this remarkable ability to split themselves in half: they can use their 'higher' moral conscience to pronounce judgment on their 'lower' animal ambitions. The greater mystery, however, is perhaps the capacity for consciousness, which the materialists have so far been unable to pin down, but which gives us the feeling that we are - how shall I put it? - housed inside our waking brains looking out upon an often hostile world.

(Conscience: That faculty within us which decides as to the moral quality of our thoughts, words, and acts. It gives consciousness of the good of one's conduct or motives, or causes feelings of remorse at evil-doing. A conscience can be educated or trained to recognise good and evil, but its action is involuntary. A good conscience is one which has no feeling of reproach against oneself, does not accuse oneself of wilful wrong. *Cruden*)

25c Jesus went unto the mount of Olives. And early in the morning he came again into the temple, and all the people came unto him; and he sat down, and taught them. And the scribes and Pharisees brought unto him a woman taken in adultery; and when they had set her in the midst, they said unto him, Master, this woman was taken in adultery, in the very act. Now Moses in the law commanded us, that such should be stoned: but what sayest thou? This they said, tempting him, that they might have to accuse him. But Jesus stooped down, and with his finger wrote on the ground, as though he heard them not. So when they continued asking him, he lifted up himself, and said unto them, He that is without sin among you, let him first cast a stone at her. And again he stooped down, and wrote on the ground. And they which heard it, being convicted by their own conscience, went out one by one, beginning at the eldest, even unto the last: and Jesus was left alone, and the woman standing in the midst. When Jesus had lifted up himself, and saw none but the woman, he said unto her, Woman, where are those thine accusers? hath no man condemned thee? She said, No man, Lord. And Jesus said unto her, Neither do I condemn thee: go, and sin no more.

John 8, 1-11

25d   There is nothing more tragic for a man who has been expecting to die than a long convalescence. After that touch from the wings of Death, what seemed important is so no longer; other things become so which had at first seemed unimportant, or which one did not even know existed. The miscellaneous mass of acquired knowledge of every kind that has overlain the mind gets peeled off in places like a mask of paint, exposing the bare skin - the very flesh of the authentic creature that had lain hidden beneath it.

He it was whom I thenceforward set out to discover - that authentic creature, 'the old Adam', whom the Gospel had repudiated, whom everything about me - books, masters, parents, and I myself had begun by attempting to suppress.. And he was already coming into view, still in the rough and difficult of discovery, thanks to all that overlay him, but so much the more worthy to be discovered, so much the more valorous. Thenceforward I despised the secondary creature, the creature who was due to teaching, whom education had painted on the surface. These overlays had to be shaken off.

And I compared myself to a palimpsest; I tasted the scholar's joy when he discovers under more recent writing, and on the same paper, a very ancient and infinitely more precious text. What was this occult text? In order to read it, was it not first of all necessary to efface the more recent one?

André Gide, *The Immoralist*

25e   With the completion of the circle of seasons, Jews all over the world would be gathering for their yearly expiation and atonement. The ritual catharsis available to Catholics at all times was theirs only on the High Holy Days. They shared a collective guilty conscience that drew enormous satisfaction from rising to confess in unison and of course to be further berated by their spiritual leader, garbed in white canonicals.

Traditionally on this occasion, the rabbi's sermon would be based on the biblical tale of Abraham being called upon to offer up his only son, Isaac, as a sacrifice to God.

But Rabbi Deborah Luria used this text merely as a point of departure. After a fleeting allusion to the piety of Abraham and the unquestioning obedience of Isaac, she continued, "Yet there are other sacrifices told of in the Bible that surpass the magnitude of Abraham's. For example," she went on, "in The Book of Judges, we find the story of Jephtha, a great hero who was obliged by a sacred oath to slay his only *daughter*."

There was a stirring among the congregants. Few, if any of them, knew the story.

"Look at some of the significant contrasts," Deborah continued. "For one, Abraham never communicated his intent to Isaac - who we know from the commentators was no mere youngster, but actually thirty-seven years old at the time."

Her audience whispered to one another ("They never taught us that at Sunday school") as she went on. "In the story of Abraham and Isaac, there is no meaningful dialogue between parent and child. But Jephtha not only discusses his oath with his daughter, she actually encourages him to fulfill it.

"Unlike the case of Isaac, no angel appears at the last minute to say. 'Do not touch that child.' Jephtha must actually kill his own daughter." She could almost feel the shiver that ran through the silent sanctuary as she continued, "I believe that this is a truer story of religious devotion, one that makes us face the realities of life: That we must be ready to serve a God who sends us no angel, neither to rescue us, nor to tell us that what we are doing is right.

"And so, tomorrow when we read of Abraham's *willingness* to sacrifice Isaac, I will be thinking of Jephtha's daughter, whose name is not even deemed worthy of mention in the Bible. For throughout history, Jewish women have always been Jephtha's daughters."

Erich Segal, *Acts of Faith*

25f   The third great issue in science which impinges on human spirituality is how we are to understand consciousness. This has always been a conundrum. *What is it to be conscious? What is human identity? What does it mean to say 'I'?*

Central to many philosophical and religious belief systems is the idea of a sharp distinction between body and mind. The mind or soul is seen as a controlling substance, not limited by the life of the body and theoretically capable of independent existence. This dualistic view has always been in contrast with the materialist view, that the mind is no more than a physical phenomenon. It is also rather different from some Jewish and Christian beliefs which stress the embodied and conditioned nature of human consciousness. There is no survival of the soul after death but the possibility of the resurrection of the body and soul.

The three views have all been important and influential in the science and religion of the Western world. But perhaps the most important has been the dualistic view. Even the arch-reductionist Jacques Monod admits that, "Objective analysis obliges us to see that this seeming duality within us is an illusion; but an illusion so deeply rooted in our being that it would be vain to ever hope to dissipate it..."

The idea that there is a sharp distinction between body and mind, or soul, was developed in the seventeenth century by the philosopher and mathematician René Descartes. He was much concerned with the question of identity, and believed that the power of reason was the most characteristically human capacity. He taught that there was a fundamental division between the mental and the material. Human beings are dual systems of mind and body. What links mind to body is the physical organ of the brain. Descartes believed that this link was located in the pineal gland, which was therefore 'the seat of the soul'. However, he was also convinced that the mind does not live in the brain. In itself it is non-material. It simply uses the brain to exercise its wishes. As the philosopher Gilbert Ryle put it, 'It (the mind in Descartes' view) is invisible, inaudible and it has no size or weight. It cannot be taken to bits...'

Ryle called this invisible governor, 'the ghost in the machine'.

Angela Tilby, *Soul*

25g The ability to face up to ourselves is the greatest test of a personal growth journey. It means, above all, being able to separate who and what we are from the rôles we may be playing at any particular time. We may be acting as mothers, fathers, employees, employers, children, wives, husbands - but these rôles are not *us* - they are only how we may be seen by certain significant other people.

Some people are terrified of losing their rôles, so closely have they identified with them. A woman who has put everything into being a mother, for instance, may be terrified at the thought that one day her children may leave home and not need her any more. A politician may find it hard to cope with life when he or she is no longer elected; a doctor may wonder what on earth to do in retirement. It is important to realise that these rôles, or any others that we might play, are not the whole of what we are, even though of course they may be an important aspect.

The journey towards getting to know ourselves may involve pain, as we have most probably denied and minimised important aspects of ourselves over the years. We may have no idea of what we are really like, especially if we have simply accepted other people's valuations of us.

Liz Hodgkinson, *Getting to Know Yourself*

Let me not be dismayed by inner conflicts: they may be a sign that something significant is about to happen.

---

26   'BEHOLD I MAKE ALL THINGS NEW'
- Powers of Invention / Creativity

26a   **The six days of creation are stages of spiritual development following an initial mental vacuum. The first thing that happens is *'the spirit of God moving over the deep'* - the implanting of benign influences in infancy. Secondly, there is a split between light and dark - what belongs to God and what belongs to man - something which seldom occurs these days without much trial and tribulation. Thirdly, the man draws on these subconscious *'tender herbs'* and starts to respect other people, but he thinks he is acting on his own initiative - *'the herb yielding seed'*. Fourthly, love and faith make themselves felt, not now because of adversity or because his conscience is giving him a hard time, but because loving and believing, those *'two great lights'* are now in place to illuminate the way forward. Then 'action stations' - the fifth stage involves movement, the man is inspired - the *'fishes of the sea'* and the *'birds of the heavens'* appear on the scene. It is time to work. In the sixth stage the man willingly exerts himself from the love of what he sees to be right: he has become a *'living soul'* - a spiritual man, and his 'good works' are the *'beasts of the earth'*. In a sense he is still earthbound, until love becomes the dominant factor, and he becomes 'celestial'.**

People these days seldom get much further than one of the in-between stages, and hardly ever does anyone reach stage seven.

Arcana Caelestia 6-13

26b   Swedenborg's revelation of the creative powers of God homes in upon his on-going preoccupation with the production of men and women fit to inhabit an angelic heaven. Who made all the rocks hurtling around in space is another matter entirely, with which he is not much concerned - nor does he confront the tricky matter of evolution.

One of the many questions which it is an impertinence to ask about the Almighty is whether he ever gets bored! Despite such pointless speculations, maybe we can marvel at the prospect of countless human souls and the processes of their *spiritual* evolution - infinitely more absorbing than the mere physics of a material universe. I have heard it suggested, as an explanation for the existence of evil, that once having created the natural world, God lost interest and abandoned it. Such a terrifying notion might actually be credible if the Creator could enjoy no possible interaction with his creation.

But plainly we ourselves have inherited creative abilities in great abundance. Even chimpanzees, it seems, have learned to use implements to crack nuts, and human creativity far exceeds that of the most intelligent animal. Having exploited Earth's resources for our material ends, we now need only to use our phenomenal inventive powers to forge loving relationships.

26c We are the master-craftsmen, God and I -
We understand one another. None, as I can,
Can creep under the ribs of God, and feel
His heart beat through those Six Days of Creation;
Enormous days of slowly turning lights
Streaking the yet unseasoned firmament;
Giant days, Titan days, yet all too short
To hold the joy of making. God caught His breath
To see the poles of the world stand up through chaos;
And when He sent it forth, the great winds blew,
Carrying the clouds. And then He made the trees
For winds to rustle through - oak, poplar, cedar,
Hawthorn and elm, each with its separate motion -
And with His delicate fingers painted the flowers,
Numberless - numberless! why make so many
But that He loved the work, as I love mine,
And saw that it was good, as I see mine?-
The supple, swift mechanics of the serpent,
The beautiful, furred beasts, and curious fish
With golden eyes and quaintly-laced thin bones,
And whales like mountains loud with spurting springs,
Dragons and monsters in strange shapes, to make
His angels laugh with Him; when He saw those
God sang for joy, and formed the birds to sing.
And lastly, since all Heaven was not enough

To share that triumph, He made His masterpiece,
Man, that like God can call beauty from Dust,
Order from chaos, and create new worlds
To praise their maker. Oh, but in making man
God over-reached Himself and gave away
His Godhead. He must now depend on man
For what man's brain, creative and divine
Can give Him. Man stands equal with Him now,
Partner and rival. Say God needs a church,
As here in Canterbury - and say He calls together
By miracle stone, wood and metal, builds
A church of sorts; *my* church He cannot make -
Another, but not that. This church is mine
And none but I, not even God, can build it.
Me hath He made vice-gerent of Himself,
And were I lost, something unique were lost
Irreparably; my heart, my blood, my brain
Are in the stone; God's crown of matchless works
Is not complete without my stone, my jewel,
Creation's nonpareil.

Dorothy L.Sayers, *The Zeal of Thy House*
(The speaker here is William of Sens, architect of Canterbury Cathedral.)

26d   The experience which we already have of how God works reminds
us that, if the possibilities of human development make a
continuation of life necessary, it is equally necessary from the
standpoint of the character of God. God is an artist and, without
being personal about some modern schools of art, the best artists do
not leave their work unfinished, or deliberately exhibit to the public
the chance sketches of their note-books. The infinite attention to
detail which is evident in the construction of a flower or the body of
an animal makes it inevitable for us to expect that God will give the
same meticulous attention to the making of a human personality.
And even God will need all eternity for that.

John Hadham, *Good God*

26e   We have hundreds of thousands of scientists busy exploring new
frontiers, and almost as many involved in the painstaking process of
retrieving old discoveries. We publish half a million scientific papers

every year. But even if all these authors were to combine in a collective effort to work out the precise mechanism that enabled any of them to put just one word down on paper, it would probably take them a hundred years.

And with all this magic and mystery everywhere around us, why do we need to look for outside sources of excitement and explanation? That is very difficult for me to understand.

I am biased. I admit it. I have spent most of my life learning a little of the way of things here, following the weft in the pattern, trying to get to know the neighbourhood. I like what I see. I enjoy the intricacy, and I feel party now to at least some of the intrigues. Damn it, I belong here and I will not see myself as some sort of heaven-sent stranger. I am an earthling and proud of our system and all its surprises. I acknowledge its weaknesses, I glory in its strengths, and I refuse to have any of them dismissed merely as gifts distributed amongst us by some patronising interplanetary tourists.

We did not come into this world. We came out of it, like buds out of branches and butterflies out of cocoons. We are a natural product of this earth, and if we turn out to be intelligent beings, then it can only be because we are fruits of an intelligent earth, which is nourished in its turn by an intelligent system of energy.

Lyall Watson, *Gifts of Unknown Things*

26f [How to increase your talent and stimulate various inventions]

Look at walls splashed with a number of stains, or stones of various mixed colours. If you have to invent some scene, you can see there resemblances to a number of landscapes, adorned with mountains, rivers, rocks, trees, great plains, valleys and hills, in various ways. Also you can see various battles, and lively postures of strange figures, expressions on faces, costumes and an infinite number of things, which you can reduce to good integrated form. This happens on such walls and varicoloured stones, (which act) like the sound of bells, in whose pealing you can find every name and word that you can imagine.

Do not despise my opinion, when I remind you that it should not be hard for you to stop sometimes and look into the stains of walls, or ashes of a fire, or clouds, or mud or like places, in which, if you consider them well, you may find really marvellous ideas. The mind of the painter is stimulated to new discoveries, the composition of battles of animals and men, various compositions of landscapes and monstrous things, such as devils and similar things, which may bring you honour, because by indistinct things the mind is stimulated to new inventions.

Leonardo da Vinci, *Trattato della Pittura*

26g [Heath Robinson] is - in my view, anyway - the one sane man in a crazy world. At a time when appallingly irresponsible things are being done on all sides and for no reason by people quite old and experienced enough to know better, the ruthless logicality of Heath Robinson's work is very heartening. Because his machines and gadgets sometimes appear rather complicated to the casual eye, it may be assumed that they are impractical; but every one of them is guaranteed to fulfil the function for which it was designed. In other words, if one had the skill and patience to construct a Heath Robinson contraption exactly on the lines laid down by the Master, *it would work* - which is more than can be said for many of the ultra-modern, labour-saving, mass-produced aids-to-living which complicate our existence today.

Much of Heath Robinson's best work derives, of course, from his theory that the longest way round is often the most entertaining way home. It is simple enough, for example, to crack a nut with nut-crackers; but how much jollier to crack it with an apparatus comprising an arm-chair, a pair of bellows, some steel springs, half a sledge-hammer and a portly relative! In a properly conducted State there would be no need to instal gramophones in factories to keep *ennui* at bay; one would simply give Heath Robinson *carte blanche* to reorganise the works.

K.R.G.Browne,
Foreword to Heath Robinson Devices

The ways in which people give form and substance to their lives are many and varied. There is no end to the things they make. Let me never lose that ability.

27   THE SPIRAL STAIRCASE
- Numbers and Degrees

27a   Every natural thing arises from some other natural thing, but the objects of the natural world don't all melt into one another: they keep their own forms, with only the finest of connections between them. Consider fruits - lemons, apples and suchlike - outside is the skin, inside is the fleshy part, and inside that the seeds. The seeds themselves have an outer casing with an inner 'soul', so to speak, from which new trees arise. These components are easily identified: they don't normally fall apart, but are connected by tiny secret passages. The mind likewise has its distinct levels, degrees or steps.

'Climbing steps' is a biblical expression for a kind of 'elevator' that takes you to new levels of awareness. Jacob saw angels using a stairway, and in the spiritual world people making progress do actually appear to be climbing steps.

Arcana Caelestia 8603, 8945

27b   The 'up and down' view of heaven and earth is 'as old as the hills'. These days 'inner and outer' is more acceptable, but still they are only diagrams. Swedenborg's particular contribution to the idea is his insistence on steps or stages. All goodness and truth is from God, he tells us, and we take in what we can at our own level - whatever, at any moment, that may be. I rather like the 'spiral stair' model myself, but it would have to be an *open* spiral - plenty of 'treads' but no 'risers', so that the connections between the steps remain a divine mystery. We need these mental plateaux so that the goodness may come to rest and be filtered out and not go rushing by, helter-skelter into the depths. Thus we are more likely to get to heaven on foot than we are by rocket.

So divine influx into the world of nature works by degrees with magic spaces in between - that's the theory. It makes some sense to me because, although I can go along with evolution, I never did understand why primeval 'soup' or whatever should have separated out into *things* in the first place.

But why clamber from one mindset to another? If it is simply so that we can enjoy a deathbed view from the topmost rung of the ladder it would scarcely seem to be worth the effort. Maybe the spiral continues.

27c   We may talk of steps, and processes, and planes of life, as though they had some existence apart from the substances which are their subjects, but in such case they would be mere figments of the imagination. Movements are substances in motion. There is no step without a stepper. There are no abstract degrees.

The doctrine of degrees may be usefully discussed in abstract ways, but it is to be clearly understood that it is neither an abstract doctrine nor a mere doctrine of abstractions. It has to do with substances and forms as they exist in both natural and spiritual worlds. It concerns the grass and the sky, the singing of birds, and the laughter of children, the sunshine that warms the body and the love that warms the heart. It is involved in the commonest experiences of life. It belongs to these things because it belongs in its fulness to man. It gives us the whole measure of a man, in the true order, and to the farthest stretch of his being.

.Henry Gordon Drummond, *Degrees*

7d   For the first part of our lives we are predominantly outgoing, externalising and developing our individual ego as a basis from which to cope with the world around us. This is the development of our first consciousness of self as a separate entity.

Starting from the pole, our initial windings are expanding. They start small, so that in the beginning it takes less time to complete one cycle. The relative speed of development and growth in a child, as seen from the outside, is prodigious in the beginning. Setting out as children, we have an enormous journey - our entire sphere to wind round - before we reach home once more. Each turn or cycle takes gradually longer to complete; objectively, the development gets slower, and the windings become gradually more stable as they approach the equator or turning-point. We can see the same development in two dimensions on the Yin Yang, where at the fulness of one cycle the seed of its opposite offsets the balance and causes a reversal of direction, after which, on the vortex as on all homeward journeys, the speed of rotation increases.

Each winding marks a containment and a completed cycle in the development of the whole; but, as each is a part of the whole, the completion is also a beginning, so that the spiral shows the enclosure and 'rounded' quality we experience, and the equivalent points reached at every new winding. The recurrent moments of crisis and decision, when understood, are growth junctures, points of initiation which mark a release or death from one state of being and a growth or birth into the next. 'How many times,' said Yeats, 'man lives and dies between his two eternities.'

Jill Purce, *The Mystic Spiral*

27e   Life produces a mind-boggling multitude of special effects, but perhaps the most extraordinary thing we have yet learned about it, is that it does so with a surprisingly small bag of tricks. Everything boils down in the end to the presence in all living things of four substances called nucleotides, which are knit together into the elegant double-helix shape of a molecule of deoxyribonucleic acid - the famous DNA.

This is the common factor. DNA occurs only in living things and it occurs in every one of them. There are differences in detail in the way in which the four nucleotides are strung together, and it is these subtle alterations that produce the variety of living organisms; but the bases are identical whether they occur in an apple or an ape, in a mouse or in a man. There is a basic unity of all metabolism and it is highly significant that DNA, the unit itself, is the molecule responsible for the control of replication.

Replication provides continuity, but that is not all it does. If it were, the world would be filled with a large number of identical replicas of one original organism. But things aren't like that, simply because no copying system can be perfect; because mistakes will always happen. Must happen, because it is these mistakes themselves that make evolution possible.

Lyall Watson, *Lifetide*

27f It is indeed a thing to marvel at that an invisible speck of protoplasm, a cell whose diameter is not more than two-thousandths of an inch, should contain within itself all that is necessary for the creation of a full-grown human being, a being who has developed the power to study the nature of the cell and of the stars from which he has derived; a being with the intellectual capacity of an Einstein, the religious insight of a Boehme or the poetic power of a Shakespeare. No wonder Macneile Dixon should exclaim, 'Miracles? For my part I see miracles everywhere. I see nothing but works of magic. Miracles are not rare birds. They fly in flocks, they darken the air in their multitudes... Nature is not natural but supernatural, delighting in marvels, in confounding us with the astounding and impossible.'*

But for the mechanist, the fewer miracles the better. His hope is that it will eventually be possible to explain all life in terms of chemistry and physics which have already accounted for so much that was once inscrutable and miraculous. The recent** exciting discovery of the chemical constituent known as deoxyribonucleic acid or DNA certainly looks like an impressive step in this direction. This astonishing chemical acts as if it were the 'brain' of the cell providing a kind of blueprint which determines the processes in the body of the cell. There is no further need of the 'agent' once postulated by the 'vitalists', still less of a Deity to give form and pattern to the flower and tree. To the poet's enquiry of the snowflake: 'What heart could have thought you?', the biochemist answers: 'deoxyribonucleic acid' for this, it is claimed, is the organising principle, the regulatory factory which guides development. But who or what guided the development of DNA?

Margaret Isherwood, *Faith Without Dogma*

* Macneile Dixon, *The Human Situation,* London, Arnold, 1935-7, p.430
** Written early in the 1960's

7g Four fundamental tools should be in the kit of every individual who strives for the good life. Of these the first is an awakened awareness of the human comedy in which we all must participate because we are human beings. The second is kindliness, the consideration and appreciation of the efforts of our neighbour, the willingness to identify ourselves with his efforts, the generosity to encourage and to help him on his way. The third is a sense of humour. We do not mean the ability to laugh at a good joke at the expense of another, less well-off than we, but the ability to laugh at ourselves, to appreciate the infinitesimal value of our own lives in the cosmic scheme, the willingness to see ourselves as very temporary fixtures in an ancient design whose nobility is beyond our complete comprehension. At the same time a sense of humour demands that we go on, courageously and optimistically, making the best of the realities of existence. Without this sterling quality, life becomes a tragedy full of unnecessary conflict and pain. Men go to war, murder their wives' lovers, suffer from nervous indigestion when the stock market goes down or their golf scores are low, because they lack this quality. Because they lack a sense of humour women slander and libel and gossip. For lack of this quality men kill each other because they disagree about God, religious rituals, or the ownership of a horse, pig, or political doctrine. It is the saving human virtue without which there is little use in living.

The fourth essential quality of the good life is zest. Zest is the correlation of healthy mind and healthy body toward a healthy goal. It implies contribution and co-operation, and the active pursuit and use of the foregoing qualities of awareness, kindliness and a sense of humour. It is the integrating character trait, an essential to life and happiness. It implies the catholic ability to thrill with a sense of belonging, both to the cosmos and to human society, in a meaningful co-operative relationship. It implies the full utilisation of all our senses, an openness to the most varied stimuli in terms of full living. Zest implies an active participation in all the discipline and the arts of human culture, work, play, the dance, music, the theatre, the graphic and plastic arts, as well as the fine arts of social and sexual intercourse. In a word, zest is the enjoyment of the art of being human.

W. Beran Wolfe, *How to be Happy though Human*

Life's ladder has many steps and I am prone to vertigo. Teach me to take one rung at a time, and to remember not to look down.

---

28   A BUNCH OF KEYS
- Doors and Barriers

8a   People can think what they like and want what they like, as
everyone knows, but it's a different story when it comes to
sounding off in public or indulging whims in practice. Thinking
and willing are spiritual, but speaking and doing are natural: so,
unless motive and manners happen to coincide, the freedom we
are talking about is only spiritual.

People can think without saying what they think, and can
want to do things without actually doing them. So spiritual and
natural are obviously separate, and to pass from the one to the
other you sometimes have to be pretty strong-minded: decisions
must be made. It is like unlocking a door. The door is already
open for reasonable law-abiding people who are not in conflict
with society: they speak their thoughts and act out their
intentions. But against the outsider the door is closed.

If you deliberately check up on your own speech and actions
and the motives behind them, you will find that, time and again,
such decisions are being made, even several times in a single
conversation. Thinking and willing may be free, but freedom of
speech and action only follow when reason is in control.

Divine Providence 71

8b   The suggestion here is that we are a lot of hypocrites, saying things
we don't really mean. Swedenborg seems to be saying that *reason* is
the key to unlock the strongroom door, so that our innermost
thoughts may flow freely into action. I wonder whether it is so
simple.

Most of us, I think the psychiatrists might agree, tend to mask
some of our deeply-held opinions so as to get by in this rather
explosive world. There's no point in upsetting the neighbours if you
don't have to, and complete honesty, we find after all, is not
necessarily the best policy. One of Swedenborg's recurrent themes is

the idea that people are constrained by society, but that the laws of the land are invariably for the common good: all very well, but it is only a provisional arrangement - and an uncomfortable one at that. We can't go on like this!

So in the spiritual world, the doors are unlocked, the masks removed, and the truth is plain to see. Life may lose some of its intrigue, and some guilty secrets may be exposed, but at least we shall be free from the frustration of having to keep them under wraps. This strikes me as a powerful *reason* for another world where things are always *precisely* what they seem.

28c   Verily, verily, I say unto you, He that entereth not by the door into the sheepfold, but climbeth up some other way, the same is a thief and a robber. But he that entereth in by the door is the shepherd of the sheep. To him the porter openeth; and the sheep hear his voice: and he calleth his own sheep by name, and leadeth them out. And when he putteth forth his own sheep, he goeth before them, and the sheep follow him: for they know his voice. And a stranger will they not follow, but will flee from him: for they know not the voice of strangers.

This parable spake Jesus unto them: but they understood not what things they were which he spake unto them. Then said Jesus unto them again, Verily, verily, I say unto you, I am the door of the sheep. All that ever came before me are thieves and robbers: but the sheep did not hear them. I am the door: by me if any man enter in, he shall be saved, and shall go in and out, and find pasture. The thief cometh not, but for to steal, and to kill, and to destroy: I am come that they might have life, and that they might have it more abundantly.

John 10, 1-10

28d   The Governor was strong upon
        The Regulations Act :
    The Doctor said that Death was but
        A scientific fact :
    And twice a day the Chaplain called,
        And left a little tract.

And twice a day he smoked his pipe,
    And drank his quart of beer :
His soul was resolute, and held
    No hiding-place for fear ;
He often said that he was glad
    The hangman's day was near.

But why he said so strange a thing
    No warder dared to ask :
For he to whom a watcher's doom
    Is given as his task,
Must set a lock upon his lips
    And make his face a mask.

Or else he might be moved, and try
    To comfort or console :
And what should Human Pity do
    Pent up in Murderer's Hole ?
What word of grace in such a place
    Could help a brother's soul ?

Oscar Wilde, *The Ballad of Reading Gaol*

8e   It is a highly significant, though generally neglected, fact that those creations of the human mind, which have borne pre-eminently the stamp of originality and greatness, have not come from within the region of consciousness. They have come from beyond consciousness, knocking at its door for admittance: they have flowed into it, sometimes slowly as if by seepage, but often with a burst of overwhelming power. This fact did not escape the keen observation of Socrates: "I soon found," he said, "that it is not by wisdom that the poets create their works, but by a certain natural power and by inspiration, like soothsayers and prophets, who say many fine things, but who understand nothing of what they say."

How comes it that the finest products of the mind are, in this sense, extra-mental? What is there outside consciousness which can produce them? They come, not only with power, but often with something exotic and other-worldly about them. Sometimes they bring with them a sense of exquisite joy.

G. N. M. Tyrrell, *The Personality of Man*

28f   It daily becomes more apparent that God's respect for the freedom of our affections, thoughts, and purposes is complete. It is part of that respect for our freedom that he never forces upon us his own gifts. He offers them, but unless we actively accept them, they remain ineffective as far as we are concerned. 'Behold, I stand at the door and knock'....He waits till we open the door of our hearts to let in his love which will call our love out. He never breaks down that door. He stands and knocks. And this is true not only of his first demand for admission to the mansion of the soul; it is true also of every room within that mansion. There are many of us who have opened the front door to him, but have only let him into the corridors and staircases; all the rooms where we work or amuse ourselves are still closed against him.

There are still greater multitudes who have welcomed him to some rooms, and hope that he will not ask what goes on behind the doors of others. But sooner or later he asks; and if we do not at once take him to see, he leaves the room where we were so comfortable with him, and stands knocking at the closed door. And then we can never again have the joy of his presence in the first room until we open the door at which he is now knocking. We can only have him with us in the room that we choose for him, if we really make him free of all the house.

William Temple, *Personal Religion and the Life of Fellowship*

28g   The 'Heavens' of materialistic religions (such as the *Valhalla* of the Norsemen or the *Elysian Fields* of the Romans) are really little more than glamourised re-creations of life on earth. At the other extreme, the 'Heaven' of the Eastern religions, like *Nirvana*, are little more than concepts - they hardly involve 'living', in any ordinary sense of the word. But the Christian Heaven avoids both extremes. It is no mere second innings of earthly existence, improved mainly by the absence of certain serious handicaps, such as pain and death; but neither is it simply a concept. In Heaven we live, and live more fully and satisfyingly than ever before. And that life involves all the really important elements of what we know as life: relationships, development, knowledge, communication... and all in the same mode as life on earth: personality expressed through a body. The differences are enormous, but do not diminish in any way the quality of life. We shall recognise our loved ones, but by who they *are*, rather than by what they look like. But better than that, we shall know them with a depth and insight and love as never before. Life will be transformed in the presence of its creator and sustainer.

David Winter, *Hereafter*

Reproduced by permission of Hodder & Stoughton Ltd

Let me keep my closely guarded secrets carefully so that they harm nobody, but may I be always ready to open up when the occasion arises.

29 WEIGHED IN THE BALANCE
- Equilibrium

29a **Heaven is sub-divided into communities of various kinds: so, too, is hell. Every social group in heaven has its counterpart in hell, so the numbers are more or less balanced. To every good there is an opposing evil, and to every truth a fallacy. Qualities of any sort can only be assessed at all by reference to their opposites.**

Thousands enter heaven or hell every day, and as the needle swings so God alone adjusts the balance, because God alone has an overall view of the situation, whilst individual angels are scarcely aware of everything that goes on in their own particular society.

Human beings owe their freewill to the equilibrium which prevails between heaven and hell. If the hellish intake increases so that evil begins to get the upper hand and human freedom is threatened, then God has no option but to judge all those in the spiritual world, sorting out all the bad apples and setting up a new heaven and a new church on earth.

Heaven & Hell, 541, 593, 594 The Last Judgment, 33, 34

29b This fascinating scenario raises a few problems. I can't help wondering, for example, whether a preponderance of goodness might also be damaging to my future prospects in the next life. However, I am mightily encouraged by Swedenborg's insistence that I shall be allowed to make up my own mind about how I might wish to spend eternity.

The likeness to a pendulum or balance is graphic enough, but the fearful drama of the human predicament, it seems to me, might have been better portrayed by the spectacle of a tug-of-war. With the angels ranged on one side, and a demonic crew on the other, I can picture the deadly contest faltering first in one direction, then the other, as I wrestle with life's daily decisions. Neither team apparently ever falls flat on its face. Till the day I die, the struggle is always kept within limits. The divine all-seeing referee has matters in hand.

29c   Early in the Christian Era, top-spinning by adults carried no disapprobation, although later it was deplored (by Basil) as a waste of time. There is a tantalising bit of medieval information from approximately A.D. 800-1200 furnished by Hone: "According to a story (whether true or false) in one of the churches of Paris, a choir-boy used to *whip a top* marked with *alleluia* written in gold letters, from one part of the choir to the other." The significance of the word and the action is elusive... The whipping of the top might be another aspect of the biblical scapegoat, that is, placing of punishment upon a substitute culprit...

Breughel's classic painting of children's games includes young top-spinners whose garb and locale seem somewhat monastic. The youth in the left archway is whipping a top; to the right, a peg-top is being spun...

The fast shrinking Stone Age culture of the Maoris does offer direct evidence of spiritual meaning ascribed to the mundane top. Songs were sung to the accompaniment of humming-tops. Words and melodies have been recorded by anthropologists. Hamilton says that the sound of the humming-top gave solace to the defeated warrior. In a culture where defeat in war was much more than a bruising of communal pride and carried with it almost certain harsh treatment, the top evidently afforded some spiritual escape from bitter reality.

D. W. Gould, *The Top*

[Would it be too far-fetched to suggest that the spinning of the top could have represented an ideal state of poise and spiritual equilibrium?]

29d   King Belshazzar made a great feast for a thousand of his lords, and drank wine in front of the thousand. Belshazzar, when he tasted the wine, commanded that the vessels of gold and of silver which Nebuchadnezzar his father had taken out of the temple in Jerusalem be brought, that the king and his lords, his wives, and his concubines might drink from them. Then they brought in the golden and silver vessels which had been taken out of the temple, the house of God in Jerusalem; and the king and his lords, his wives, and his concubines drank from them. They drank wine, and praised the gods of gold and silver, bronze, iron, wood, and stone.

Immediately the fingers of a man's hand appeared and wrote on the plaster of the wall of the king's palace, opposite the lampstand; and the king saw the hand as it wrote. Then the king's colour changed, and his thoughts alarmed him; his limbs gave way, and his knees knocked together....

Then Daniel answered before the king.... "I will read the writing to the king and make known to him the interpretation. O king, the Most High God gave Nebuchadnezzar your father kingship and greatness and glory and majesty; and because of the greatness that he gave him, all people, nations, and languages trembled and feared before him; whom he would he slew, and whom he would he kept alive; whom he would he raised up, and whom he would he put down. But when his heart was lifted up and his spirit was hardened so that he dealt proudly, he was deposed from his kingly throne, and his glory was taken from him; he was driven from among men, and his mind was made like that of a beast, and his dwelling was with the wild asses; he was fed grass like an ox, and his body was wet with the dew of heaven, until he knew that the Most High God rules the kingdom of men, and sets over it whom he will. And you his son, Belshazzar, have not humbled your heart, though you knew all this, but you have lifted up yourself against the Lord of heaven; and the vessels of his house have been brought in before you, and you and your lords, your wives, and your concubines have drunk wine from them; and you have praised the gods of silver and gold, of bronze, iron, wood, and stone, which do not see or hear or know, but the God in whose hand is your breath, and whose are all your ways, you have not honoured.

"Then from his presence the hand was sent, and this writing was inscribed. And this is the writing that was inscribed: MENE, MENE, TEKEL, and PARSIN. This is the interpretation of the matter: MENE, God has numbered the days of your kingdom and brought it to an end; TEKEL, you have been weighed in the balances and found wanting; PERES, your kingdom is divided and given to the Medes and Persians."

Then Belshazzar commanded, and Daniel was clothed with purple, a chain of gold was put about his neck, and proclamation was made concerning him, that he should be the third ruler in the kingdom. That very night Belshazzar the Chaldean king was slain. And Darius the Mede received the kingdom, being about sixty-two years old.

Daniel 5, 1-6, 17-30

29e   If the force of gravity were very slightly weaker, or the force of electromagnetism very slightly stronger, the nature of the universe would be very different from what it is. All stars would be of the variety known as red dwarfs. (These stars are smaller and cooler than average.) Red dwarfs are believed not to be able to have planets. By contrast, if gravity and electromagnetism were slightly stronger than they are, all stars would be blue giants (large stars, from which heat energy escapes mainly by radiation). In either case, the universe would be very different from what it is. *It is remarkable that the fine balance between these two forces of nature seems to make it possible for stars like our sun to exist.....*

The emergence of human consciousness, the ability to survey and reason about the universe of which we form an insignificant part, the capacity for personal freedom and personal relationships and the ability to appreciate the values of truth, goodness and beauty - these do seem to me to provide good grounds for assigning to man a central and privileged place within this vast universe. despite its billions of stars and galaxies and enormous regions of interstellar space.

Hugh Montefiore, *The Probability of God*

29f   Across the wide field lay two broad bands of furrowed brown earth, and down the side of one of them two horses pulled steadily at a plough. They were both strong, well-built animals, the one brown and the other white. Their shapely heads with well-combed manes worked in rhythm with their feet. Behind them the ploughman whistled as he followed, and yet again a vast company of sea-gulls searched the newly-turned furrows.

Autumn had tinted the surrounding trees, still full of foliage, and the sunshine made the most of each red and golden leaf. The light breeze seemed to whisper "Peace," and over all the scene brooded the charm and mystery which the sight of the plough ever evokes, for it sums up for us all the processes by which we obtain our daily bread, and, by its suggestion of man's co-operation with nature, is a link binding the seen with the unseen.

The very horses carried themselves with a dignity and measured energy which seemed to betoken a consciousness of their share in the production of the yearly harvest and of what it portends to all living beings.

As the ploughman turned his team by the hedge the sound of horses' feet in the lane arrested his attention, and presently two strange horses raised their heads that they might contemplate the others in the field. Well-groomed were the newcomers, and carefully covered with blanket-cloths. Their heads looked narrow and small by the side of the massive heads of the ploughman's horses, and their legs were longer and more delicately formed. Their restless movements, however, and impatient efforts to continue their canter as soon as their curiosity was satisfied, were in direct contrast to the complacence with which the others took their unexpected leisure, for they were race-horses of high pedigree.

And the ploughman told the groom of all the doings at the farm: the value of the late harvest, the building of a barn, and the new crops to be raised; and in return the groom spoke of the news at his stables, the chances of his horses at the Derby, the latest betting tips, the scandals in society, and the prospects of the hunting season.

The horses would wait no longer. They resumed their exercise with much goodwill. The ploughman called to his four-footed helpers: they started a new furrow, and the seagulls once again followed in the wake of the plough.

L. Wemyss Rhodes, *On the Top of the Pillars*

144

Dozens of my books were purchased with money which ought to have been spent upon what are called the necessaries of life. Many a time I have stood before a stall, or a bookseller's window, torn by conflict of intellectual desire and bodily need. At the very hour of dinner, when my stomach clamoured for food, I have been stopped by sight of a volume so long coveted, and marked at so advantageous a price, that I *could* not let it go; yet to buy it meant pangs of famine. My Heyne's *Tibullus* was grasped at such a moment. It lay on the stall of the old bookshop in Goodge Street - a stall where now and then one found an excellent thing among quantities of rubbish. Sixpence was the price - sixpence! At that time I used to eat my mid-day meal (of course, my dinner) at a coffee-shop in Oxford Street, one of the real old coffee-shops, such as now, I suppose, can hardly be found. Sixpence was all I had - yes, all I had in the world; it would purchase a plate of meat and vegetables. But I did not dare to hope that the *Tibullus* would wait until the morrow, when a certain small sum fell due to me. I paced the pavement, fingering the coppers in my pocket, eyeing the stall, two appetites at combat within me. The book was bought and I went home with it, and as I made a dinner of bread and butter I gloated over the pages.

George Gissing, *My Books*

Always to be perfectly balanced would be very dull, but never let life's see-saw pitch so low that it can't be righted.

30 THE HUMAN FACE
- An Infinity of Expression

30a **The first and most eloquent 'language' was simply a matter of facial expression, especially around the eyes and mouth. The human face was designed to mirror the mind within - to project its thoughts and feelings. People of long ago were so open and spontaneous, it didn't worry them in the least that every look was a giveaway. So long as everything and everyone was 'on the level' then their thoughts and feelings in all their subtlety were evident for all to see - far better than words. The difference was rather like the difference between reading about some place, and actually being there. These ancient people thus shared directly in the language of the angels by allowing the whole face to 'speak'. Words, by comparison, are a very roundabout long-winded means of communication: they have to be invented, learned and applied.**

Everything was fine until people started to think one thing and pretend another, which happens with self-love: then the voice began to take over from the facial features. The face was no longer animated from within: much of its real life faded away, leaving only an appearance.

Worlds in Space, 52

30b I take some comfort from the infinite variety evident in the human face. I know that to an Englishman, all Chinamen look the same, and the reverse no doubt applies, but it is plainly not so. We know people by their faces, and there are lots of people around. We may have a problem with twins, but even 'identical' twins aren't quite. No two people in all the course of human history have ever been *totally* alike: the divine identikit is inexhaustible.

We can still guess, more or less, how people are feeling by the looks on their faces, but we may well be mistaken. Actors, of course, exploit a whole range of facial expression deliberately to mislead us, but we know it is only a game - a game which Swedenborg's ancients would presumably have found rather difficult to play - not many Oscars for them!

The brain, it seems, is programmed from earliest infancy to lock on to faces. Babies recognise faces, and tones of voice, but not words. As I peer into the foliage outside my window, or gaze at passing clouds, the shapes of faces are usually the first to present themselves to my imagination. Maybe we can see in this the shadows of a long-lost visual language that linked us once with the heavens.

30c We all have a very distinct idea of Christ's physical appearance, and it is natural to suppose that there is an authentic portrait from which our knowledge is derived and on which the representations of Christ in art are based. Yet when we go back in history we find that man's idea of the Saviour's person has changed very much through the ages. And when we enquire whether there is any representation or description that dates from the time of Christ himself and can therefore claim to be authentic we find that there is none, and that even the most venerable of his portraits were produced by later generations.

The Christ face as we know it is therefore entirely an achievement of the human imagination. It is precisely this fact which makes it such an interesting subject for study. For in its varying shapes it reflects the changes which man's conception of the Saviour has undergone during a period of seventeen centuries.

It is certainly very strange that the outcome of this development should be a portrait which is commonly looked upon as authentic and 'real'. One may well wonder how an image purely imaginary in origin should in course of time have acquired all the rights and honours of an authentic record. The history of the Christ figure in art provides an answer to this question.

Ernst Kitzinger / Elizabeth Senior, *Portraits of Christ*

30d There is the 'Mona Lisa', the portrait of the lovely wife of Signor
Zanobi del Giocondo (hence her popular name of 'La Gioconda').
Everybody knows that picture, which is frequently held up as the
ideal example of the Eternal Feminine. For does not the lady smile
that wistful smile which betrays that she knew all the secrets of
perfect womanhood? Perhaps so. Perhaps she also smiled because
she was the third wife of a husband who was years older, and whose
will had made her the exclusive heir to his entire estate, so that some
day she would have a chance to return to her native Naples as a
beautiful widow with an unlimited fortune.

Whatever the cause, that face attracted more than usual attention,
even when it was being painted. Pietro Aretino, the social columnist
of the fifteenth century, still remembered for his attempt to
blackmail Michelangelo and as fine a gossip scavenger as any of his
tribe living today, pounced upon this picture with glee. He hinted
that Leonardo had used this picture as an excuse to make the lovely
lady sit for him for four long years. He told how the artist used to
hire musicians to fill his client's heart with a soft glow of happiness
which thereupon reflected itself in the lustre of her drooping eyes. It
made good copy, but the only definite fact we know in connection
with the picture is the price - four thousand golden florins.

Hendrik van Loon, *The Arts of Mankind*

30e In 1977 Elisabeth* told me a story about her own encounter with a
deceased acquaintance. As I recall the story, Elisabeth was walking
in a hallway toward her office one day when she happened to notice
a woman standing in the corridor.

The two women struck up a conversation, and Elisabeth led the
woman into her office. After a while Elisabeth leaned toward the
woman and, with considerable amazement, said, "I know you!" She
had recognised the woman to be a 'Mrs.Schwartz', a patient to
whom she had been close and who had died some months earlier.
Mrs.Schwartz acknowledged her identity, and the two continued to
talk for some period of time.

When Elisabeth told me this story, I remember protesting loudly.

"Elisabeth, give me a break!" I said. "If this was someone you knew so well, how could it be that you didn't recognise her from the beginning?"

Now, all these years later, I can say that I understand. From my own experience and those of others I can confirm that apparitions of the deceased don't look exactly as they did before they died. Strangely - or perhaps not so - they look younger and less stressed in their apparitional state, but still they are recognisable as who they are.

Raymond Moody, *Reunions*

* Dr. Elisabeth Kübler-Ross

Oddly, the best of Marian's drawings, she thought now, was one of the most rapidly made - a five-minute pose. And however minimal the merits of this piece of work, it had defined the task for her. The nature of the task was to discern the exact position of the intersection between a physical object and the light, and draw a line round it. She had always supposed, in all those years as Stella's daughter, that the difficulty - an insuperable difficulty for anyone but the most crazed devotee - was in the drawing, or the painting, come to that; that the difficulty was technical. A mere two hours trying it had taught her that what came first was seeing. The model's nakedness had dazzled her like the rising sun. She had had to struggle not to avert her eyes, to look steadily at the pensive face, the soft breast, the complex magenta cavity in the pubic hair, to look unflinching, until she saw enough to move the pencil on the paper. What was hard was to see the shape of another person, uncovered whole, as an absolute in the light, like a bare rock in the tides of the shore. She struggled to keep her feet in waves of misplaced emotion, feeling and rejecting embarrassment, admiration, jealousy, repulsion, curiosity - curiosity most of all - before arriving at something cool and hard: simple attention.

'Could one - could anyone - 'Marian wondered, 'look at themselves like that? Could I look at myself like that? And what would I see if I did?'

Jill Paton Walsh, *The Serpentine Cave*

30g The phenomenon of a face that returns our gaze is a main feature of iconographic religious art. By the symbolic perfection of its particular visage, the icon can appear to look back at the beholder. When eye meets eye, the beholder's heart and imagination open, and the emerging reality is flooded with emotional fullness.

Iconic gazing is practised in many of the great religious traditions. Diana Eck describes the Hindu darshan:

"The central act of Hindu worship, from the point of view of the lay person, is to stand in the presence of the deity and to behold the image with one's own eyes to see and be seen by the deity."

In Western Christian contemplative tradition, the gnostic spark of divine knowledge experienced within the heart is founded on this primal interactional gaze. Meister Eckhart, a fourteenth-century Rhineland mystic, describes "the eye of the heart" by saying that "the eye with which I see God is the eye with which God sees me."

Walter R. Christie, *The Icon of Sophia*

Though I may seek the company of the like-minded, let me be for ever thankful that I need fear no spiritual double.

---

31   THE HEALING TOUCH
- Feeling and Sensation

1a   **The senses - taste, smell, hearing and sight are just 'long-distance' versions of the major sense of touch. These *external* contacts with the outside world exist to serve different kinds of *internal* awareness or perception, formed by what seems good and true. The several varieties of sensory experience all reflect spiritual qualities of goodness and truth because perception starts *within*, and is sparked off by what people know and want. The sense of touch thus has a general overall meaning to do with giving and receiving.**

In the next life, incompatible people seem to be physically far apart; those who get along pretty well live together as neighbours, and those who actually get to shaking hands share their lives completely. Handling or touching suggests the transmission of personal power.

Innocence and affection may be conveyed by touch as between mothers and babies, or between lovers. Even mental concepts can sometimes be conveyed by touch. So Jesus touched infants and invalids, and to this day priests are still initiated by the symbolic laying on of hands.

Arcana Caelestia 3528, 10023, 10199
Conjugial Love 393

1b   So even smelling, hearing and seeing are forms of touching: they are the feelers whereby we explore what's 'out there' - our contacts with the outside world.

Close bodily contact between living creatures can be the most powerful, albeit the least articulate, of our means of communication. That must be why people like stroking cats, or holding babies, or walking hand-in-hand. But we must be careful not to take liberties - 'handle with care' is a label that applies to most of us. Swedenborg is saying, however, that the senses are, after all, only channels, and awareness begins within. How we perceive the world depends upon who we think we are, inside.

The sad thing about bereavement is that our dear departed are, quite literally, beyond our reach. In rare cases, it seems, they may appear in visions, or speak to us in dreams, but we are always denied the reassurance of holding our loved ones in our arms. This tenuous state of affairs is very worrying, but I suppose it does fit with Swedenborg's spiritual world-view. Trapped in earthly bodies we simply lack the necessary sensors: tactile comforts only work within their own plane, either in this world or, more intensely, in the next.

31c   Side by side, their faces blurred,
The earl and countess lie in stone,
Their proper habits vaguely shown
As jointed armour, stiffened pleat,
And that faint hint of the absurd -
The little dogs under their feet.

Such plainness of the pre-baroque
Hardly involves the eye, until
It meets his left-hand gauntlet, still
Clasped empty in the other; and
One sees, with a sharp tender shock,
His hand withdrawn, holding her hand.

They would not think to lie so long.
Such faithfulness in effigy
Was just a detail friends would see:
A sculptor's sweet commissioned grace
Thrown off in helping to prolong
The Latin names around the base.

They would not guess how early in
Their supine stationary voyage
The air would change to soundless damage,
Turn the old tenantry away:
How soon succeeding eyes begin
To look, not read. Rigidly they

Persisted, linked, through lengths and breadths
Of time. Snow fell, undated. Light
Each summer thronged the glass. A bright
Litter of birdcalls strewed the same
Bone-riddled ground. And up the paths
The endless altered people came,

Washing at their identity.
Now, helpless in the hollow of
An unarmorial age, a trough
Of smoke in slow suspended skeins
Above their scrap of history,
Only an attitude remains:

Time has transfigured them into
Untruth. The stone fidelity
They hardly meant has come to be
Their final blazon, and to prove
Our almost-instinct almost true:
What will survive of us is love.

Philip Larkin, *An Arundel Tomb*

1d   By mid-afternoon the tide was lapping again at his right flipper, but
      even when it reached its peak, the water was no more than two feet
      deep around the body.

      At that moment the whale's eyes were just beneath the surface,
      and he seemed to realise that it was now or never. He made a mighty
      effort, lifting his fins and tail flukes as high as they would go,
      straining the whole spine into a tight arc and then slapping
      everything down together in what should have been a great leap free
      of the surface.

      But gravity and inertia were too much for him, and after half a
      dozen further attempts, he collapsed and didn't move again. We
      knew then that it was hopeless. He was going to die. I couldn't bear
      to watch any more and walked as fast as I could on round the
      eastern shore to the bay of Telok Ketjil, working off my anger and
      despair in physical effort.

By the time I returned it was well after dark, but the moon was coming up behind me and I could see everything very clearly. I was calm now, but filled with hopeless sorrow like a doctor forced to watch a patient die for lack of the appropriate vaccine. The whale was abandoned again by the tide and by all the people except Tia, who knelt on the sand beside the massive head and gently stroked his skin. She was singing to him. Singing one of the soft, sad songs in the old language. A song of friends long dead and times now past, of children grown and gone. A sound like a mother's sigh.

I couldn't understand the words any more than the whale could, but there was no mistaking the meaning. She was keeping him company in the dark hours of his long and lonely death. Sitting in for the other whales who, if he had been dying in the deeps, would have borne him to the surface on their fins, helping him to breathe and see, easing his passage with their sympathy and song.

This child, in her innocence, was doing the proper thing. I in my rage and futility, and Marduk in his righteous propriety, had missed the point altogether. So bound up in the petty intricacies of our politics and technology, we couldn't see that all the situation required was compassion. Not how to move the whale, or how to move the people; but how to be kind and to keep in touch. A way of reaching out in empathy to the biggest brain on the planet. I hung back in the shadows and watched them for a while, a child and a whale in communion.

Lyall Watson, *Gifts of Unknown Things*

31e And there was a woman who had had a flow of blood for twelve years, and who had suffered much under many physicians, and had spent all that she had, and was no better but rather grew worse. She had heard the reports about Jesus, and came up behind him in the crowd and touched his garment. For she said, "If I touch even his garments, I shall be made well." And immediately the haemorrhage ceased; and she felt in her body that she was healed of her disease. And Jesus, perceiving in himself that power had gone forth from him, immediately turned about in the crowd, and said, "Who touched my garments?" And his disciples said to him, "You see the

crowd pressing around you, and yet you say, 'Who touched me?'"
And he looked around to see who had done it. But the woman,
knowing what had been done to her, came in fear and trembling and
fell down before him, and told him the whole truth. And he said to
her, "Daughter, your faith has made you well; go in peace, and be
healed of your disease."

Mark 5, 25-34

31f   You will find, in fact, that the concept of truth was originated by the
senses and that the senses cannot be rebutted. The testimony that we
must accept as more trustworthy is that which can spontaneously
overcome falsehood with truth. What then are we to pronounce more
trustworthy than the senses? Can reason derived from the deceitful
senses be invoked to contradict them, when it is itself wholly derived
from the senses? If they are not true, then reason in its entirety is
equally false. Or can hearing give the lie to sight, or touch to
hearing? Can touch in turn be discredited by taste or refuted by the
nostrils or rebutted by the eyes? This, in my view, is out of the
question. Each sense has its own distinctive faculty, its specific
function. There must be separate discernment of softness and cold
and heat and of the various colours of things and whatever goes with
the colours; separate functioning of the palate's power of taste;
separate generation of scents and sounds. This rules out the
possibility of one sense confuting another. It will be equally out of
the question for one sense to belie itself, since it will always be
entitled to the same degree of credence. Whatever the senses may
perceive at any time is all alike true. Suppose that reason cannot
elucidate the cause why things that were square when close at hand
are seen as round in the distance. Even so, it is better, in default of
reason, to assign fictitious causes to the two shapes than to let things
clearly apprehended slip from our grasp. This is to attack belief at its
very roots - to tear up the entire foundation on which the
maintenance of life is built. It is not only reason that would collapse
completely. If you did not dare trust your senses so as to keep clear
of precipices and other such things to be avoided and make for their
opposites, there would be a speedy end to life itself.

Lucretius, *The Nature of the Universe*

155

31g It was absolutely forbidden that male Zen monks should touch females. Two monks came to a stream bank where a woman desperately needed to cross to get to her child on the other side. One monk simply picked her up and carried her across and put her down on the other side. The two monks walked on and it appeared the other monk was troubled. Finally after six miles, the troubled monk blurted out, "How could you pick up and carry a woman. You know it is forbidden?" The helpful monk just said, "I put her down on the stream bank. *You* are still carrying her."

This stressful tearing apart of thought occurs to all who try to control thought. It was an experience known to most saints. Those who never tried to control anything find it hard to fathom. It is a very useful process. It directly overcomes the vanity of the thought that one can control all thoughts. You quickly find you are involved in forces larger than yourself.

Wilson van Dusen, *Emanuel Swedenborg's Journal of Dreams*

What matters is how I *interpret* the evidence of my senses - they may be telling me half-truths. Teach me to respect the intangible.

---

32   FRIENDS AND NEIGHBOURS
- Community and Companionship

32a   **God loves everything that he has made - and that includes people, good and bad alike. Love is the wish to be close to and to be part of another. God likes people to be happy.**

This all-pervading divine love crops up again and again - it's universal. We find it in the way parents care for their children, and in the way birds and animals cherish their young. Even deadly serpents look after their little ones. God's love affects everything and everyone, especially those who themselves believe in him and are charitably disposed toward their neighbour - we may call it friendship.

When you invite someone to dinner, you shake hands, serve the best you can, and try to be helpful. When like-minded people get together that's another instance of divine love in operation. It can even be seen in the way that plants and trees respond to the warmth of the sun and become fruitful. The sun's heat is an expression of spiritual heat which is love itself.

True Christian Religion 43, 44

32b   Those who already believe in a loving God will have no difficulty here. Those who are not so sure may find this piece rather glib and one-sided. It has, after all, been taken out of context.

Swedenborg's particular contribution is the idea that the love of God is an all-pervasive innate *conatus* that causes even things, as well as humans, to gravitate together. I'm not sure how this squares with the galaxies which - so I'm informed - are flying apart at immense speed, but I can see that it does tend to work with people. It's abundantly clear that the general run of mankind likes nothing better than to gang together for one purpose or another. We have suffered enough down the centuries from cults and combines of various kinds: regiments and warring factions have often torn the world apart, but even these instruments of greed and aggression might, I suppose, be regarded as examples of divine love, but of divine love perverted.

At the same time, we may take great comfort from the many charitable institutions where people have pooled their resources to support and care for others. Togetherness works both ways, but hermits are scarce these days, and few of us can do without company completely.

32c 'Now what is history? Its beginning is that of the centuries of systematic work devoted to the solution of the enigma of death, so that death itself may eventually be overcome. This is why people write symphonies, and why they discover mathematical infinity and electromagnetic waves. Now, you can't advance in this direction without a certain upsurge of spirit. You can't make such discoveries without spiritual equipment, and for this, everything necessary has been given us in the Gospels. What is it? Firstly, the love of one's neighbour - the supreme form of living energy. Once it fills the heart of man it has to overflow and spend itself. And secondly, the two concepts which are the main part of the make-up of modern man - without them he is inconceivable - the ideas of free personality and of life regarded as sacrifice. - Mind you, all this is still quite new. There was no history in this sense in the classical world. There you had blood and beastliness and cruelty and pock-marked Caligulas untouched by the suspicion that any man who enslaves others is inevitably second-rate. There you had the boastful dead eternity of bronze monuments and marble columns. It was not until after the coming of Christ that time and man could breathe freely. It was not until after Him that men began to live in their posterity and ceased to die in ditches like dogs - instead, they died at home, in history, at the height of the work they devoted to the conquest of death, being themselves dedicated to this aim. - Ouf! I'm sweating like a pig. I might as well be talking to a blank wall.'

'That's metaphysics, my dear fellow. It's forbidden me by my doctors, my stomach won't take it.'

Boris Pasternak, *Doctor Zhivago*

2d   I see the clubs*, as they are called, coming down the village; a
procession of its rustic population all in their best attire. In front of
them comes bearing the great banner, emblazoned with some fitting
scene and motto, old Harry Lomax, the blacksmith, deputed to that
office for the brawny strength of his arms, and yet, if the wind be
stirring, evidently staggering under its weight, and finding enough to
do to hold it aloft. There it floats its length of blue and yellow, and
on its top nods the huge posy of peonies, laburnum flowers, and
lilacs, which our own garden has duly furnished. Then comes
sounding the band of drums, bassoons, hautboys, flutes, and
clarionets: then the honorary members - the freeholders of the place
- the sage apothecary, and the priest whose sermon says "be merry"
- literally, for years, his text being on this day the words of Solomon
- "Let us eat and drink, for tomorrow we die"; and then the simple
sons of the hamlet, walking as stately and as gravely as they can for
the nods and smiles of their neighbours who do not join in the
procession, but are all at door and window to see them go by.

There they go, passing down the shady lane with all the village
children at their heels, to the next hamlet, half a mile off, which
furnishes members to the club, and must therefore witness their
glory. Now the banner and the gilded tops of their wands are seen
glancing between the hedgerow trees; their music comes merrily up
the hill; and as it dies away at the next turn, the drumming of distant
villages becomes audible in half a dozen different quarters. Then
come, one after another, the clubs of the neighbouring hamlets.

William Howitt, *The Rural Life of England, Vol.II (1838)*

* Friendly Societies, forerunners of trade unions.
' The older societies formed bonds of fellowship, and tended to bring men into
social contact, a benefit that village life can ill afford to lose.'
(Government Report 1919)

2e   And Jesus answering said, A certain man went down from Jerusalem
to Jericho, and fell among thieves, which stripped him of his
raiment, and wounded him, and departed, leaving him half dead.

And by chance there came down a certain priest that way: and
when he saw him, he passed by on the other side. And likewise a

Levite, when he was at the place, came and looked on him, and passed by on the other side.

But a certain Samaritan, as he journeyed, came where he was: and when he saw him, he had compassion on him. And went to him, and bound up his wounds, pouring in oil and wine, and set him on his own beast, and brought him to an inn, and took care of him. And on the morrow when he departed, he took out two pence, and gave them to the host, and said unto him, Take care of him; and whatsoever thou spendest more, when I come again, I will repay thee.

Now which of these three, thinkest thou, was neighbour unto him that fell among the thieves? And he said, He that shewed mercy on him. Then said Jesus unto him, Go, and do thou likewise.

Luke 10, 30-37

32f   "Had he and I but met
            By some old ancient Inn,
    We should have sat us down to wet
            Right many a nipperkin!

    "But ranged as infantry
            And staring face to face,
    I shot at him as he at me,
            And killed him in his place.

    "I shot him dead because -
            Because he was my foe,
    Just so: my foe of course he was;
            That's clear enough; although

    "He thought he'd list, perhaps,
            Offhand like - Just as I -
    Was out of work - had sold his traps -
            No other reason why.

"Yes; quaint and curious war is!
    You shoot a fellow down
You'd treat if met where any bar is,
    Or help to half-a-crown."

Thomas Hardy, *The Man He Killed*

2g   The causes of the disaster are not due to faulty organisation, but to
misfortune in all risks which had to be undertaken... But it would do
your heart good to be in our tent, and to hear our songs and the
cheery conversation... We have decided to die naturally in the track...
We could have got through if we had neglected our sick...

We are weak, writing is difficult, but for my own sake I do not
regret this journey, which has shown that Englishmen can endure
hardships, help one another, and meet death with as great a fortitude
as ever in the past. We took risks, we knew we took them; things
have come out against us, and therefore we have no cause for
complaint, but bow to the will of Providence, determined still to do
our best to the last... Had we lived, I should have had a tale to tell of
the hardihood, endurance and courage of my companions which
would have stirred the heart of every Englishman. These rough notes
and our dead bodies must tell the tale...

To Mrs. E A Wilson

My Dear Mrs.Wilson, -
If this letter reaches you Bill and I will have gone out together.
We are very near it now and I should like you to know how splendid
he was at the end - everlastingly cheerful and ready to sacrifice
himself for others, never a word of blame to me for leading him into
this mess. He is not suffering, luckily, at least only minor
discomforts.

His eyes have a comfortable blue look of hope and his mind is
peaceful with the satisfaction of his faith in regarding himself as part

of the great scheme of the Almighty. I can do no more to comfort you than to tell you that he died as he lived, a brave, true man - the best of comrades and staunchest of friends.

My whole heart goes out to you in pity. Yours, R. Scott.

Scott of the Antarctic - *last notes*

Let us not forget that infant humans are among the most dependent of creatures, and even when they grow up they seldom survive for long alone.

---

33   GARDENS OF CONTENTMENT
- An Eloquent Environment

3a   **Those who pride themselves on their erudition in support of
fallacies don't employ the faculty of true reason, but simply
revel in the ability to put up a good argument, which is not the
same thing at all. Indulging in polemics for its own sake is by no
means rational: it's often a matter of 'proving' whatever takes
one's fancy. The real truth remains hidden. Genuine rationality
is like a garden: seeds of truth, planted in the memory sprout
and flower in the warmth and light of heaven. Angels get very
upset when clever academics tend to attribute everything to
'nature' and deny all heavenly influence. Such characters in the
other life lose their powers of argument, lest they mislead the
simple-minded, and are banished into the desert.**

   **Heavenly gardens are a living expression of the faculty of
reason. When the spirit of God with its celestial power stirs the
rational mind, then the paradise gardens appear in all their
marvellous beauty and abundance surpassing every imagination.
What is so moving is not so much the loveliness of the gardens
themselves, but the heavenly motives that inspire them.**

Heaven and Hell 464 Arcana Caelestia 1588

3b   This is a typical example of Swedenborg making a 'pre-emptive
strike' - putting a stop to the debate before it has even begun. By
flouting dialectic skills he effectively puts any opposing argument in
a no-win situation. However, it's easy to see what he's getting at.
The mastermind mentality tends to treat argument as some kind of
competitive sport concerned only with scoring points. Political
slanging matches, for example, seldom arrive at lasting solutions.

   I'm sure, however, that Swedenborg doesn't really regard debate
as the work of the devil. I certainly don't. Reasoned argument is
surely a mark of civilisation, provided it is informed by love - its
intention to woo, not to win. So the image of a garden is apt - a
place where lovely things *grow* and are not merely fabricated, where

163

intelligence weaves organic patterns rather than the brittle intricacies contrived by man alone.

33c   Around Swedenborg's house was a large garden, with many fruit trees and flowers. Here at times he was to be found entertaining his visitors, giving some little attention to the plants, or walking up and down the paths, his mind deep in thought, his face lit up with a cheerful smile and his grey hairs peeping out in all directions from under his wig. With him, on the small estate, dwelt an old gardener and his wife who were deeply attached to him. While the gardener was occupied with the fruit and vegetables, all of which he was allowed to use for himself, his wife attended to the few and simple needs of the master of the house...

While at work, Swedenborg needed complete quiet. But at other times it delighted him to show children round the garden. In one corner he had made a maze from which the children, having once entered, had great difficulty in finding the way out. He also arranged in one of the garden buildings a 'blind door'. Behind the door was nothing but a large mirror. When one of the children opened the door, supposing it led out into the garden, he saw in front of him the reflection of the flower beds and bushes which were really behind him. The arrangement was skilfully made and gave the children endless amusement.

Eric A.Sutton *The Happy Isles*

33d   All gardens that are tended pay tribute to the unconquerable spirit of man, for he embarks on a labour that can have no end and knows that he is fighting Nature all the time. She does not want an ordered beauty, she is an experimenter; she does not preserve life, but is prepared to squander it without remorse; there is no step you can take along the road to beauty without learning that she is waiting to trip you up.

My first garden, only a few yards long, was given to me more than sixty years ago; since then I have cultivated acres of garden and miles, literally miles, of grass paths, and acres of orchard and vegetable ground. Looking back on my work there is only one word that can be used to describe it - failure...

We can keep a space of garden ground clear by hand weeding, and see order come back and remain in attendance until the first heavy shower drives it away, and here such visitations are rare. We can keep certain greatly favoured trees and bushes from wilting by making trenches in the sandy soil round them, and turning on the hose or carrying cans of water. Not much good as war-work* you may say, and rightly, but if you can't sustain any effort however excellent your intention, surely it is good to keep a little space of God's shattered world clean and productive?

S.L.Bensusan, *Gardener's Path*

* Written during time of war 1942-4

3e   Here in a quiet and dusty room they lie,
Faded as crumbled stone or shifting sand,
Forlorn as ashes, shrivelled, scentless, dry -
Meadows and gardens running through my hand.

Dead that shall quicken at the trump of spring,
Sleepers to stir beneath June's morning kiss,
Though bees pass over, unremembering,
And no bird seeks here bowers that were his.

In this brown husk a dale of hawthorn dreams;
A cedar in this narrow cell is thrust
That will drink deeply of a century's streams;
These lilies shall make summer on my dust.

Here in their safe and simple house of death,
Sealed in their shells, a million roses leap;
Here I can blow a garden with my breath,
And in my hand a forest lies asleep.

Muriel Stuart, *The Seed Shop*

33f Cottage garden plants are enjoying renewed interest among gardeners, but they have never been out of fashion in churchyards. Many species planted on graves are brought from local gardens and the introduced plants of the churchyard may be as representative of the domestic flora of the parish as the wild flowers are of the surrounding countryside. Many of them are native wild plants that grow truly wild only in restricted locations or conditions, but have been widely grown in gardens and churchyards. Common Solomon's seal, with its arch of wing-like leaves and creamy flower bells, is a plant of southern woodlands, but it is well established and widespread as an introduction. It shares its churchyard habitat with a hybrid that is the most common garden form. Solomon's seal has had biblical associations since at least the first century AD. Its root is supposed to resemble the seal of Solomon, the magic pentacle which was supposed to point to the five wounds of Christ. It has an alternative English name, 'ladder to heaven' and it is often planted upon graves. In favourable conditions it can spread to form a most attractive small forest of foliage, which arises suddenly as if from nowhere in spring.

Francesca Greenoak, *God's Acre*

33g In the middle of the garden the Lord God had planted two very special trees - the Tree of Life and the Tree of the Knowledge of Good and Evil. Adam is commanded *not* to eat the fruit of the second tree - the Tree of Knowledge, for short, - "for when you eat of it, says the Lord, you will surely die". The fruit of all other trees, however, Adam is free to eat and enjoy.

The two 'special' trees in the middle of the garden represent the two central ways the psyche can mentally see and understand its experience of life. The first way - the Tree of Life, is to experience its life and its world as it is in reality - 'Life made manifest', that is, as an expression of omnipresent divine life.

The second way - the Tree of the Knowledge of Good and Evil, is for the psyche to perceive its world as a *separate* explorable domain, existing independently from itself - as, in fact, it always so *appears*.

In effect, the Divine Source provides the means for the psyche to be aware of two ways of 'seeing' or interpreting its experience of life: one according to deeply intuited reality, the other according to sensed appearance.

According to the first way, it is recognised that true knowledge is to be found in the hidden depths of spirit or Life itself.

According to the second way, it appears that knowledge of truth about life can be discovered and gained 'for oneself' through exploration and experience in the outer world of forms. But the psyche has the deep intuitive knowledge of the divine warning that actually to *experience* this path leads to losing touch with its Divine Source and reality, which is 'spiritual death'.

Michael Stanley, *Eve, the Bone of Contention*

Let us listen to one another's arguments, and not be too upset if by any strange chance the other person should turn out to be right after all.

---

34   HAPPY AND GLORIOUS
- The Awesome Face of Wonderment

34a   **The clothing of the angels matches their intelligence, the brighter the angel the more glittering and flamboyant the outfit. Some appear in luminous apparel; lesser intelligences are attired in shining white, and some in coloured gear of various kinds. The innermost angels, in their innocence, need no clothes at all. You could say these denote levels of 'divine truth' - some garments are ablaze with goodness and light, while others reflect a whole spectrum of truthful ideas - white light splintered into its several colours. These are not optical tricks, but real costumes that can be put on or taken off as befits the mood of the wearer.**

I have seen palaces in heaven that defy description, they are so grand, their upper storeys gleaming like pure gold, and the lower floors sparkling like gems. The interior decoration is beyond any human language. In the radiant parkland round-about there are flowers gleaming with all the colours of the rainbow: the leaves shine like silver and golden fruits adorn the trees.

The light of the world and the light of heaven are incomparable. The intelligence of heaven has nothing to do with the wit of man, but is a kind of intuitive perception springing from a love of truth itself - the source of all heavenly light. Thus the glories of heaven exist, not for their own sake, but as an automatic illumination of the truth within.

Heaven and Hell, 178, 179, 181, 185, 347

34b   I am not, myself, cut out for this sort of heaven. The prospect makes me profoundly uneasy. I can do without the bright lights and the extravaganza. In the unlikely event that I should ever attain to a place among the blessed, I'd gladly settle for more homely surroundings. Let me awaken in a corner of some cosy downtown celestial tavern with a comely angelic barmaid in attendance. As for clothing, give me a comfortable tweed jacket and a warm pair of twill trousers without any holes in the pockets.

Frankly, Swedenborg's description surprises me. After all, his own lifestyle was pretty frugal, and his lodgings made no pretence at grandeur. I can only think that he is trying here to convey some ecstatic experience way beyond all normal human comprehension. It is perhaps unfortunate that he chose imagery which has dated somewhat since the 18th.century, but what else could he do ? He says as much when he tells us that the light of heaven is by no means the same as the light of the world. I draw comfort from that, and from his insistence elsewhere that angels are still real people and not some dazzling mutation.

4c   He carried me away in the spirit to a great and high mountain, and shewed me that great city, the holy Jerusalem, descending out of heaven from God, having the glory of God: and her light was like unto a stone most precious, even like a jasper stone, clear as crystal; and had a wall great and high, and had twelve gates, and at the gates twelve angels, and names written thereon, which are the names of the twelve tribes of the children of Israel. On the east three gates; on the north three gates; on the south three gates; and on the west three gates. And the wall of the city had twelve foundations, and in them the names of the twelve apostles of the Lamb. And he that talked with me had a golden reed to measure the city, and the gates thereof, and the wall thereof. And the city lieth foursquare, and the length is as large as the breadth: and he measured the city with the reed, twelve thousand furlongs. The length and the breadth and the height of it are equal. And he measured the wall thereof, an hundred and forty and four cubits, according to the measure of a man, that is, of the angel. And the building of the wall of it was of jasper: and the city was pure gold, like unto clear glass. And the foundations of the wall of the city were garnished with all manner of precious stones. The first foundation was jasper; the second, sapphire; the third, a chalcedony; the fourth, an emerald; the fifth, sardonyx; the sixth, sardius; the seventh, chrysolite; the eighth, beryl; the ninth, a topaz; the tenth, a chrysoprasus; the eleventh, a jacinth; the twelfth, an amethyst. And the twelve gates were twelve pearls; every several gate was of one pearl: and the street of the city was pure gold, as it were transparent glass.

And I saw no temple therein: for the Lord God Almighty and the Lamb are the temple of it. And the city had no need of the sun, neither of the moon, to shine in it: for the glory of God did lighten it, and the Lamb is the light thereof. And the nations of them which are saved shall walk in the light of it: and the kings of the earth do bring their glory and honour into it. And the gates of it shall not be shut at all by day: for there shall be no night there. And they shall bring the glory and honour of the nations into it. And there shall in no wise enter into it any thing that defileth, neither whatsoever worketh abomination, or maketh a lie: but they which are written in the Lamb's book of life.

Revelation 21, 10-27

34d   'Look! Look at that!' exclaimed voices. 'She's going to dance! That blind girl's going to dance! Fancy that!'

'Ain't it a bleedin' wonder!' said Rosy Starling scornfully. 'And me with me disability!'

She tossed her head and leaned, lightly as a feather, on Turtle's strong left arm.

He watched, with infinite care, the ground before her feet; he guided her away from the looser cobbles, he wove her in and out of the moving dancers, drawing her away from the wilder ones and taking her gently into the current of the maypole dance.

She followed as effortlessly as his shadow.

'Quicker - quicker!' she breathed. 'I can go quicker...only - only just keep hold of me hand!'

Turtle obeyed. He danced well, and he knew it. Music of any description excited and exhilarated him; but he had never before felt it so strongly as now, when he moved to the ragged banging and scraping of the sweeps' three fiddles and tambourine.

'Like King David before the Ark of the Covenant,' muttered the ancient pedlar to his boy as they watched from the fringe of the crowd. 'By my life and soul!'

Turtle was indeed dancing with a rare skill and ecstacy, as he stared and stared at Rosy Starling who seemed insensible of his tethering hand and flew like a bird.

Walls were melting before her and crowding bars were proving no more substantial than bad dreams. The darkness was expanding and stretching till it was an infinite green space through which, she felt, she could dance and fly for ever. There was no loneliness in it, no red of pain nor white of death; all was green, as far as the inner eye could see.

'On me own! On me own! Let me try! Let me spin!'

Turtle hesitated, then let her go. She swayed a little, then she began to turn. Every part of her expressed amazement and delight. Turtle stepped back, as did other dancers till there was a moving circle of space about her. Everyone felt the strange nature of the blind girl's escape into space.

Leon Garfield, *Rosy Starling*

4e   It is a great adventure to contemplate the universe, beyond man, to contemplate what it would be like without man, as it was in a great part of its long history and as it is in a great majority of places. When this objective view is finally attained, and the mystery and majesty of matter are fully appreciated, to then turn the objective eye back on man viewed as matter, to view life as part of this universal mystery of greatest depth, is to sense an experience which is very rare, and very exciting. It usually ends in laughter and a delight in the futility of trying to understand what this atom in the universe is, this thing - atoms with curiosity - that looks at itself and wonders why it wonders. Well, these scientific views end in awe and mystery, lost at the edge in uncertainty, but they appear to be so deep and so impressive that the theory that it is all arranged as a stage for God to watch man's struggle for good and evil seems inadequate.

Richard P.Feynman, *The Uncertainty of Values*

4f   It is difficult to find a religion which has not, at some stage in its history, inspired in the breasts of at least certain of its followers those transports of mystical exaltation in which man's whole being seems to fuse in a glorious communion with the divinity. Transcendental experiences of this kind, typically conceived of as states of 'possession', have given the mystic a unique claim to direct experiential knowledge of the divine and, where this is acknowledged by others, the authority to act as a privileged channel of communication between man and the supernatural. The accessory phenomena associated with such experiences, particularly the 'speaking with tongues', prophesying, clairvoyance, the transmission of messages from the dead, and other mystical gifts, have naturally attracted the attention not only of the devout but also of sceptics. For many people, in fact, such phenomena seem to provide persuasive evidence for the existence of a world transcending that of ordinary everyday experience.

I.M.Lewis, *Ecstatic Religion*

34g   The angelic nature in number doth extend
        So far beyond the range of mortal mind,
        No tongue or thought has ever reached the end.

And in the Book of Daniel thou wilt find,
        For all the thousand thousands he there states,
        No fixed and final figure is assigned.

The Primal Light the whole irradiates,
        And is received therein as many ways
        As there are splendours wherewithal it mates.

Since, then, affection waits upon the gaze
        And its intensity, diversely bright
        Therein the sweets of love now glow, now blaze.

Consider well the breadth, behold the height
        Of His eternal Goodness, seeing that o'er
        So many mirrors It doth shed its light,

Yet One abideth as It was before.

Dante Alighieri, *Paradise,* Canto XXIX 130-145, Tr. Barbara Reynolds

---

I do enjoy the occasional firework display, and stately homes are fine for a day out, but when the show is over may there always be a comfortable home-coming and a well-worn easy chair.

---

35 ON A PERSONAL NOTE
- The Gifts and Curses of Heredity

35a **Perceptive people suspect, in their wisdom, that the story of Adam and Eve must have some meaning, but what that meaning is no-one seems prepared to say. Obviously the Almighty would scarcely have planted a couple of trees in a garden simply to trip up the unwary. The idea that two people, just because they took a bite from the wrong tree, were thereby cursed and that the curse plagued everyone ever after is plainly daft, especially since no real offence took place. If God was so concerned about his precious trees why didn't he take steps to keep Adam out of harm's way, and why didn't he keep the talking serpent under control?**

The story is, in fact, about the freewill which people enjoy when confronted by the malignant longings which they inherit from their parents. Under no circumstances will God ever take away that freewill. Persistent mindsets can be traced through many generations, but everyone can always decide for himself whether to go for the tree of life, or the tree of the knowledge of good and evil.

The True Christian Religion, 469

35b Swedenborg's view of heredity is rather simplistic. After all, genetics hadn't been mooted, and Gregor Mendel wouldn't be born until another fifty years after Swedenborg's death. Even so, Swedenborg's grasp of the subject is tenable so far as it goes. He is, of course, preoccupied with hereditary *evil*. (Hereditary goodness, which he mentions briefly elsewhere - AC 6208 - is only a very poor substitute for the real thing.) To some extent we do seem to be stuck with the cards we are dealt at birth. I get the odd impression that we are each given a salutary injection of evil, administered by fate, in order to stimulate our defences and so to immunise the soul - that is, if our better nature wins the ensuing battle.

At all events, I am glad that genetically we do turn out as individuals. Our genes may determine what happens to us *physically.* When it comes to life everlasting, however, they don't have the last word - we do.

35c That lunchtime it was Janácek's *Sinfonietta* for orchestra at the Albert Hall, with a brass section like the band of the Grenadier Guards. In 1864, at the age of ten, Leos Janácek joined the choir school at the monastery of the Augustinians in Brno where he studied under the choirmaster Pavel Krizkovsky. Thus said the programme notes.

Like Mendel, Janácek was from northern Moravia. They would have shared the accent. Like Mendel, Janácek was fascinated by the countryside and by wildlife. He must have walked round the monastery garden with the friar; he must have seen the mice in their cages and the bees in the hives on the slope behind the chapter house; he must have played with the pet vixen, an orphaned animal that had been rescued as a cub by a friend of Mendel's; he must have heard the fat friar's stories about animals and lectures condemning catapults. Mundane things, the matters of childhood that etch themselves more deeply into the memory than any adult experience.

Genetics is of scant interest to musicians, and music of rare concern to geneticists (although tone-deafness [dysmelodia] and perfect pitch are probably autosomal dominant traits with imperfect penetrance*); so biographies of Mendel never mention Janácek and biographies of the composer of *The Cunning Little Vixen* never mention Mendel. Such is the narrow way we perceive the past. When, at the age of nineteen, Janácek was appointed to the position of choirmaster in place of Father Pavel Krizkovsky it was Abbot Gregor Mendel who appointed him.

Simon Mawer, *Mendel's Dwarf*
* Kalmus and Fry. *Annals of Human Genetics 43*, 1980

35d And an angel of the Lord came up from Gilgal to Bochim, and said, I made you to go up out of Egypt, and have brought you unto the land which I sware unto your fathers; and I said, I will never break my covenant with you. And ye shall make no league with the inhabitants of this land; ye shall throw down their altars: but ye have not obeyed my voice: why have ye done this?

Wherefore I also said, I will not drive them out from before you; but they shall be as thorns in your sides, and their gods shall be a snare unto you.

And it came to pass, when the angel of the Lord spake these words unto all the children of Israel, that the people lifted up their voice, and wept. And they called the name of that place Bochim: and they sacrificed there unto the Lord.

And when Joshua had let the people go, the children of Israel went every man unto his inheritance to possess the land. And the people served the Lord all the days of Joshua, and all the days of the elders that outlived Joshua, who had seen all the great works of the Lord, that he did for Israel.

And Joshua the son of Nun, the servant of the Lord, died, being an hundred and ten years old. And they buried him in the border of his inheritance in Timnath-heres, in the mount of Ephraim, on the north side of the hill Gaash. And also all that generation were gathered unto their fathers; and there arose another generation after them, which knew not the Lord, nor yet the works which he had done for Israel.

Judges 2, 1-10

5e   Most mothers would not wish to pass on haemophilia, or other diseases that carry with them deformity and painful death for their children. But what about short-sightedness? A harmless disability - but a genetically passed one, and one that tends to be dominant. If we do not stop short-sighted people from 'breeding', it is only a matter of time before normally-sighted people will die out, and short-sightedness will be normal. We have by-passed natural selection, which would have guaranteed the early death of short-sighted people before they had had time to breed. By inventing glasses we have tampered with nature, and brought on ourselves a problem which will become increasingly acute. The same must be true for many other conditions. Our knowledge has brought us responsibilities that animals are not bothered with. This is the price of our humanity...

...there is another alternative, which may possibly embrace both the other biological ones - and that is the notion of *behaviourism.* Lamarck had hinted at this, but had not fully worked out the implications - the idea that skills acquired in a lifetime could be passed on to future generations. We have already seen how genetically this does not seem to be possible - for example, if you practise ten hours a day and become a concert pianist, your child will not be born any one whit more loose-fingered than the child next door. But the chances are high that he *will* grow up to be more musical, because of his background and the accepted pattern of musical training in the house. One might counter this by supposing that he will be *less* interested because he has had too much of it 'thrust down his throat'...

Our consciousness leads to behaviour, and our behaviour alters the future. And what scope lies there for man! It would take too long to argue whether or not animals have original ideas, and certainly we know that they don't have many. Man does.

Rosalyn Kendrick, *Does God Have a Body?*

35f   The congregation in Tollamore Church were singing the evening hymn, the people gently swaying backwards and forwards like trees in a soft breeze. The heads of the village children, who sat in the gallery, were inclined to one side as they uttered their shrill notes, their eyes listlessly tracing some crack in the old walls, or following the movement of a distant bough or bird, with features rapt almost to painfulness.

In front of the children stood a thoughtful young man, who was plainly enough the schoolmaster; and his gaze was fixed on a remote part of the aisle beneath him. When the singing was over, and all had sat down for the sermon, his eyes still remained in the same place. There was some excuse for their direction, for it was in a straight line forwards; but their fixity was only to be explained by some object before them. This was a square pew, containing one solitary sitter. But that sitter was a young lady, and a very sweet lady was she.

Afternoon service in Tollamore parish was later than in many others in that neighbourhood; and as the darkness deepened during the progress of the sermon, the rector's pulpit-candles shone to the remotest nooks of the building, till at length they became the sole lights of the congregation. The lady was the single person besides the preacher whose face was turned westwards, the pew that she occupied being the only one in the church in which the seat ran all round. She reclined in her corner her bonnet and dark dress growing by degrees invisible, and at last only her upturned face could be discerned, a solitary white spot against the black surface of the wainscot. Over her head rose a vast marble monument, erected to the memory of her ancestors, male and female; for she was one of high standing in that parish. The design consisted of a winged skull and two cherubim, supporting a pair of tall Corinthian columns, between which spread a broad slab, containing the roll of ancient names, lineages, and deeds, and surmounted by a pediment, with the crest of the family at its apex.

Thomas Hardy, *An Indiscretion in the Life of an Heiress*

35g   The cloning of humans is on most of the lists of things to worry about from Science, along with behaviour control, genetic engineering, transplanted heads, computer poetry, and the unrestrained growth of plastic flowers.

Cloning is the most dismaying of prospects, mandating as it does the elimination of sex with only a metaphoric elimination of death as compensation. It is almost no comfort to know that one's cloned, identical surrogate lives on, especially when the living will very likely involve edging one's real, now ageing self off to side, sooner or later. It is hard to imagine anything like filial affection or respect for a single, unmatched nucleus; harder still to think of one's new, self-generated self as anything but an absolute, desolate orphan. Not to mention the complex interpersonal relationship involved in raising one's self from infancy, teaching the language, enforcing discipline, instilling good manners, and the like. How would you feel if you became an incorrigible juvenile delinquent by proxy, at the age of fifty-five?

The public questions are obvious. Who is to be selected, and on what qualifications? How to handle the risks of misused technology, such as self-determined cloning by the rich and powerful but socially objectionable, or the cloning by governments of dumb, docile masses for the world's work? What will be the effect on all the uncloned rest of us of human sameness? After all, we've accustomed ourselves through hundreds of millennia to the continual exhilaration of uniqueness; each of us is totally different, in a fundamental sense, from all the other four billion. Selfness is an essential fact of life. The thought of human nonselfness, precise sameness, is terrifying, when you think about it.

Well, don't think about it, because it isn't a probable possibility, not even as a long shot for the distant future, in my opinion. I agree that you might clone some people who would look amazingly like their parent cell doners, but the odds are that they'd be almost as different as you or me, and certainly more different than any of today's identical twins.

Lewis Thomas, *The Medusa and the Snail*

Don't hold me responsible for my genes, they are not of my making. Family trees are for climbing rather than fruit-picking.

---

36   A RIGHT MIND
- The Pursuit of Reason and Omens of Madness

36a **When religious ideas come up in conversation, the 'celestial' angels simply affirm or deny: they don't argue - they *know*. 'Spiritual' angels, on the other hand, will discuss whether something is true or not.**

The mind is like a house with three floors - the angels live at the top, some rather worldly people live in the middle, and some very dodgy characters live in the basement. Anyone in their right mind has the run of the whole house and can even, to some extent, keep some order in the lower levels.

When a judge has listened to a lot of legal argument, he assembles the evidence in the lofty regions of his mind in order to make a detached assessment of the situation. He then comes down to earth and explains matters. We are surely all aware that we can sometimes grasp in a moment what may take an hour to spell out in detail.

The New Jerusalem 140 The True Christian Religion 395, 603

36b Swedenborg was *not* a philosopher, whatever people may say. Philosophers are good at formulating questions, but Swedenborg's speciality lay in giving answers - telling us what he had "seen and heard" - take it or leave it. His so-called 'arguments' are often bewildering: for example, something is reasonable if it is true, but unreasonable if it is false - which gets us precisely nowhere. Reason, he seems to say, is the reward of obedience, not the result of dispute. The highest angels enjoy God-given awareness rather than powers of argument. 'Spiritual' angels of a slightly lower rank may discuss theology, but the 'celestial' ones are way above that sort of thing. This is bad news for people like me who like to use their brains. After all, if the celestial angels don't discuss religion, what *do* they talk about, I should like to know? But actions speak louder than words, and I suppose all this is a warning for those of us who try to raise ourselves by our intellectual bootlaces. Heavenly entrance

179

requirements may be exacting, but intelligence tests are not included.

36c Philosophers often warn against confusing ontological questions with epistemological questions. What exists is one thing, they say, and what we can know about it is something else. There may be things that are completely unknowable to us, so we must be careful not to treat the limits of our knowledge as sure guides to the limits of what there is. I agree that this is good general advice, but I will argue that we already know enough about minds to know that one of the things that makes them different from everything else in the universe is the *way* we know about them. For instance, you know you have a mind and you know you have a brain, but these are different kinds of knowledge. You know you have a brain the way you know you have a spleen: by hearsay. You've never seen your spleen or your brain (I would bet), but since the textbooks tell you that all normal human beings have one of each, you conclude that you almost certainly have one of each as well. You are more intimately acquainted with your mind - so intimately that you might even say that you *are* your mind. (That's what Descartes said: he said he was a mind, a *res cogitans*, or thinking thing.) A book or a teacher might tell you what a mind is, but you wouldn't have to take anybody's word for the claim that you had one. If it occurred to you to wonder whether you were normal and had a mind as other people do, you would immediately realise, as Descartes pointed out, that your very wondering this wonder demonstrated beyond all doubt that you did indeed have a mind.

Daniel C.Dennett, *Kinds of Minds*

36d To be conscious, is, first of all, to be aware. Consciousness seems to be what we know and remember. It is the space in which we live that we call our own, or at least the one within which we move, breathe, and have our being. To be conscious in this sense means not only to recognise that we are aware, but to recognise that there are fluctuations in our level of awareness. Some days we are very sensitive; other days we are completely insensitive. Some days we remember things; other days we are completely forgetful. All of this happens within our awareness. When we are not aware, most of us presume that we are not conscious. Thus, consciousness seems to expand and contract.

Eugene Taylor, *A Psychology of Spiritual Healing*

Eugene Taylor is quoting here (loosely, I think) from William James, *Principles of Psychology*

6e From the very beginning Yegor Timofeyevich realised that he was in a lunatic asylum, but this did not worry him as he was convinced that he could shed his body whenever he felt like it and could then fly and wander all over the world. The first days he flew every morning to his government office, but later he was deflected to more important occupations. He was tall and very lean; his hair, which was still very black and wavy, stuck out good-naturedly in all directions, and so did his beard. He wore spectacles with very thick lenses, and when he laughed he bared his gums, so that it looked as if the whole of him was laughing, both outside and inside, and that even his hair was laughing too. He laughed very often. His voice was low - a gurgling bass that sounded as though someone was sitting on him and bouncing up and down; but when he laughed very much it changed to a high tenor.

He soon made friends with all the other patients and assumed a prominent and definite position among them - that of protector. He knew vaguely that he was somebody very exalted, but his ideas on the subject were not very clear and therefore changed frequently: sometimes he felt he was Count Almaviva or a Councillor of the Provincial Administration, and at others, a saint performing miracles and a benefactor of mankind. This awareness of his stupendous strength, boundless power and dignity never deserted him; and made him very considerate in his dealings with others, only on rare occasions did he become stern or aggressive. This was when someone called him Yegor instead of 'Georgi'. With tears of indignation he then shouted that he was the victim of intrigue and wrote voluminous complaints to the Holy Synod and the Chapter of the Order of the Knights of St.George. Dr.Shevyrev would immediately send him a formal reply that his application had been granted, and he calmed down at once and poked fun at the doctor and his consternation at receiving an official document.

'I used to write hundreds of similar documents daily,' he would say laughing, 'and I could do the same now, if I wanted to.'

Leonid Andreyev, *Phantoms* Translated by Walter Morison

36f   The first humans, settled among the primal uplands of early Earth, were afflicted by a plague which destroyed their reason and left them, men women and children, dying beside the embers of their hard-won fires. The same plague still affects mankind, still rages unchecked among the peoples of the world - counting its victims in millions.

There seems to be no cure for the deadly fever, no vaccination or other control as there is for bacterial and viral diseases.

This plague is not spread by germs but by man to man, from parent to child, from nation to nation, as easily as words pass from mouth to ear.

Early symptoms are readily seen. Temples throb, faces redden, voices become angry shouts until its destroying arm, the arm of man himself, wields the killing machine of the age. The primal generators of this age-old infection continue to be religious belief and nationalism - widely accepted as banners to be carried boldly through life yet both manifest absurdities masquerading as absolutes.

In every community the vulnerable young are indoctrinated into the local faith by sincere adults and are never told that at the same time, in other communities, equally vulnerable young people are being instructed into quite different faiths by equally sincere and dominant adults.

Neither are they made aware that particular religions and nationalism bear no ultimate validity, being mere geographical accidents of birth.

After this indoctrination we are commonly surprised and even amused by the beliefs and ceremonies of other religions, while apparently not being aware of the patent absurdities of our own. This would be a harmless exercise if its followers did not use it as an excuse to hate and even make war against followers of other faiths.

Presumably most of those who read this are not atheists or supranationalists as I am and will already feel the maggots gnawing at their reason.

Rod Burnham, *The Hate that Plagues Mankind*

6g   In the winter time, when deep snow lay on the ground, a poor boy was forced to go out with a sledge to fetch wood. When he had gathered it together and piled it he wished, as he was so frozen with cold, not to go home at once but to light a fire and warm himself a little. So he scraped away the snow and as he was thus clearing the ground, he found a tiny gold key. So he thought that where the key was the lock must be too, and dug in the ground and found an iron chest. "If only the key fits it!" thought he; "no doubt there are precious things in that little box." He searched, but no keyhole was there. At last he discovered one, but so small that it was hardly visible. He tried it, and the key fitted it exactly. Then he turned it once round, and now we must wait until he has quite unlocked it and opened the lid, and then we shall learn what wonderful things were inside that box.

The Brothers Grimm, *The Golden Key*

May I know my own mind, & heed the minds of others.

37   A COSMIC TREASURE CHEST
- Jewels, Gold and Silver - Minerals

37a   Stones stand for truths - the sort of information you can rely on for support, like stepping stones. *Precious* stones are special kinds of truth: they express by their clarity and colour varieties of truth made luminous by the good intention behind them.

Stones that have been shaped for building (rather like bricks), however, may represent truths with which man has tinkered about for his own ends, so that they end up as falsities.

A craftsman who works with *precious* stones, however, engraving them and exploring every translucent facet, is more like someone who is prompted by a genuine love of truth, whose motives are good.

No-one, up to now, seems to have twigged that all the metals in the Bible - not to mention stone and wood - have inner meanings. Gold, for example, means celestial goodness, silver means spiritual truth, bronze means natural goodness, and iron means natural truth.

Arcana Caelestia, 425, 3858[9] 8941 9846

37b   It's marvellous what the universe is made of - tons of rock and debris whirling around in space. Earth was once, so they tell me, a seething mass of molten stuff. When it had cooled down a bit, fire and lava continued to gush out, forming volcanoes which, to this day, spew forth from time to time their primaeval pyro-technics over the surface of the globe. Now, magically, if we dig in just the right places, we find all manner of most useful and beautiful substances. This surprises me. We might so easily have found ourselves slopping about in some universal cosmic sludge.

Swedenborg tends to make us dizzy with vast abstract terms like goodness, truth, faith and charity - or their Latin equivalents - we find them on almost every page. They are space shots - attempts to categorise whatever it may be that makes people tick. At ground level, however, the basic qualities of minerals - Biblical ones anyway - may help us to identify some of our own buried motives as we poke around in life looking for gemstones.

87c   Intentionally coloured glassware, often in strong hues, both translucent and opaque, was caused by the addition of metallic oxides originally discovered by trial and error but perfected by every major ancient industry. Copper, for instance, produced blue, green or opaque red glass, depending on the conditions of the furnace. Manganese under the right circumstances yielded a purple glass and cobalt an attractive dark blue, Perhaps the most sophisticated use of such additives was achieved by the Roman industry of the fourth century AD, when producing dichroic (two- coloured) glass. The recipes called for the addition of powdered gold and silver which caused the glass to show a different colour depending on whether light was reflected from its surface or transmitted through it. The Rothschild Lycurgus Cup, presently housed in the British Museum, is the most celebrated example of such a technique. The cup is a striking jade-green colour in reflected light and a vivid magenta in transmitted light. Among translucent colours, royal blue, purple, yellow and several greens were common; and among opaque colours, red, white, yellow, light blue, turquoise and peacock blue, orange, diverse greens and even 'flesh-colour' were known. Frequently the most desirable colours resembled natural stones such as lapis lazuli and agate or synthetic materials like faience and enamels. Indeed, many of the first uses of glass were as substitutes for other substances, and in several ancient languages glass is actually referred to as 'man-made stone'. The iridescent gold and silver surfaces now associated with so much ancient glass are the result of weathering and devitrification and were never intentional. This rainbow-like effect occurs when thin layers of the alkali in the glass are slaked out over time by moisture and chemical agents, especially when the glass has lain in the earth for many years.

David F.Grose, *The Origins and Early History of Glass*

Why include this rather technical piece here? If we apply Swedenborg's 'correspondences' - 'truth' for light, 'love' and 'wisdom' for gold and silver, and so on, then some interesting psychological ideas emerge.

37d   Men are but children still and guard their toys
Most jealously. Is not the buffalo
Of coolest jade what engines are to boys,
And breaking it imparts an equal blow?
Is not the diamond pendant on the breast
A daisy chain writ larger with the years?
And all the rubies in an aunt's bequest
A cause of infant jealousy and tears?
Yet when the inventory has been made
And all our dear possessions laid on end,
We cannot take beyond the grave our jade
Or profit us our broken toys to mend.
Nor does the diamond in the darkness shine.
What shimmers there comes not from any mine.

Somerset de Chair, *Toys*

37e   We are only just beginning to rediscover the power of the mineral kingdom. I believe knowledge is contained within stones such as those at Stonehenge, Avebury, Machu Pichu in Peru, the Mayan temples in Guatemala, the pyramids of Egypt and Mexico, the stone temples in Angor Wat, Cambodia and many other well-known sites. I feel this knowledge was imprinted by wise men, just as we imprint information on to micro-discs today. Through science as well as religion we are beginning to read these stones. Crystals provide a bridge between right and left brain, yin and yang, positive and negative, male and female, science and spirit, and will in future, I believe, enable them to merge...

Stones, gems and crystals are magical and mysterious, a law unto themselves. They appear and disappear, lose their lustre when we are ill and sparkle when we are happy. They can be used to amplify thought, impart information, focus and transmit energy, generate love. Crystals are a rainbow bridge by which we can freely and joyously participate in the dance of life.

Soozi Holbeche, *The Power of Gems and Crystals*

87f The stones stand
in a rough circle
under the mountain's
coning shadow:
they lean and sag,
slowly bowing
back into the earth,
above the thin wedge
of level land
that tapers
and drops to where
the sea grinds in
to the land's heart.
These were the
royal tombs
of nameless kings
who ruled by
the slurring edge
of bronze, bringing
the ships from
the blue southern
seas in search

of gold and ores.
Once buried
by vast mounds,
they stand bare
under the lash
of the endless rain,
the soil drifting
away, year by year,
until, skeletal,
gray as the ages,
they wrench free
of the earth's clutch,
cancered by
spreading patches
of lichen, to tell
of the lost rituals
in one last
leaping song
of dumb praise
before they bow
back into the earth
again.

Bryn Griffiths, *Cerrig Y Gof*

7g According to several classical authors the Celts were a proud people, fond of displaying their wealth and status. In particular they had an obsession with gold. To some Roman and Greek writers, this was their major weakness. The Greek geographer Strabo, for example, wrote about what he called the Gaulish Celts' childish 'love of decoration. They wear ornaments of gold, torcs on their necks and bracelets on their arms and wrists, and their nobles adorn themselves with dyed garments sprinkled with gold. It is this vanity which makes them so unbearable in victory and so downcast in defeat....'

The pagan Celts took their most treasured possessions into the grave and the finest examples of Celtic art have been discovered in aristocratic tombs. Clothing accessories for both men and women, such as brooches, neck collars, torcs and armlets, were of rich metals. Gold, silver and bronze were cast in flat moulds and sometimes plaited to create more complex forms; some torcs consist of hollow tubes. Colour was provided by enamel inlays. Bronze hand-mirrors have been mainly found in women's graves, their backs incised with Celtic designs. Finely decorated metal horse-tackle, drinking bowls, swords, shields and helmets reflect the fighting and feasting of the myths.

Author unknown, *The Celts - Artists and Storytellers*

The mind has many workings. When one seam has been worked out, there is usually another.

---

38   HILARITY AND HOLINESS
- Laughter - Happiness - Joy

38a **When gladness wells up in the mind, the grey matter is, so to speak, released from its habitual straitjacket. The face lights up and the whole body seems to expand. We wake up and take a rosier view of life: the blood flows freely and the whole balance of mind and body is restored. Through gladness, all the anatomical paths of communication are opened...**

The brain is refreshed and experiences again a youthful vitality. Then joyful tremors arise - laughter shakes the body and gladdens the face, because brain and lungs alike dance to the same tempo. But outward laughter cannot exist without inner perception, so it is only found in mankind: its tremulous effects spring from the capacity to envisage present or future happiness. The first stage is contentment, the second is hilarity, the third gladness, and the fourth laughter.

The more a man is in tune with the Almighty the happier he becomes. States of blessedness intensify when the spiritual and celestial levels of the mind are opened up. They continue to expand for ever.

Rational Psychology, 201 Divine Providence, 37

38b So laughter is good for you, as medical opinion seems to confirm. Swedenborg's *Rational Psychology* is an early work. Later on, after his so-called 'illumination', he is more straight-faced and dwells more on the moral implications. The important thing *then* is what prompts the laughter in the first place. To laugh at another's misfortune, for example, is not what we would normally expect of angelic behaviour.

If there is laughter in heaven it bubbles up from purer springs, but without a lively sense of the ridiculous, the prospect is scarcely inviting. Does God allow himself the occasional chuckle? Religious movements have usually been pretty po-faced, but the remarkable thing about human beings is that they are the only species capable of laughing at themselves: I wish they would do so more often.

In order to appreciate the funny side of life you do, of course, have to detach yourself and look at the situation from a very long way off: only then can you see what amusing little creatures we humans are. It's not easy, but the fact that it's just *possible* gives cause for optimism.

38c   And they said unto him, Where is Sarah thy wife? And he said, Behold, in the tent. And he said, I will certainly return unto thee according to the time of life; and, lo, Sarah thy wife shall have a son. And Sarah heard it in the tent door, which was behind him.

Now Abraham and Sarah were old and well stricken in age; and it ceased to be with Sarah after the manner of women. Therefore Sarah laughed within herself, saying, After I am waxed old shall I have pleasure, my lord being old also? And the Lord said unto Abraham, Wherefore did Sarah laugh, saying, Shall I of a surety bear a child, which am old? Is anything too hard for the Lord? At the time appointed I will return unto thee, according to the time of life, and Sarah shall have a son. Then Sarah denied, saying, I laughed not; for she was afraid. And he said, Nay; but thou didst laugh.

Genesis 18, 9-15. 21, 5-6.

38d   I've wisdom from the East and from the West,
        That's subject to no academic rule;
You may find it in the jeering of a jest,
        Or distil it from the folly of a fool.
I can teach you with a quip, if I've a mind;
        I can trick you into learning with a laugh;
Oh, winnow all my folly, and you'll find
        A grain or two of truth among the chaff!

I can set a braggart quailing with a quip,
        The upstart, I can wither with a whim;

He may wear a merry laugh upon his lip,
    But his laughter has an echo that is grim.
When they're offered to the world in merry guise'
    Unpleasant truths are swallowed with a will -
For he who'd make his fellow-creatures wise
    Should always gild the philosophic pill!

W. S. Gilbert, The Philosophic Pill

8e   The Emergence of The Fool : The fool is holy. The fool contains
within its symbol the image of a being of deep humility, he is not a
king, but a simpleton, one who stands apart from the rest because of
his unworldliness, he calls us to sympathy, to pity, for the fool is
vulnerable. He is not glamorous, has no worldly trappings and his
path is one that few would want to imitate, for he becomes easily the
subject of ridicule, as he wanders through a hostile world with little
in the way of possessions or power. And yet Cecil felt that this was
an apt symbol for his work, for the fool is like the new born baby
who has just started on his quest, his journey through life. In the fool
is a certain wisdom, and a certain lack of fear, for he approaches
every day afresh, and gradually builds his wisdom as he goes along.
His quest is the inner journey, he must understand and bring to
others the meaning behind his existence.

Linda Anne Landers, On Cecil Collins

8f   Those of us who are Anglicans know well that the language of the
Book of Common Prayer, its extraordinary beauties of sound and
rhythm, can all too easily tempt us to delight in the sheer sound
without thinking what the words mean or whether we mean them. In
the General Confession, for example, what a delight to the tongue
and ear it is to recite 'We do earnestly repent and are heartily sorry
for these our misdoings; and the remembrance of them is grievous
unto us; the burden of them is intolerable.' Is it really intolerable?
Not very often.

W. H. Auden, Secondary Worlds

38g   The moral and religious life is not really bound to be joyless - I
        know plenty of men and women who live it joyfully - but deep
        within most of us lies the gloomy conviction that being good and
        God-fearing rules out having fun. This is partly the fault of the
        church, with its ancient heresy that whatever delights the flesh must
        distract the soul from total devotion to God. We are told that God
        manifests himself to us in his earthly gifts; but have not the holiest
        people denied themselves every bodily comfort to reach the heights?
        Their example has entrenched the belief that the religious life must
        be set apart from the world, a rigour which most of us do not want
        and could not manage if we wished it, because of our
        responsibilities to others. Partly also our conviction does reflect our
        awareness that we are sinful and that many of the things that please
        us will turn out wrong. We might do better if we chose to; but
        choosing can be tiresome and so we slip into the assumption that
        morality brings misery and that pleasure lies outside it.

        This is very poor theology. If we believe in a Creator God, it
        hardly seems likely that he will have endowed us (and the innocent
        beasts) with pleasant sensations which are inherently evil. Even the
        sense of having done right is a pleasure. It is our motive for seeking
        these pleasures and the use we make of them - in two words, our
        choice - that raises the moral issue and the possibility of
        unhappiness.

                                              Gerald Priestland, *Enjoy, Enjoy!*

Let us take life seriously - but not too seriously

---

39   LAW AND ORDER
- A Quiet Life

9a   **There are two areas where people need to be kept in order - 'ecclesiastical' to do with heaven, and 'civil' to do with the world. Order cannot be preserved on Earth unless there is always someone in command to keep an eye on things, to reward the virtuous and punish the wayward. Otherwise civilisation would disintegrate. Everyone inherits a propensity to order other people around, and to help himself to their belongings, resulting in all sorts of anti-social behaviour. So unless good people are rewarded with honours and possessions, and bad people are deprived of them, we shall all be done for.**

    So there is a need for wise, God-fearing lawyers to take charge. To guard against corruption in high places there should be higher and lower ranking offices to regulate affairs.

    While magistrates deal with worldly justice however, priests are supposed to point the way to heaven according to the tenets of the church and holy writ: but this is futile unless people adjust their lives accordingly. God only knows the real character of a person, so the priest has no business to go pontificating about a man's actual chances of angelhood. Nevertheless, priests do deserve our respect, not on their own account, but because of their holy office. Priests should be truthful and should teach folk to lead good lives. Compulsion won't work because, whatever people may pretend outwardly, in their hearts they believe what they believe. Never mind if someone disagrees with the priest: leave the rebel alone so long as he makes no fuss: but if he gets troublesome turn him out.

The New Jerusalem and its Heavenly Doctrine, 311-318

9b   Swedenborg got it all sorted: here he is laying down the law, and making it all sound quaintly unambiguous. I doubt whether today's judiciary would find it very helpful.

Where *spiritual* progress is concerned, Swedenborg had no time for the 'sticks and carrots' approach - *"Those who do good hoping for reward don't act from God, but from themselves."* He *does* approve of such incentives, however, as primitive instruments of government - as the means of harnessing self-interest simply to keep the whole show on the road.

But the real courtroom drama is, all the while, being quietly played out in secret, and God alone knows what the final verdict may be.

39c   Men are taught to be decent citizens. Were it not the case, few people would end up by being so. Let your son as a young child take anything that comes to hand and at fifteen he will be a highway robber; praise him for having told a lie and he will become a false witness; flatter his desires and he will end up for certain as a debauchee. Men are taught everything, virtue, religion.

Voltaire, *On the Pensées of Pascal*

[The piece is in refute of Pascal's observation that: *'Men cannot be taught to be decent citizens, but they are taught everything else; yet they pride themselves on that more than anything else. Thus they only pride themselves on knowing the one thing they cannot learn.'*]

39d   The *Rule of St. Benedict* is fundamental... It is very easy to read, very simple and specific. Every monk must have known it practically be heart, and for real insight into the purpose and function of monastic buildings it is more valuable than any number of guide-books. It has two basic principles: work and prayer. Life is completely communal. Private property is abolished. Everyone is equal. Each man has his task and does it: 'Here! Work, and be sad no longer.'...

While reading the *Rule* one can almost see the monastic layout taking shape. Like a castle, its form grows out of its function. The monks need a church, readily accessible - each of them has to go in and out of it eight times a day. They need a big room to eat together; another in which to sleep. They need a kitchen, an infirmary, storehouse and meeting place. All these rooms have to be in easy communication with one another, and there has to be plenty of passageway since everybody in a monastery is perpetually on the move. So the standard plan, with the various buildings grouped round a square cloister protected from the weather, seems to evolve spontaneously. And this layout hardly changed for the next thousand years.

Ian Richards, *Abbeys of Europe*

9e   Almighty God, who alone can bring order to the unruly wills and passions of sinful humanity: give your people grace so to love what you command and to desire what you promise, that, among the many changes of this world, our hearts may surely there be fixed where true joys are to be found.

The Collect for the third Sunday before Lent

9f   The Lord governs the entire universe by laws of order. We may discover these laws of order by looking for them in nature. We find that things happen in fixed, unchangeable ways, over and over again: day is followed by night; winter is followed by spring; the planets go around the sun; under favourable conditions, seeds grow; and animals, too, go through a regular pattern of birth and growth. All these things happen over and over again in a way which is consistent and orderly. It is this constant order in nature which proclaims that all things are ruled by the Lord.

What would happen if there were no order? Suppose things did not happen the same way over and over again? Could we possibly discover anything? Could we learn and progress? If there were no repetition in nature, if things happened differently each time, would experience tell us anything?

No! Without order everything would be confused and jumbled. It would be like trying to play a game in which the rules were changed every day. It would be impossible for us to learn anything to make progress, or in fact to live, if the universe were not ruled by consistent laws, for order is the foundation of everything. In order we see the "Spirit of the Lord." In the things which he makes and sustains we see reflected the constancy of his love and the order of his wisdom.

David R. Simons, *Unity in the Universe*

39g   Newtonian gravity has features, such as elliptical orbits, that match our universe. Relativity has other features that Newton's system lacks. The universe probably uses neither to go about its business; Newton's and Einstein's are models for human brains, not ultimate truths. Rather good models, to be sure, but few scientists nowadays seriously believe that their laws are true. (Only cosmologists and particle physicists do, perhaps, and both ought to know better, since they work in precisely those fields in which the perceived laws have changed most dramatically in the last fifty years.)

Laws are not timeless truths. They are context-dependent regularities, and we bring out different laws by asking different questions. Despite this, the glass menagerie of science works brilliantly, precisely because different points of view illuminate different features of the world. There is no reason to suppose that buried within it there lies a single ultimate law - and no reason to want one in any case.

Jack Cohen & Ian Stewart, *The Collapse of Chaos*

Constrained by all the checks and balances of this mortal life, at least let me dream of a world where love prevails, free from irritating rules and regulations.

40 THE MUNDANE AND THE MIRACULOUS
- A Magic Roundabout

40a **You can't argue with miracles: they leave you no choice, no room to manoeuvre. The mind is baffled, and the reasoning faculties numbed. Supernatural events may be very impressive, but they demand a kind of lifeless acceptance: the spectator is not improved by them, he is simply petrified, and made no better as a result.**

A miraculous occurrence tends to dominate the mind and preclude any possibility of turning matters over rationally, so any 'faith' thus induced is entirely superficial. There's nothing spiritual about it. That's why miracles don't happen these days.

Think of the miracles witnessed by the Jews in Egypt, at the Red Sea, in the desert and on Mount Sinai. Yet within a month they had set up a golden calf and begun to worship that. There were other miracles in Canaan but they had no lasting effect. The Jewish people in those days were a ritualistic lot, and any attempt to inspire them from within would have been a waste of time.

Divine Providence, 129-132

40b Miracles are a problem. As Swedenborg seems to be saying, they amount to a kind of spiritual blackmail; that is if, in fact, they ever actually happened. There are plenty of plausible explanations going around for those of us who are naturally suspicious of the magical.

Whether Biblical miracles took place in history is maybe beside the point: the interesting question is whether they *mean* anything. Swedenborg tells us elsewhere that there are good psychological reasons behind them - like dreams, they typify some rather surprising things that go on in people's minds.

In that sense the divine conjurer is still in business - it's just that we now have the audacity to peer up his sleeve, or, if you prefer the official jargon - "Now it is permitted to enter intellectually into the mysteries of faith." *('True Christian Religion No.508 ³)* Most of us, I imagine, are not really very comfortable with the miraculous - we prefer marvellous things to happen slowly and predictably, which, more often than not, they do.

40c   Lister's* kindness and consideration for his patients was unbounded. They, in turn, adored and revered him, and trusted him implicitly. The familiar doll story related to an incident during the Glasgow period. Here it is, as told by one of his house-surgeons:

"A little girl was suffering from an abscess of the knee. As Lister came to her bed he greeted her with his accustomed and delightful smile. They understood each other perfectly, and he dressed the joint.

"When all was finished she produced her doll which had lost a leg; a fumble under her pillow brought out the limb, and holding dolly in one hand and the leg in the other, gravely handed them to Lister. With seriousness and concern he received the case, shook his head ominously, for it was very serious, fitted them together, asked for a needle and cotton, and carefully and securely stitched on the limb, and with quiet delight handed her back to her mother. Her large brown eyes spoke endless gratitude, but neither uttered a word."

Douglas Guthrie, *Lord Lister, His Life and Doctrine*

* Joseph Lister, Pioneer surgeon in the field of antisepsis

40d   Fowling in the swamps of the Nile was a sport practised by the Egyptian nobles from early times. As a desirable occupation in the Next World it was represented on the walls of their tombs, the deceased owner being shown in the act of throwing his boomerang at birds rising from the swamp. One of the finest illustrations of the scene...shows a high official, who lived about a hundred years earlier than King Tutankhamun, standing in a boat made of papyrus stems, accompanied by his wife and daughter. In one hand he holds three live birds and in the other a serpent-boomerang. His tame goose stands in the prow of the boat and his cat leaps at a bird. It is uncertain whether the cat is retrieving a bird which has been stunned by a blow from Nebamun's boomerang or making its own capture, the purpose of the cat in the latter case being to disturb the birds so that they would rise above the papyrus flowers, thereby enabling the fowler to throw his boomerang at them without obstruction.

Among the magical spells written on the sides of the wooden coffins of nobles, five hundred years before the time of Tutankhamun, is an assurance to the deceased that the wadis of the Next World will be full of water, so that he may 'pluck papyrus flowers and marsh flowers, lotus and lotus buds. Waterfowl will rise by the thousand as (he) passes by. When (he) directs his boomerang against them a thousand will fall through the rush of air, geese, duck and many other kinds of fowl'. Both the wording of this spell and the painted representations on the walls of tombs would suggest that the deceased person was concerned only with providing himself with magical means for ensuring a continuance of his earthly pleasures and supplies of food in the Next World, but it is also possible that, by the time of Tutankhamun, the scene had acquired a symbolic significance without, however, necessarily excluding its original purpose. If the latter be true, the birds would represent marsh-dwelling demons of the Next World, who were a menace to the safety of the tomb-owner in the Afterlife.

Author unknown,
Catalogue to the Treasures of Tutankhamun Exhibition.
British Museum 1972

0e Upon New Year's Day a great host of knights met together, But none as yet could draw forth the sword out of the stone. Then they all went a little way off, and pitched tents, and held a tournament or sham-fight, trying their strength and skill at jousting with long lances of wood, or fighting with broad-swords.

It happened that among those who came was the good knight Sir Ector, and his son Kay, who had been made a knight not many months before; and with them came Arthur, Sir Kay's young brother, a youth of scarcely sixteen years of age.

Riding to the jousts, Sir Kay found suddenly that he had left his sword in his lodgings, and he asked Arthur to ride back and fetch it for him.

'Certainly I will,' said Arthur, who was always ready to do anything for other people, and back he rode to the town. But Sir Kay's mother had locked the door, and gone out to see the tournament, so that Arthur could not get into the lodgings at all.

This troubled Arthur very much. 'My brother Kay must have a sword,' he thought, as he rode slowly back. 'It will be a shame and a matter for unkind jests if so young a knight comes to the jousts without a sword. But where can I find him one?... I know! I saw one sticking in an anvil in the churchyard, I'll fetch that: it's doing no good there!'

So Arthur set spurs to his horse and came to the churchyard. Tying his horse to the stile, he ran to the tent which had been set over the stone - and found that all ten of the guardian knights had also gone to the tournament. Without stopping to read what was written on the stone, Arthur pulled out the sword at a touch, ran back to his horse, and in a few minutes had caught up with Sir Kay and handed it over to him.

Arthur knew nothing of what sword it was, but Kay had already tried to pull it from the anvil, and saw at a glance that it was the same one. Instantly he rode to his father Sir Ector, and said:

'Sir! Look, here is the sword out of the stone! So you see I must be the true-born King of all Britain!'

But Sir Ector knew better than to believe Sir Kay too readily. Instead, he rode back with him to the church, and there made him swear a solemn oath with his hands on the Bible to say truly how he came by the sword.

'My brother Arthur brought it to me,' said Kay, with a sigh.

Roger Lancelyn Green, *King Arthur and his Knights*

The light ahead was growing stronger. Lucy saw that a great series of many-coloured cliffs led up in front of them like a giant's staircase. And then she forgot everything else, because Aslan himself was coming, leaping down from cliff to cliff like a living cataract of power and beauty.

And the very first person whom Aslan called to him was Puzzle the Donkey. You never saw a donkey look feebler and sillier than Puzzle did as he walked up to Aslan; and he looked, beside Aslan, as small as a kitten looks beside a St Bernard. The Lion bowed down his head and whispered something to Puzzle at which his long ears went down; but then he said something else at which the ears perked up again. The humans couldn't hear what he had said either time. Then Aslan turned to them and said:

'You do not yet look so happy as I meant you to be.'

Lucy said, 'We're so afraid of being sent away, Aslan. And you have sent us back into our own world so often.'

'No fear of that,' said Aslan. 'Have you not guessed?'

Their hearts leaped and a wild hope rose within them.

'There was a real railway accident,' said Aslan softly. 'Your father and mother and all of you are - as you used to call it in the Shadowlands - dead. The term is over: the holidays have begun. The dream is ended: this is the morning.'

And as He spoke He no longer looked to them like a lion; but the things that began to happen after that were so great and beautiful that I cannot write them. And for us this is the end of all the stories, and we can most truly say that they all lived happily ever after. But for them it was only the beginning of the real story. All their life in this world and all their adventures in Narnia had only been the cover and the title page: now at last they were beginning Chapter One of the Great Story which no one on earth has read; which goes on for ever; in which every chapter is better than the one before.

C. S. Lewis, *The Last Battle*

40g   At the time when St. Francis dwelt in the city of Gubbio, there appeared in the neighbourhood an enormous wolf, terrible and ferocious, which devoured not only animals but even men also, insomuch that all the citizens stood in great terror, because many times he had approached the city. And all carried arms when they went out of the city, as though they were going to battle; yet with all this if any one met him alone he could not defend himself against him. And for fear of this wolf it had come to such a pass that no one had the courage to go out of the city. Therefore St. Francis had compassion on the men of the place, and desired to go out to this wolf, although all the citizens together counselled him not to do so: and making the sign of the most holy Cross he went out into the fields, he and his companions, all his confidence resting in God. And the others hesitating to go any further, St. Francis took his way to the place where the wolf was.

And behold! seeing the many citizens who had come out to witness the miracle, the wolf made at St. Francis with open mouth. And when he had come near, St. Francis made on him the sign of the most holy Cross, and called him to him, saying: "Come along, Brother Wolf, I command thee on the part of Christ, that thou do no harm, neither to me, nor to any one." And O wonder! immediately St. Francis had made the holy sign, the terrible wolf shut his mouth, and ceased to run, and did as he was commanded, coming gently as a lamb, and lay down to rest at the feet of St. Francis. Then St. Francis spoke to him thus: "Brother Wolf, thou hast done much damage in these parts, and many evil deeds, ravaging and killing the creatures of God, without His permission; and not only killing and devouring the cattle, but having the hardihood to destroy men made in the image of God, for which cause thou dost deserve to be hung upon the gallows like a convict, as being a thief and the worst of murderers; and all the people cry out and murmur because of thee, and the whole neighbourhood is hostile to thee. But, Brother Wolf, I would make peace between them and thee, so that thou offend no more, and they shall pardon thee all past offences, and neither men nor dogs shall persecute thee more."

At these words, the wolf, by the motions of his body and his tail and his eyes, and by inclining his head, showed that he accepted what St. Francis had said, and was ready to observe it. Then St.

Francis said again: "Brother Wolf, since it pleaseth thee to make and to keep this peace, I promise thee that I shall have thy food given to thee continually by the men of this place, as long as thou shalt live, so that thou shalt suffer no more hunger, for I know well that it is hunger which made thee do all this evil. But since I have obtained for thee this grace, I desire, Brother Wolf, that thou promise me never more to harm man or beast; dost thou promise me this?" And the wolf by inclining his head made evident signs that he promised. And St. Francis said to him: "Brother Wolf, I would have thee pledge me thy faith that thou wilt keep this promise, without which I cannot well trust thee." And St. Francis holding out his hand to receive his faith, the wolf immediately lifted up his right paw and gently placed it in the hand of St. Francis, thus giving him such pledge of faith as he was able.

Then St. Francis said: "Brother Wolf, I command thee in the Name of Jesus Christ that thou come now with me, without doubting of anything; and let us go and confirm this peace in the name of God." And the wolf obediently went with him like a mild and gentle lamb; which the citizens saw, and marvelled greatly.

And immediately the news spread over the whole city, and all the people, men and women, great and small, young and old, thronged to the piazza to see the wolf with St. Francis. And all the people being gathered together, St. Francis got up to preach, telling them amongst other things, how it was on account of sin that God permitted such calamities, and also pestilences. "Much more terrible," he said, "are the flames of hell, which the damned will have to endure eternally, than the fangs of the wolf, which cannot destroy more than the body. How much more then are the jaws of hell to be feared, when we see so many held in terror by the jaws of a little animal! Turn therefore, beloved, to God, and do worthy penance for your sins, and God will deliver you now from the fires of hell."

And the sermon ended, St. Francis said: "Listen, my brethren: Brother Wolf, who is here before you, has promised, and has pledged me his faith to make peace with you, and never to offend again in anything; and you will promise to give him every day that which is necessary; and I make myself surety for him, that he will faithfully observe the treaty of peace." Then all the people promised with one voice to feed him continually. And St. Francis, before them all, said to the wolf: "And thou, Brother Wolf, dost thou promise to observe and to keep the treaty of peace that thou wilt not offend either man or beast, or any creature?" And the wolf knelt down and inclined his head, and by gentle movements of his body and his tail and his ears, showed as well as he could that he was willing to keep all he had promised them. Then said St. Francis: "Brother Wolf, I desire that as thou hast pledged me thy faith to this promise outside the gates, thou wilt pledge me thy faith again before all the people, and not deceive me in the promise and guarantee which I have given for thee." Then the wolf, lifting up his right paw, placed it in the hand of St. Francis.

Whilst this and the rest that has been told above was taking place, there was such joy and admiration amongst all the people, both through devotion to the Saint, and through the novelty of the miracle, and also on account of the peace made with the wolf, that all began to cry to Heaven, praising and blessing God for sending to them St. Francis, who by his merits had delivered them from the jaws of the cruel beast. And after this, the said wolf lived two years in Gubbio; and went sociably into the houses, going from door to door without doing harm to any one, or any one doing harm to him, and was continually entertained by the people. And thus, as he went through fields and lanes, never did any dog bark at him. Finally, after two years, Brother Wolf died of old age; at which the citizens grieved much; for whilst he went so gently about the town, they remembered the virtue and sanctity of St. Francis.

Unknown (14th.century?) author,
The Little Flowers of Saint Francis of Assisi

Things assembled by magic need more than technology to take them apart. Let me not be too ready to dismantle the miraculous.

204

41 HOME SWEET HOME
- The Delights of Domesticity

41a **After death, people find themselves with those whose love of life is similar to their own. In any other spiritual company they would feel like fish out of water, so like-minded people are attracted to one another as if they were life-long friends and neighbours. They may meet in the open, but everyone feels most at home in his own house. A visitor in another person's house knows intuitively where to sit, and would be speechless and uncomfortable anywhere else.**

The Biblical phrase 'building a house' or 'setting up home' can mean (among other things) nurturing all those everyday qualities with which we feel snug and easy - hopefully, a mental framework of goodness, and a respect for the truth, which implies, of course, that we have some regard for other people.

The 'house of Pharaoh', on the other hand, means a house of facts or scientific information which *could* provide a basis for intelligence, even wisdom. Also, a whole man is sometimes referred to as 'a house'.

Divine Providence, 338[4] Arcana Caelestia 1488[3], 4390

41b I suppose one definition of a sound mind might be one within which we feel 'at home'. In mental illness we sometimes find a situation where the ideas by which someone lives have collapsed like a house of cards. If, however, we can live comfortably 'inside our own heads' then, for good or ill, we are equipped to face the world. One's prejudices and preconceptions form, so to speak, a mental crash-helmet - but Swedenborg would not, of course, know what I am talking about.

His timeless image of the spiritual home is probably more useful - and certainly more Biblical: we read, after all, about wise and foolish builders and their choice of various substrata for their ways of life.

The idea that there are 'many mansions' in the spiritual world, and that we all might qualify for a plot in the heavenly property market is perhaps still a comfort, but Swedenborg puts a fresh spin on the concept with his reminder that 'home' is of our own making.

41c   We do not live in the physical world. We live inside our heads. When a baby is born, his brain is virtually an empty house, with the plaster still drying on the walls. He immediately proceeds to furnish it with various items of knowledge. And eventually, it becomes a fairly comfortable residence, so that when he lies awake on a dark night, he can amuse himself for hours by wandering through its rooms. Still, a child's mental house has far less furniture than an adult's, which is why children are so much more easily bored, and so much more dependent on what goes on around them.

Throughout my life I gain experience and knowledge of the universe around me by means of 'attention'; by directing the jets of water at external objects. Having done that, I store the information on a kind of microfilm and put it in its appropriate place in my 'house'. So when I come to live in a new town, I have first of all to find my way around by means of a street map; but in no time at all, the map is inside my head. My library of microfilms also contains far more complicated maps with such labels as 'French', 'Counting', 'English language', 'English literature' - in fact, every subject you would find on a school curriculum, and hundreds more.

Colin Wilson, *Mysteries*

41d   Because the new suburban Winterstoke has its exact counterpart in every sizeable town in England, there is no need for us to linger in this prim world of privet hedge and raw red tile, of pebble-dash and mock-Tudor timbering, of grinning bay window, artificial stone bird bath and aubretia-covered rockery of sooty stone. It was a strange half-world of compromise and pretentious make-believe created by a people who imagined they could combine the advantages of town and country life without the disadvantages of either and succeeded in destroying both. How hygienic were these new 'all-electric homes', how convincing a demonstration of the blessings which material progress had showered upon mankind! How consoling to shut out the realities of life's mysterious and terrible adventure behind a ring fence of the office desk, the golf club, the bridge party, the wireless set, the weekly visit to the cinema and the week-end car ride! Compared with the old crowded courts of Camp, Hangar Lane or Darley Bank, life in these new suburbs was so eminently respectable and law-abiding, so disinfected and dehydrated, that they seemed almost as dead as the cemetery in Lower Leasowe.

L. T. C. Rolt, *Winterstoke*

1e   The old rectory is an important house in the village, and ranks next to the manor-house. It consists of a fine hall, the lower part divided off by a screen, a solar of two storeys at one end, and a kitchen at the other. It is built of oak framework, filled in with wattle and daub.

The duty of entertaining strangers and travellers was duly recognised by the clergy. There were rooms set apart for guests, and the large stables attached to rectories and vicarages were not for the purpose of providing accommodation for the rector's hunters, but for the steeds of his visitors.

The interior of the rectory speaks of learning and books. Books line the walls of the study; they climb the stairs; they overflow into dining-room and drawing-room. The light that shines from the study window is always there. Country-folk retire early to bed, and the village lights are soon extinguished; but that study light is always burning far into the night, and is scarcely put out before the approach of dawn calls the labourer from his couch to begin his daily toil.

P.H.Ditchfield, *The Charm of the English Village*

1f   The house was Winifred's. Her father was a man of energy, too. He had come from the north poor. Now he was moderately rich. He had bought this fair stretch of inexpensive land, down in Hampshire. Not far from the tiny church of the almost extinct hamlet stood his own house, a commodious old farm-house standing back from the road across a bare grassed yard. On one side of this quadrangle was the long, long-barn or shed which he had made into a cottage for his youngest daughter Priscilla. One saw little blue-and-white check curtains at the long windows, and inside, overhead, the grand old timbers of the high-pitched shed. This was Prissy's house. Fifty yards away was the pretty little new cottage which he had built for his daughter Magdalen, with the vegetable garden stretching away to the oak copse. And then away beyond the lawns and rose-trees of the house-garden went the track across a shaggy, wild grass space, towards the ridge of tall black pines that grew on a dyke-bank, through the pines and above the sloping little bog, under the wide, desolate oak trees, till there was Winifred's cottage crouching unexpectedly in front, so much alone, and so primitive.

It was Winifred's own house, and the gardens and the bit of common and the boggy slope were hers: her tiny domain.

D. H. Lawrence, *England, my England*

41g "My dear fellow", said Sherlock Holmes, as we sat on either side of the fire in his lodgings at Baker Street, "Life is infinitely stranger than anything which the mind of man could invent. We would not dare to conceive the things which are really mere commonplaces of existence. If we could fly out of that window hand in hand, hover over this great city, gently remove the roofs, and peep in at the queer things which are going on, the strange coincidences, the plannings, the cross-purposes, the wonderful chain of events, working through generations, and leading to the most *outré* results, it would make all fiction with its conventialities and foreseen conclusions most stale and unprofitable."

Conan Doyle, *The Adventures of Sherlock Holmes*

May there never be any shortage of material to build a lasting refuge, fit to share with friends.

42   MOTHERS AND FATHERS
- The Perils of Parenthood

42a   **Partners support one another in various ways, some appropriate to the woman, and some appropriate to the man. But what really brings them together is their concern for the children. Each partner has a proper rôle, the woman usually attending to babies and keeping an eye on growing girls, and the man dealing with the boys. Working together or in close harmony, they are thus united and inspired by parental love, and a homely sphere prevails.**

Sinners and saints can be equally good at caring for their infants. Wild animals are often better than domesticated ones when it comes to rearing their young: likewise, even with some crooks, because they see themselves in their offspring and are prompted by self-love, which is a perversion of divine influx, without which they would just die out. When the infants lose their innocence, however, parental love subsides and the youngsters may be thrown out.

The appealing innocence of little toddlers is God-given. It is evident when they smile, in their guileless gestures and their early gurgling speech. They have learned no cunning. They are unassuming and look to their parents for everything. They are easily pleased with simple gifts, don't worry about the future, nor expect worldly treasures. They love their parents and their playmates. They are easily led. They listen and obey. Such is the innocence of infancy.

Conjugial Love, 176, 329, 395, 398

42b   Swedenborg has a rosy view of early childhood: he is not speaking from personal experience, though it is known that he liked children and got along well with them. The innocence of infants is, of course, well-known. Anyone who has ever pushed a baby in its buggy knows that they radiate something very special, and bring out the best in people.

If this were not so, the human race would probably not last very long. What we have to decide, I suppose, is whether it is Divine Love that makes the world go round, or whether it is simply some kind of inbuilt species survival mechanism. Darwin no doubt had some thoughts on the matter.

Somehow, it seems to me, despite Swedenborg's naive and idealistic view of the nursery, the deep emotions of millions of parents over the centuries speak more eloquently about the chances of our eternal happiness.

42c   And as for the pretty lady, I cannot tell you what the colour of her hair was, or of her eyes: no more could Tom; for, when anyone looks at her, all they can think of is, that she has the sweetest, kindest, tenderest, funniest, merriest face they ever saw, or want to see. But Tom saw that she was a very tall woman, as tall as her sister: but instead of being gnarly, and horny, and scaly, and prickly, like her, she was the most nice, soft, fat, smooth, pussy, cuddly, delicious creature who ever nursed a baby; and she understood babies thoroughly, for she had plenty of her own, whole rows and regiments of them, and has to this day. And all her delight was, whenever she had a spare moment, to play with babies, in which she showed herself a woman of sense; for babies are the best company, and the pleasantest play-fellows in the world; at least, so all the wise people in the world think. And therefore when the children saw her, they naturally all caught hold of her, and pulled her till she sat down on a stone, and climbed onto her lap, and clung round her neck, and caught hold of her hands; and then they all put their thumbs into their mouths, and began cuddling and purring like so many kittens, as they ought to have done. While those who could get nowhere else sat down on the sand, and cuddled her feet - for no-one, you know, wears shoes in the water except horrid old bathing-women, who are afraid of the water-babies pinching their horny toes. And Tom stood staring at them; for he could not understand what it was all about.

"And who are you, you little darling?" she said.

"Oh, that is the new baby!" they all cried, pulling their thumbs out of their mouths; "and he never had any mother," and they all put their thumbs back again, for they did not wish to lose any time.

"Then I will be his mother, and he shall have the very best place; so get out all of you, this moment."

Charles Kingsley, The Water Babies

2d Let's look at both sides of the child's ambivalent feelings. First, a child needs to feel free of his parents. In the years of middle childhood he dethrones his parents. Not only does he dethrone his parents, but he becomes disillusioned about them. To his parents these may seem like bad things for a child to do. And yet, for a child to be disillusioned about parents, he must first cherish illusions about them. For a child to dethrone his parents, he must first place his parents unrealistically on a throne. And the pre-school child does both of these. He places his parents on a throne and cherishes illusions that they are all-knowing and all-powerful.

This was brought home most clearly to me when my youngest son Rusty was about three years old and asked a question about something. I have forgotten the exact question, but I recall that it was something I didn't know the answer to. So I told him, 'Rusty, I don't know the answer to that question.' Just as if he hadn't heard my reply, he asked me the question again. Again I said, 'Rusty, I told you already; Daddy doesn't know the answer to that question.' 'Yes you do, Daddy,' he said emphatically, 'you know everything! Now tell me the answer!'

Flattering as it may be to have such godlike qualities ascribed to us, our children must give up these ideas and replace them with a more realistic assessment. And yet, how difficult it is for us to take when our middle-childhood children see us as human beings after all, with the faults, foibles, psychological warts, and inconsistencies of human beings!

Fitzhugh Dodson, How to Father

42e The earliest education is most important and it undoubtedly is
woman's work. If the author of nature had meant to assign it to men
he would have given them milk to feed the child. Address your
treatises on education to the women, for not only are they able to
watch over it more closely than men, not only is their influence
always predominant in education, its success concerns them more
nearly, for most widows are at the mercy of their children, who show
them very plainly whether their education was good or bad. The
laws, always more concerned about property than about people,
since their object is not virtue but peace, the laws give too little
authority to the mother. Yet her position is more certain than that of
the father, her duties are less trying; the right ordering of the family
depends more upon her, and she is usually fonder of her children.
There are occasions when a son may be excused for lack of respect
for his father, but if a child could be so unnatural as to fail in respect
for the mother who bore him and nursed him at her breast, who for
so many years devoted herself to his care, such a monstrous wretch
should be smothered at once as unworthy to live. You say mothers
spoil their children, and no doubt that is wrong, but it is worse to
deprave them as you do. The mother wants her child to be happy
now. She is right, and if her method is wrong, she must be taught a
better. Ambition, avarice, tyranny, the mistaken foresight of fathers,
their neglect, their harshness, are a hundredfold more harmful to the
child than the blind affection of the mother.

Jean Jacques Rousseau (1712-1778), *Emile*
Reprinted with permission of Everyman Publishers plc

42f She was my mother's mother and must have been nearly seventy
when I first became conscious of her in about 1915. At that time, my
father was serving in France with H Battery of the Royal Horse
Artillery, and my mother was carrying on his job as an insurance
agent. My elder sister and I were left with Grandma Read, who lived
nearby, for most of the day.

She was small and neat, with a very smooth skin and dark hair
parted in the middle and taken back behind her ears into a bun. Her
hair remained dark and glossy until her death at seventy-six. It was
generally believed that she had a Portuguese forbear and her looks
would certainly bear this out.

She dressed well. Her frocks were of dark silk, usually brown or black, trimmed with lace and made with a high neck. She was particularly fond of prettily-trimmed bonnets worn tied under the chin with ribbons. As children, we often gave her bonnet trimmings of feathers or velvet for her birthday or Christmas presents. One particular bonnet I remember clearly, trimmed with velvet pansies of different colours which framed her face and delighted my admiring eye.

An older cousin of mine remembers her as 'a very happy lady. She had a nice smile, and her eyes smiled too.' That too is how I remember her.

She was a wonderful companion to young children, cheerful, spritely and not over-anxious, as so many adults are, about the niceties of correct behaviour or the awful consequences of such daring feats as jumping off low walls or down the conservatory steps. Having had twelve children of her own, she was probably past worrying over much.

Miss Read, A Fortunate Grandchild

2g   I don't think you should need a protocol or religion to encourage parenting skills. If you can get it through to prospective parents, the advice is quite simple really. Don't have children unless you're going to enjoy them. Easier said than done, I know, but think first.

Whether their existence was intended or not, treat them as you would treat a guest, except of course that they didn't have the option of declining your invitation to come into the world! Be prepared to put yourself out for them as you would for a guest. Having said that, you should also get them to help you about the home, but never make chores a punishment.

Don't just dump them in front of the television, give them plenty of attention but don't spoil them. Encourage them to take an interest or a hobby and to be proactive. Be realistic about their capabilities. Don't ignore children's fashions and crazes but don't be a slave to them either. Encourage them to take plenty of exercise. Don't ferry them around everywhere in the car. Have your meals together at the same time, preferably at the table. Do plenty of things together as a family.

Be empathetic; try to see things from their view point, physically and mentally. Be prepared to answer whatever questions they ask. Don't be judgemental. Be factual but at the same time don't worry too much about make-believe things, especially when they're tiny. Reality will come to them gradually and shouldn't come to them later as a shock or a disappointment.

Be polite. Most people, including babies and children, are reasonable if you are nice to them. If they do wrong be stern but never lose your temper. Respect their dignity. Stand up for them when they need it but don't be over-protective; encourage them to stand up for themselves as well.

Be aware of what other people say and do and write about bringing up children and attend to these as necessary, but at the end of the day do what you think feels right for you.

Remember a baby or a child is not going to be like that for ever - though it might seem an eternity at the time!

With any luck your child will grow up to be a friend for life.

Martin Fletcher, *Sundry thoughts on problems of parenthood.*

With the coming of children arises the opportunity to review our*selves*. May we seek to perpetuate the old, not only when it suits *us*, but when it suits *them*.

---

43   ON TOP OF THE WORLD
- In Ascending Order

43a   There are six sorts of truth. The first and second levels, as they proceed directly from God, are so profound they are even beyond the angels. The third level is perceived in the innermost (or uppermost) heaven, but it is completely beyond the likes of you and me. The fourth level operates in the second heaven, but that doesn't make any sense to ordinary mortals either. The fifth level works in the third heaven - the outermost (or lowest) and it is just possible that a few supremely enlightened people here might see some glimmering of it, but they would be hard-pressed to put it into words. Only when it forms specific ideas are people likely to recognise truth for what it is. The sixth level, however, is better adapted to human view, so, though clouded, it forms the substance of a lot of Biblical material. Inner truths are 'the glory *in* the cloud' so God's appearances to the Israelites are always cloudy.

Visual and auditory experience is all in the mind. Sense impressions reach the understanding by way of eyes and ears: thoughts then turn into intentions, and so into speech and action. There is a cycle of events, and everything revolves around the *will*. A good person, though he may not know it, is prompted by God: his motives spring from a heavenly source.

Arcana Caelestia, 8443, 10,057

3b   We have absolutely no means of verifying this information: we simply have to take it on trust - or not, as the case may be. The same has to be said of anything presented to us as 'revelation'. Whether it rings true is a matter of gut-feeling.

It's pretty obvious, however, that most people have a passion for seeking promotion. They love hierarchy - slotting human achievement into league tables and awarding 'grades'. We live our lives as though we are all hoping for a place in some glorious cup-final in the sky. So Swedenborg's 'levels of truth' strikes a familiar chord.

He tells us, however, that there is a two-way traffic. We cannot begin the upward climb unless there is first some heavenly impulse. The first move is always *from* on high. There is 'influx' from the spiritual into the natural, but never the other way round. But abstract terms like 'truth' mean nothing to the natural mind unless they are *applied* to something we can get hold of - the truth has to be *about* something specific. And the truth is, that a lot of people do like the feeling that life is a progression.

43c   And Jacob went out from Beersheba, and went toward Haran. And he lighted upon a certain place, and tarried there all night, because the sun was set; and he took of the stones of that place, and put them for his pillows, and lay down in that place to sleep. And he dreamed, and behold a ladder set up on the earth, and the top of it reached to heaven: and behold the angels of God ascending and descending on it. And behold, the Lord stood above it, and said, I am the Lord God of Abraham thy father, and the God of Isaac: the land whereon thou liest, to thee will I give it, and to thy seed; And thy seed shall be as the dust of the earth, and thou shalt spread abroad to the west, and to the east, and to the north, and to the south: and in thee and in thy seed shall all the families of the earth be blessed. And, behold, I am with thee, and will keep thee in all places whither thou goest, and will bring thee again into this land; for I will not leave thee, until I have done that which I have spoken to thee of. And Jacob awaked out of his sleep, and he said, Surely the Lord is in this place; and I knew it not. And he was afraid, and said, How dreadful is this place! this is none other but the house of God, and this is the gate of heaven. And Jacob rose up early in the morning, and took the stone that he had put for his pillows, and set it up for a pillar, and poured oil upon the top of it. And he called the name of that place Bethel: but the name of that city was called Luz at the first. And Jacob vowed a vow, saying, if God will be with me, and will keep me in this way that I go, and will give me bread to eat, and raiment to put on, So that I come again to my father's house in peace; then shall the Lord be my God: And this stone, which I have set for a pillar, shall be God's house: and of all that thou shalt give me I will surely give the tenth unto thee.

Genesis 28, 10-22

3d It is an interesting semantic coincidence that sage and thyme are often used to flavour our food. In its other sense, 'sage' means 'the wisdom of experience...a profoundly wise man (sorry ladies, but that's what the dictionary says)...any of the ancients, traditionally reputed wisest of their times'. As for thyme - or time, as the case may be - is it 'on our hands' or 'on our side'? Does it 'hang heavily' or 'fly'? Sage and time are what it's all about. It's about using time happily and productively, and about discovering and rediscovering uses for the sagacity of accumulated wisdom, experience and knowledge which we all possess.

In Britain today the popular image of elderly people does not show them as sages. There is not the tradition of respect that we understand to be common in other cultures. But a revolution is already under way. Older adults are becoming more active and more vociferous in their own cause. They are beginning to earn respect and admiration by a more productive and creative use of their time and talents.

Dianne Norton, *Adding Spice to Life*

3e

Holy Father, cheer our way
With thy love's perpetual ray:
Grant us every closing day
Light at evening time.

Holy Saviour, calm our fears
When earth's brightness disappears;
Grant us in our latter years
Light at evening time.

Holy Spirit, be thou nigh
When in mortal pains we lie;
Grant us, as we come to die,
Light at evening time.

Holy, Blessèd Trinity,
Darkness is not dark with Thee;
Those Thou keepest always see
Light at evening time.

R. Hayes Robinson, *Hymns Ancient and Modern No.22*

43f   The painter ought always to consider, when he has a wall on which he has to represent a story, the height at which he will locate his figures, and when he draws from nature for this composition, he ought to take a position with his eye as much below the object that he is drawing, as the object, when inserted into the composition, will be above the eye of the observer. Otherwise the work will be reprehensible.

Why groups of figures one above another are to be avoided:

This practice, which is universally adopted by painters on the walls of chapels, is by reason strongly to be condemned seeing that they represent one scene at one level with its landscape and buildings, and then they mount to the stage above this to represent another scene and so vary the point of sight from that of the first, and then make a third and a fourth scene in such a way that on one wall there are four points of sight, which is extreme folly on the part of such masters.

We know that the point of sight is opposite the eye of the spectator of the scene, and if you were to ask how I should represent the life of a saint divided into several scenes on one end of the same wall I answer to this that you must set the foreground with its point of sight on a level with the eye of the spectator of the scene. And on this plane represent the first episode on a large scale. And then by diminishing gradually the figures and buildings upon the various hills and plains you can represent all the events of the story. And on the rest of the wall up to the top you will make trees of sizes proportioned according to the figures or angels if these are appropriate to the story, or birds or clouds or similar things; otherwise do not put yourself to the trouble for all your work will be wrong.

Leonardo da Vinci, *Trattato della Pittura,*
MS 2038 in the Bibliothèque Nationale

43g   In general we are taught in the New Revelation that there are three discrete degrees of life. These are called, "the natural", "the spiritual" and "the celestial", or "heavenly." But each of these general levels may be subdivided into a more particular trine of planes. Thus, there are three levels in the natural state, three in the spiritual, and three in the celestial. The regeneration or spiritual evolution of the human mind simply involves the successive elevation of the ruling love from one plane to the higher through all these distinct degrees or stages of life. After passing through the three natural stages, and then through the three spiritual stages, a man first reaches the celestial stage in the seventh state, that symbolised by the seventh or Sabbath day, after the six days of Creation, described in the first chapter of Genesis. The new creation, described in the second chapter of Genesis, involves the still further formation of the celestial man. It is especially in the transition process from one of these levels to the higher, that a man undergoes temptations and existential anxiety, for this involves in every case a certain death followed by a resurrection and elevation to a higher plane of life, or what is the same, a withdrawal of the heart or ruling love from one level and its establishment upon a higher level. The most grievous temptations occur in the transition from a natural to a spiritual state, thus between the third and fourth days, and then again in the transition from a spiritual to a celestial state, thus between the sixth and seventh days.

Harry W. Barnitz, *Existentialism and the New Christianity*

They tell me the world looks beautiful from outer space. If, when I die, anyone can see my life from the perspective of eternity, I hope they will not be too disappointed.

44   PEACE AND PERFECTION
- Peace Within and Peace Without

44a   Peace on earth can give us clues regarding peace in heaven, which is what keeps the hells in their place. After war, for instance, in time of peace everyone feels safe in his home town and in his own house and grounds: they enjoy protection from their enemies: or, as Micah put it, 'They sit, each man, under his vine and under his fig tree, unafraid.'

Other examples are when you put your feet up after a hard day, or the solace experienced by mothers after childbirth, when maternal feelings bring comfort and relief. Likewise, sunshine after stormy weather, or the coming of spring after a severe winter, or a safe landfall after a perilous voyage.

Wisdom follows three stages - natural, spiritual and celestial. In this world someone might aim at *natural* perfection, but they won't get any further until they die; then, at the spiritual stage they could try for *spiritual* perfection. Finally they might embark on the *celestial* stage, but the limitless wisdom of the angels is ineffable. So there is no seamless progression, but a set of quantum leaps.

True Christian Religion, 304, Divine Providence, 34[2]

44b   *Requiescat in pace* - rest in peace - how boring! There is a very subtle distinction between being 'at rest' and being 'at peace' - I'm not too sure what it is, but it has something to do with idleness, inactivity, inertia - fine, provided that it doesn't go on too long. The nice thing about Swedenborg is that his system always leaves us with something else to look forward to. His use of the term 'peace' here seems to denote an *untroubled* condition.

'Perfection' is another of those bewildering terms which are quite meaningless until you say precisely what it is you are talking about. The dinner in the oven may be 'done to perfection', but if you are discussing perfect wisdom that's something else entirely. Perfection at one level, Swedenborg informs us, is provisional - complete only so far as it goes, but that is not the end of the story. Utter perfection, thank God, is beyond us.

4c   There will come a supreme moment in which there will be care neither for ourselves nor for others, but a complete abandon, a *sans souci* of unspeakable indifference. and this moment will never be taken from us; time cannot rob us of it but, as far as we are concerned, it will last for ever and ever without flying. So that, even for the most wretched and most guilty, there is a heaven at last where neither moth nor rust doth corrupt and where thieves do not break through nor steal. To himself every one is an immortal: he may know that he is going to die, but he can never know that he is dead.

If life is an illusion, then so is death - the greatest of all illusions. If life must not be taken too seriously - then so neither must death.

Samuel Butler, from *The Notebooks*

4d   What is unbearable in life, I think, is the sense that what we are doing and suffering is meaningless - that there will be no adequate outcome from it, only more pain; that it all somehow is ended at death. But the gospel teaches us that, depending on us and our relationship with the Lord, even our worst struggles can be sanctifying, glorifying, and perfecting. It is a strange thing, is it not, that the same phenomenon - namely, pain - can have opposite effects, depending on one's attitudes and responses. For some it can lead to bitterness, the shriveling of the soul, hostility, and shaking the fist at God and all men; and to others it can lead to deeper love, deeper compassion, a more radiant exposure and expression, and eventually exaltation.

Truman G. Madsen, *The Radiant Life*

4e   The gambling instinct, so often perverted and used for unworthy ends, is one of the most valuable instincts possessed by man, and nowhere does it find a truer or more complete outlet and fulfilment than in religion. As Donald Hankey once said to us, writing from the trenches in France, "Religion is betting your life there is a God." I decided to bet my life that there is a God, and more and more as the years go by I find that in so far as I yield up my will to God, and open my heart to his in-dwelling, in so far as I try to live out my everyday life in the Christ spirit, *the experiment works !* Peace and serenity come to the soul and harmony and balance to conflicting instincts. It seems to me that by one road or another we are all coming back to the Christ, not so much the Christ of dogma and ritual but to a "layman's Christ," the Christ of Galilee and Gethsemane. What does he stand for to us lay folk who try to follow him, not only in his relationship with other people but also in his relationship with the All-Father ?

'The Unknown Man', *My Religion*

44f　Lord, make me an instrument of thy peace. Where there is hatred, let me sow love; where there is injury, pardon; where there is doubt, faith; where there is despair, hope; where there is darkness, light; where there is sadness, joy.

O divine master, grant that I may not so much seek to be consoled, as to console; to be understood, as to understand; to be loved, as to love. For it is in giving that we receive, it is in pardoning that we are pardoned; it is in dying that we are born to eternal life.

St. Francis of Assisi

44g　All night the roar of the surf sounded in their ears, and with teeth chattering violently they saw the east begin to grey.

With the coming of the dawn the wind showed no signs of abating and the waves were as huge as ever. They saw the far bank; sloping fields dotted with pheasant coverts, round spinneys of fir, and pleasant parkland. All their fishing tackle had been swept away and their stores washed overboard, but their sleeping- bags were intact (with the exception of the third sleeping-bag, which had done duty for a sail) and these they carried up the shore.

They were feeling far too ill to do anything more. What with the thrashing of the trees and the roaring of the surf on the shingle they were quite mazed. After a while, as the light increased, the effects of the night's ordeal wore off and Sneezewort, who was a better sailor than the others and the first to recover, at last pulled himself together and ventured out from under the bushes.

He soon made the surprising discovery that they had not, as he had first thought, been driven aground on the bank of the lake. They were on Poplar Island, and nearly half a mile of storm-tossed water separated them from the mainland. Unless the waves and winds subsided they would have to stay there for the rest of the day. So he went back to the others and fell fast asleep again, which, under the circumstances, was the best possible thing to do.

Denys Watkins Pitchford ('BB'), *The Little Grey Men*

Grant me that perfect peace which doesn't bring everything to a standstill.

---

45 THE PLENTEOUS GLOBE
- Poverty and Population

45a **God's influence can be seen wherever you care to look - in the universe, in living things, and in the way that everything serves some purpose. The fertile landscapes of the *spiritual* world moreover are formed in a moment: abundant plants and fruit trees sprout spontaneously as an outward expression of angelic productivity. The angels engage in elevating conversation and enjoy all sorts of good things entirely free of charge simply because they lead useful lives.**

Persistent loafers, however, have a hard time until they finally give in. If that doesn't do the trick they are banished, and eke out a meagre existence in barren outposts, where there are few grassy fields. The idle rich run the risk of ending up in this way.

Spiritual uses defy description, but there are some parallels in the natural world. The entire globe is an arena of uses. The mineral world supports the vegetable, which in turn supports the animal, and human beings rely on all these in their service to God and to one another.

You have only to look at what goes on inside the human body to see that everything - every tiny fibre, every muscle and organ - is there for a purpose. The complete *person* likewise has a use to perform. After death, anyone who does nothing useful is considered worthless.

God, Providence, Creation, 112

45b Swedenborg does not concern himself here with worldly famine, or population explosion, poverty or conflict: he is only interested in the original divine blueprint, and does not dwell upon the fact that it all seems to have gone horribly wrong. Never mind! It will all get sorted in the hereafter.

He's right of course. If it were not for man's greed and stupidity there *would* be enough to go round. With up-to-date transport and communications it needn't be *so* difficult to share out the world's resources. Even the problem of too many babies need not, I suppose, be insurmountable, though it's odd that most living creatures do have the capacity to multiply at an alarming rate.

Swedenborg seems to dodge the issues that affect us most urgently: they are not his province. What he *does* say is that the system is basically sound, despite all appearances: the natural world is an amazing complex composed of millions of 'uses'. It's not God's fault that they are constantly breaking down, and our own greatest satisfaction must lie in knowing that we have tried to do *something*.

45c As for the money vortex that drives the global economy, this may be best regarded for the time being as a quasi-natural phenomenon. Individual corporations and banks are increasingly alert to environmental issues. Enlightened self-interest nowadays includes averting the costs and opprobrium of avoidable pollution or land degradation, and anticipating the circumstances most propitious for business in a greenhouse or anti-greenhouse world. But markets have their own compulsions, revolving around money itself, and their effects on the distribution of wealth and economic activity may be inherently ungovernable, like hurricanes or volcanoes.

Hope lies with ordinary people minding their own business in their own localities, where their prosperity and even their survival depend on striking the shrewdest possible bargains with Nature. A key human number is population, and that is set mainly by the private decisions of billions of individual parents. For new scientific discoveries about the Earth system to have any practical payoff, they will have to be understood, interpreted and acted upon by those same ordinary people. They are the true watchkeepers of Spaceship Earth.

Nigel Calder, *Spaceship Earth*

45d The materialist creed by which a large part of humanity has sought to live during the last few centuries confused the needs of survival with the needs of fulfillment; whereas man's life requires both. For survival, the physiological needs are uppermost; and the most imperative, obviously, are the needs for air and water: then food and shelter against extremes of temperature, and so by degrees one passes to those social needs for communication and co-operation that never wholly limit themselves to life-preservation in the narrow sense. Within the life-span of a generation, the needs for sexual intercourse and parental care are as imperative as those for air and water.

In terms of life-fulfillment, however, this ascending scale of needs, from bare physical life to social stimulus and personal growth, must be reversed. The most important needs from the standpoint of life-fulfillment are those that foster spiritual activity and promote spiritual growth: the needs for order, continuity, meaning, value, purpose and design - needs out of which language and poesy and music and science and art and religion have grown. The deepest, the most organic, of these higher needs is that for love: all the stronger because it is rooted in survival. Neither group of needs is in a watertight compartment: lovers must eat and even greedy eaters have been known to share their food with the starving.

Lewis Mumford, *The Condition of Man*

45e God in his love for us lent us this planet,
     gave it a purpose in time and in space:
     small as a spark from the fire of creation,
     cradle of life and the home of our race.
     Thanks be to God for its bounty and beauty,
     life that sustains us in body and mind:
     plenty for all, if we learn how to share it,
     riches undreamed-of to fathom and find.

     Long have our human wars ruined its harvest;
     long has earth bowed to the terror of force;
     long have we wasted what others have need of,
     poisoned the fountain of life at its source.
     Earth is the Lord's: it is ours to enjoy it,
     ours, as his stewards, to farm and defend.
     From its pollution, misuse, and destruction,
     good Lord, deliver us, world without end!

Frederick Pratt Green,
from *'Songs for Worship'*

Reproduced by permission of Stainer & Bell Ltd

226

45f   Perhaps the most important advantage of "useless" knowledge is that it promotes a contemplative habit of mind. There is in the world much too much readiness, not only for action without adequate previous reflection, but also for some sort of action on occasions on which wisdom would counsel inaction. People show their bias on this matter in various curious ways. Mephistopheles tells the young student that theory is grey but the tree of life is green, and everyone quotes this as if it were Goethe's opinion, instead of what he supposes the devil would be likely to say to an undergraduate. Hamlet is held up as an awful warning against thought without action, but no-one holds up Othello as a warning against action without thought. Professors such as Bergson, from a kind of snobbery towards the practical man, decry philosophy, and say that life at its best should resemble a cavalry charge.

For my part, I think action is best when it emerges from a profound apprehension of the universe and human destiny, not from some wildly passionate impulse of romantic but disproportioned self-assertion. A habit of finding pleasure in thought rather than in action is a safeguard against unwisdom and excessive love of power, a means of preserving serenity in misfortune and peace of mind among worries. A life confined to what is personal is likely, sooner or later, to become unbearably painful; it is only by windows into a larger and less fretful cosmos that the more tragic parts of life become endurable.

Bertrand Russell, *"Useless" Knowledge*

5g   Pottery is at once the simplest and the most difficult of all arts. It is the simplest because it is the most elemental; it is the most difficult because it is the most abstract. Historically it is among the first of the arts. The earliest vessels were shaped by hand from crude clay dug out of the earth, and such vessels were dried in the sun and wind. Even at that stage, before man could write, before he had a literature or even a religion, he had this art, and the vessels then made can still move us by their expressive form. When fire was discovered, and man learned to make his pots hard and durable; and when the wheel was invented, and the potter could add rhythm and uprising movement to his concepts of form, then all the essentials of this most abstract art were present. The art evolved from its humble origins until, in the fifth century before Christ, it became the representative art of the most sensitive and intellectual race that the world has ever known. A Greek vase is the type of all classical harmony. Then eastward another great civilisation made pottery its best loved and most typical art, and even carried the art to rarer refinements than the Greek had attained. A Greek vase is static harmony, but the Chinese vase, when once it has freed itself from the imposed influences of other cultures and other techniques, achieves dynamic harmony; it is not only a relation of numbers, but also a living movement. Not a crystal but a flower.

Herbert Read, *The Meaning of Art*

In a restless world like this, may I always know when to move, and when to be moved.

46   POWERS, HEAVENLY AND EARTHLY
- Inspiration and Influx

6a **Some people expect angels to be so pure and powerless, and so spiritual that you can't see them, whereas, in fact, they have powers which can even be transmitted to *us*. Without understanding and motivation you cannot move a muscle. What your spirit thinks, your mouth speaks: what your spirit asks, your body obeys. Power is from God by means of angels: you cannot take a single step without some spiritual input.**

You wouldn't believe what I have seen of the sheer strength of the angels. In the spiritual world, if anything gets in the way of divine order, the angels can topple it with a look. I have seen mountains shaken and the devils upon them swallowed up: I've seen hordes of evil spirits scattered and banished into hell. The angels can never be outwitted or outnumbered. There are several Biblical references to their great powers.

Their strength is not their own, however: all power is from God, as the angels are well aware. If one of them were to forget, and tried to muscle in on the Almighty he would immediately become too feeble to resist even a solitary evil straggler. But the angels claim nothing for themselves: they ascribe all their powers to the glory of God.

Heaven and Hell, 228, 229, 230.

5b This is Swedenborg at his most dramatic. There are two strands here - in *this* world, we are told, life comes to us from God, with the angels as intermediaries: in the *next* world the angels exercise divine powers to spectacular effect.

So we have the suggestion - nay, assertion - that all human movement is 'spiritual' in origin - reasonable enough since dead bodies don't usually move about on their own. Then God is identified as the motive power behind all action - human and superhuman. I have no alternative explanation. There is, though, some difference between a *driving* force which propels us willy-nilly, and a *life* force to which we may 'plug in' as required.

I am not so happy about all those violent goings on in the spiritual world: I would have preferred a more diplomatic scenario. Angelic task forces carrying out mopping up operations are hard to take. I shall keep well out of the way. Nor do I find anything here about the power behind natural disasters, but I'm sure Swedenborg deals with the matter pretty thoroughly somewhere else.

46c   The greatest revival of interest in angels since the Renaissance was in the Victorian age, when angels reappeared in poetry, hymns and painting, particularly in Pre-Raphaelite art, and angel monuments proliferated in the cemeteries. This was the beginning of their prevalence in popular culture, which has never diminished, until today they are found in the modern media of films, and popular music, as well as being the favourite motif of Christmas cards.

The First World War was the height of angel sightings. Previously, at least since the Middle Ages, such sightings had been private affairs communicated only to family, if at all. But in the mass slaughter of trench warfare such stories became more public and even commonplace...

After the First World War, not much was heard of angels for a long time, except at Christmas. Now they have suddenly made a reappearance on an unprecedented scale, in the lives of the thousands of people who have encountered them, and in the even greater numbers of people with no personal experience but who nevertheless believe in them and long to develop their own capacities to see these beings and receive their help.

Glennyce S. Eckersley, *An Angel at my Shoulder*

46d   *In the time of War and Tumults*
O Almighty God, King of all kings, and Governor of all things, whose power no creature is able to resist, to whom it belongeth justly to punish sinners, and to be merciful to them that truly repent; Save and deliver us, we humbly beseech thee, from the hands of our enemies; abate their pride, asswage their malice, and confound their devices; that we, being armed with thy defence, may be preserved

evermore from all perils, to glorify thee, who art the only giver of all victory...

For Peace and Deliverance from our Enemies
O Almighty God, who art a strong tower of defence unto thy servants against the face of their enemies; We yield thee praise and thanksgiving for our deliverance from those great and apparent dangers wherewith we were compassed: We acknowledge it thy goodness that we were not delivered over as a prey unto them; beseeching thee still to continue such thy mercies towards us, that all the world may know that thou art our Saviour and mighty Deliverer...

For restoring Publick Peace at Home
O Eternal God, our heavenly Father, who alone makest men to be of one mind in a house, and stillest the outrage of a violent and unruly people; We bless thy holy Name, that it hath pleased thee to appease the seditious tumults which have been lately raised up among us; most humbly beseeching thee to grant to all of us grace, that we may henceforth obediently walk in thy holy commandments; and, leading a quiet and peaceable life in all godliness and honesty, may continually offer unto thee our sacrifice of praise and thanksgiving for these thy mercies towards us...

The Book of Common Prayer

If the mind of man is non-physical, it is possible to formulate a hypothetical picture of a non-physical system or world made up of all such minds existing in some sort of relationship to each other. This leads to speculative views of a kind of psychical oversoul, or reservoir, or continuum, or universe, having its own system of laws and properties and potentialities. One can conceive of this great total pattern as having a transcendent uniqueness over and above the nature of its parts that some might call its divinity...

It is shocking but true that we know the atom today better than we know the mind that knows the atom. If we could arrive at half as good an understanding of the mind as physics has achieved with the elements of matter, we should probably be able to release and utilise guiding principles of inconceivable significance to human life and society. The researches on the atomic bomb have set a standard for us. They have shown us something of what we might have a right to expect from highly concentrated research when mankind really wants to know something.

It is only a question, then, as to how urgently we want to find out about 'nuclear psychology'. The comparison with atomic physics is forced upon us by events. So I ask: Are we yet willing to give the necessary priority to the human problem? Do we appreciate what it would be worth to discover enough of the inner resources of man's psychical nature to generate the ethical power and social feeling that would free his mind for ever from fear of his fellow-men?

J. B. Rhine, *The Reach of the Mind*

46f   Power is a new preoccupation, in a sense a new idea, in science. The Industrial Revolution, the English revolution, turned out to be the great discoverer of power. Sources of energy were sought in nature: wind, sun, water, steam, coal. And a question suddenly became concrete: Why are they all one? What relation exists between them? That had never been asked before. Until then science had been entirely concerned with exploring nature as she is. But now the modern conception of transforming nature in order to obtain power from her, and of changing one form of power into another, had come up to the leading edge of science. In particular, it grew clear that heat is a form of energy, and is converted into other forms at a fixed rate of exchange. In 1824 Sadi Carnot, a French engineer, looking at steam engines, wrote a treatise on what he called *'la puissance motrice du feu'*, in which he founded, in essence, the science of thermodynamics - the dynamics of heat. Energy had become a central concept in science; and the main concern in science now was the unity of nature, of which energy is the core.

Jacob Bronowski, *The Ascent of Man*

46g   The eruption must have started between 10 and 11 o'clock on the morning of the 24th, and by the evening of that day some 6 feet of ash had already fallen on Pompeii. Here the first 8 or 9 feet of deposit consist of a thin scatter of lava pebbles (*lapilli*), the debris of the plug of solidified basalt which had for so long sealed the volcano, followed by successive layers of almost pure pumice. This represents the body of volcanic magma which was ejected up the throat as soon as it was clear, under conditions of great heat and enormous pressure, to a height of several thousand metres (the trunk of the 'pine tree'); on reaching the upper atmosphere the drops of magma were able to expand, releasing some of the gases which they contained, and to fall as a dense, spreading cloud of incandescent, gaseous pumice. More than two thirds of the deposits at Pompeii represent this first, cataclysmic series of events, after which the gases of the interior were free to escape upwards with a much smaller admixture of pure magma, its place being taken by increasing quantities of alien material, as the old volcanic matter of the existing cone collapsed inwards upon itself, causing a series of convulsive blockages and explosions. This was the peak moment of the eruption, involving a tremendous release of gaseous pressure and causing the earthquakes which destroyed Pomponianus's villa at Stabiae and spread panic at Misenum. But although the deadly rain of gas and cinders continued, the body of actual solid matter that fell was already tailing off rapidly. In terms of its power to destroy, by the afternoon of the 25th the eruption had done its worst.

The city of Pompeii had ceased to exist, buried beneath twelve feet of lethal ash. We have no means of estimating the casualties, but in the town itself and the immediate countryside they must have run into many thousands. Those who got away did so in the first few hours, the lucky ones by sea, the rest striking inland before the roads were blocked and the air became unbreathable. Those who dallied to collect their valuables or who took shelter in the houses and cellars died miserably, some when the roofs and upper storeys collapsed upon them under the weight of the ash, most of them suffocated by the steady accumulation of deadly sulphurous fumes. The ash solidified round their bodies, leaving for posterity the pathetic record of their death agonies amid the darkness of that terrifying August day.

John Ward-Perkins & Amanda Claridge, *Pompeii AD79*

When I am just running on batteries, let me not forget that they are the rechargeable sort.

47   REWARDS
- An Equitable God

47a   **People who really love one another actually *enjoy* being helpful. Their delight is their reward. So when they perform any service they are in their heaven. As soon as they start wondering what they can get out of it for themselves true happiness flies out of the window because they are no longer thinking about others. Heavenly blessedness is thus diverted. They are like things that absorb light instead of reflecting it.**

The 'hired servants' that we read about in the Bible mean those who do good but who are in it for the money - or some other worldly benefit, or they may expect some pay-off in the next world.

'Strangers' in the Bible mean those who are prompted to good works for no better reason than that they were born with good intentions. They may, of course, be ill or feeble minded. Their 'goodness' is merely instinctive: they work 'in the dark'. Those who are motivated by religious principles, however, act from conscience, like the angels.

Arcana Caelestia 6388, 8002

47b   Swedenborg is in danger of being misunderstood here. As a one-time 'Assessor of Mines' he had, in fact, sufficient experience of practical business administration to know that workers should be paid in the currency of this world. In a state of heavenly bliss no doubt we could happily depend upon the voluntary efforts of our fellows, but in this life, whether by banking systems or barter, we need payment of some sort, simply to keep the wheels of industry ticking over; otherwise everything would grind to a halt - good works and all. Sometimes I get paid, sometimes I don't. The important thing, presumably, from a spiritual point of view, is what I do with the money - how much I plough back into the business, how much I tuck away for my old age, how much I give away, how much I spend on having fun, and how much I need to survive.

The angels, if they concern themselves at all, must think this all rather pathetic, makeshift and unreliable - a tedious expedient. So I am reminded that consumerism has serious limitations: in the long run it is a somewhat 'unrewarding' pastime. Let us hope that it is only a temporary arrangement.

7c   Take heed that ye do not your alms before men, to be seen of them: otherwise ye have no reward of your Father which is in heaven. Therefore when thou doest thine alms, do not sound a trumpet before thee, as the hypocrites do in the synagogues and in the streets, that they may have glory of men. Verily, I say unto you, they have their reward, but when thou doest alms, let not thy left hand know what thy right hand doeth: That thine alms may be in secret: and thy Father which seeth in secret himself shall reward thee openly.

And when thou prayest, thou shalt not be as the hypocrites are: for they love to pray standing in the synagogues and in the corners of the streets, that they may be seen of men. Verily I say unto you, They have their reward. But thou, when thou prayest, enter into thy closet, and when thou hast shut thy door, pray to thy Father which is in secret: and thy Father which seest in secret shall reward thee openly. But when ye pray, use not vain repetitions, as the heathen do: for they think that they shall be heard for their much speaking. Be not ye therefore like unto them: for your Father knoweth what things ye have need of, before ye ask him.

After this manner therefore pray ye: Our Father which art in heaven, Hallowed be thy name. Thy kingdom come. Thy will be done in earth, as it is in heaven. Give us this day our daily bread. And forgive us our debts, as we forgive our debtors. And lead us not into temptation, but deliver us from evil: For thine is the kingdom, and the power, and the glory, for ever. Amen.

Matthew 6, 1-13

7d   Happy the man whose wish and care
              A few paternal acres bound,
      Content to breathe his native air,
              In his own ground,

Whose herds with milk, whose fields with bread,
    Whose flocks supply him with attire,
Whose trees in summer yield him shade,
    In winter fire.

Blest, who can unconcern'dly find
    Hours, days, and years slide soft away,
In health of body, peace of mind,
    Quiet by day,

Sound sleep by night; study and ease,
    Together mixt; sweet recreation;
And Innocence, which most does please
    With meditation.

Thus let me live, unseen, unknown,
    Thus unlamented let me die,
Steal from the world, and not a stone
    Tell where I lie.

Alexander Pope, *Happy the Man*

47e   Once on a time a poor pious peasant died, and arrived before the gate of heaven. At the same time a very, very rich lord came there who also wanted to get into heaven. Then Saint Peter came with the key, and opened the door and let the great man in but apparently did not see the peasant, and shut the door again. And now the peasant outside heard how the great man was received in heaven with all kinds of rejoicing, and how they were making music and singing within. At length all became quiet again, and Saint Peter came and opened the gate of heaven and let the peasant in. The peasant, however, expected that they would make music and sing when he went in also, but all remained quite quiet; he was received with great affection, it is true, and the angels came to meet him, but no-one sang.

    Then the peasant asked Saint Peter how it was that they did not sing for him as they had done when the rich man went in, and said that it seemed to him that there in heaven things were done with just

as much unfairness as on earth. Then said Saint Peter, "By no
means, thou art just as dear to us as anyone else, and wilt enjoy
every heavenly delight that the rich man enjoys, but poor fellows
like thee come to heaven every day, but a rich man like this does not
come more than once in a hundred years!"

The Brothers Grimm, *The Peasant in Heaven*

7f   It is an ancient and profound truth that education should teach men
to love and to hate the right things; but the aphorism must not lead
us into the error of supposing that love and hate are of co-ordinate
value. A love, since it urges one to explore and develop the riches of
its object, is a principle of growth, of expansion; a hate, since its aim
is to destroy relations with its object, is, so far, doomed to sterility.
Hate is fruitful only when made to subserve a love, by eliminating
hindrances to its growth or purging it of elements that deface its
nobility. Thus the 'patriotism' whose core is the hatred of other
nations is a poor and fruitless thing, but hatred of the deeds that
stain our country's history is one of the surest safeguards of her
honour. Similarly - to compare a smaller thing with a greater -
hatred of 'sloppiness' and inexactitude is a necessary element in
every type of 'scholarship.'

We conclude that the central duty of school teaching is to
encourage loves, and that it should use hates only as the gardener
uses his pruning knife to remove the rank growth that wastes the sap
of the tree, and spoils its beauty.

Percy Nunn, *Education, Its Data and First Principles*

7g   At the more naive mythical levels, the good place may be simply the
place of the dead in general. Everybody goes there, to an improved
version of earthly life. The spirit realm of the Tumbuka, in Malawi,
is an underworld where the departed are always young and never
hungry or sad. Such beliefs occur also in New Guinea and New
Caledonia. Some American Indians, the Ojibways and Choctaws for
example, have kindred hopes about the region of sunset, or a happy
hunting-ground in some secret country. These places are paradises

and the homes of the dead, but scarcely heavens, because they are not selective. The goodness of the good place is not therefore in itself a reward.

When selectivity does come in, it may still not take an ethical form. Admission may depend upon social rank. In the Leeward Islands in the Caribbean, aristocratic spirits go to 'sweet-scented Rohutu' and the commoners go to 'foul-scented Rohutu'. In Peru, the mansions of the sun were reserved for the Incas and their nobles. Even when conduct is a passport, and the good place has to be earned, the demands are not always moral. Entry may depend on having performed a ritual, or gone through an initiation.

The motif of achieving the good place for one's afterlife through merit appears crudely in the Norse Valhalla, which was reached by martial prowess. Further refinement of selectivity accompanies the development of imaginative power, which tends to locate the good place in the sky rather than on earth. Celestial dwellings for the dead are nearly always selective; the wicked and ignoble seldom go upward. In Egypt during the 3rd millennium BC, the pharaohs hoped to join the sun god and attend him on his journeys through space. While this is another instance of privilege through rank, early texts show that the god's attitude to a deceased ruler could depend partly on his virtues. Later, when similar hopes were extended to lesser men, this idea of judgement became more prominent.

In the ancient Vedic religion of India the monarch of the dead was called Yama, and he reigned in the outer sky, a realm of light, over all the worthy departed. Their life was an enhancement of earthly life (as in most paradises of myth) with music, sexual fulfilment, and many more pleasures of the same type, and with no pain or care.

Author unknown, *Encyclopedia of World Mythology*

In an award-winning world, doing good is a dicey business. I shall try to keep in mind that intangible rewards are more gratifying. There are no Oscars in Paradise.

---

48 FASHIONABLE GEAR
- Secret Garments

48a *"The soldiers took his garments, and made four parts, one for each of them; also his tunic. But the tunic was without seam, woven from top to bottom; so they said, 'Let us not tear it, but cast lots for it.'"*

Anyone who has not considered that there might be some detailed spiritual symbolism in the Bible, sees nothing remarkable in the above information. The soldiers divided the clothes, but not the tunic - so what? The fact is, however, that in every reported detail of the crucifixion story there is a secret inner meaning.

Thus Jesus's clothes mean 'divine truth' which is to be found in all the inspired parts of the Bible (i.e. most of it). The outer coverings which were divided mean the literal stories, but the tunic is the *inner* meaning. Stories can be bandied about and garbled, especially by militant ecclesiastics (the soldiers). The truth within is not so easily dispersed.

Apocalypse Explained, 64

8b   Swedenborg's interpretations of scripture do sometimes seem a bit far-fetched, but here we have a very neat example of what he calls 'correspondences'. He tells us of inner meanings, and actually uses one to support the truth about which he is trying to convince us. The inner meaning is that there is an inner meaning. It is a curious kind of 'argument'. We are invited, however, to apply the system in countless other Biblical situations - the proof of the divine pudding lies in the eating.

If it works, as it appears to do in this instance, then it opens up the Bible and imparts a timeless psychological credibility to what might otherwise be just an unreliable old history book: irrelevant details could become spiritually eloquent. Most great literature, of course, functions on different levels, but Swedenborg's claim is a bold one. Seamless truths might thus be shielded from the vagaries of fashion.

48c   Sitting down on the edge of his couch, Demetrius reverently
       unfolded it across his knees. Again he had the strange sensation of
       tranquillity that had come to him when he had handled the robe in
       Jerusalem. It was a peculiar sort of calmness; not the calmness of
       inertia or indifference, but the calmness of self-containment. He was
       stilled - but strengthened.

       There had never been any room in his mind for superstition. He
       had always disdained the thought that any sort of power could be
       resident in an inanimate object. People who believed in the magical
       qualities of insensate things were either out-and-out fools, or had got
       themselves into an emotional state where they were the easy victims
       of their own inflamed imagination. He had no patience with
       otherwise sensible men who carried lucky stones in their pockets. It
       had comforted him to feel that although he was a slave his mind was
       not in bondage.

       Well, be all that as it might, the solid fact remained that when he
       laid his hands upon the Galilean's robe, his agitation ceased. His
       nervous anxiety vanished. After the previous occasion when he had
       sensed this, he had told himself that the extraordinary experience
       could be accounted for in the most practical, common-sense terms.
       This robe had been worn by a man of immense courage; effortless,
       inherent, built-in, automatic courage! Demetrius had seen this Jesus
       on trial, serene and self-assured with the whole world arrayed
       against him, with death staring him in the face, and not one
       protesting friend in sight. Was it not natural that his robe should
       become a symbol of fortitude?

                                                  Lloyd C. Douglas, *The Robe*

48d   It might be assumed and is often accepted that the story of clothes
       and the story of fashion are the same, but this is not so. Fashion in
       clothes is a freak among the arts in that its existence as we
       understand it is limited to the Western World and to the period from
       the later Middle Ages onwards. Mankind has for innumerable
       centuries been drawing, painting, carving and sculpting, building,
       telling stories, dancing, singing songs and making music - in all
       sorts of ways such as these expressing himself and adjusting himself

to the world around him by that exercise and projection of his feelings, thoughts and aspirations which we define in general as the arts.

But while these arts were continually changing and developing and taking on different forms from one era and one part of the world to another, men and women dressed in very much the same way generation after generation, century after century, even in one civilisation after another.

The history of clothing is usually, and reasonably, regarded by most people as dating from the time when mankind discovered how to spin and weave and therefore how to make fabrics that were durable and washable. This was many thousands of years ago, and the materials used were wool, flax or cotton, according to the part of the world concerned. In China from early days it was silk; the process of manufacture was until only a few centuries ago cherished as a closely guarded secret by that country.

It is impossible to say for certain which clothing material came first and from where, or how the method was first discovered of how to twist the raw materials together so as to produce continuous threads from which cloth could be woven by criss-crossing them at right angles on an elementary loom. But having produced lengths of fabric, people, men and women alike, draped them around their bodies in various ways and went on doing so.

Elizabeth Ewing, *Dress and Undress*

8e   I speak of aspirations because those alone are what fashion plates disclose, not realities. They take us into a rarefied world peopled with the young and good-looking and carefree, where all clothes are clean and new, all ladies and gentlemen polite, all children well brought up; where not only are tailors' and dressmakers' bills of small consequence but there is an abundance of delightful opportunities for wearing our finery. In this charmed sphere it never rains at garden parties, never blows our hats off at a race meeting (where we always, needless to say, have tickets for the grandest grandstand). There is someone else to make beds and wash saucepans. The beasts painlessly yield their fur, and the birds their feathers, for our adornment. Violence, crime, starvation, are unknown. War itself is merely an occasion for wearing coquettish little military symbols or attractive mourning.

Doris Langley Moore, *Fashion through Fashion Plates*

48f   Contemporary culture is plagued by the passion to possess. The unreasoned boast abounds that the good life is found in accumulation, that 'more is better'... Furthermore, the pace of the modern world accentuates our sense of being fractured and fragmented. We feel strained, hurried, breathless. The complexity of rushing to achieve and accumulate more and more frequently threatens to overwhelm us; it seems there is no escape from the rat race.

Christian simplicity frees us from this modern mania. It brings sanity to our compulsive extravagance, and peace to our frantic spirit... It allows us to see material things for what they are - goods to enhance life, not to oppress life. People once again become more important than possessions. Simplicity enables us to live lives of integrity in the face of the terrible realities of our global village.

Turn your back on all high-pressure competitive situations that make climbing the ladder the central focus. The fruit of the Spirit is not push, drive, climb, grasp and trample. Don't let the rat-racing world keep you on its treadmill. There is a legitimate place for blood, sweat and tears; but it should have its roots in the call of God; not in the desire to get ahead. Life is more than a climb to the top of the heap.

Richard Foster, *Freedom of Simplicity*

48g   I hold, as firmly as St Thomas Aquinas, that all truths, ancient or modern, are divinely inspired; but I know from observation and introspection that the instrument on which the inspiring force plays may be a very faulty one, and may even end, like Bunyan in The Holy War, by making the most ridiculous nonsense of his message.

However, here is my own account of the matter for what it is worth.

It is often said, by the heedless, that we are a conservative species, impervious to new ideas. I have not found it so. I am often appalled at the avidity and credulity with which new ideas are snatched at and adopted without a scrap of sound evidence. People will believe anything that amuses them, gratifies them, or promises them some sort of profit. I console myself, as Stuart Mill did, with the notion that in time the silly ideas will lose their charm and drop out of fashion and out of existence; that the false promises, when broken, will pass through cynical derision into oblivion; and that after this sifting process the sound ideas, being indestructible (for even if suppressed or forgotten they are rediscovered again and again) will survive and be added to the body of ascertained knowledge we call Science. In this way we acquire a well tested stock of ideas to furnish our minds, such furnishing being education proper as distinguished from the pseudo-education of the schools and universities.

Bernard Shaw, *Preface to The Black Girl in Search of God*

In my wardrobe there may be garments for every social and spiritual occasion, but grant me also a never-ending supply of clean underwear.

---

49   DREAMS AND VISIONS
- The Mystery of Sleep

49a   There are holy visions and unholy visions, but nobody is any the better for them because they leave no room for argument. Devilish visions are conjured up in hell, but holy visions are symbolic projections from heaven - they don't happen now-a-days because nobody would have any idea what to make of them. Even the old Biblical prophets only saw visions when they were in a 'spiritual' state, not when fully awake in this world. Sometimes demented people also see weird things but they are not worth taking seriously.

There were some cases of 'infernal apparitions' caused by mad spirits who had got it into their heads that they were '*Holy* Spirits', but they have now been safely fenced off in a private hell of their own. The only visions worth studying for improvement are those recorded in the Bible.

Conversations with the dead are not much help either: they might induce a kind of pseudo-piety but it's only a flash in the pan: the person's own thoughts are simply stifled. They soon re-assert themselves, and then they profane whatever they may have learned. Spirits may insinuate religious notions into the minds of men, but angels never go in for this kind of thing.

Divine Providence, 134, 134a

49b   Since Swedenborg was perhaps the greatest visionary of all time, it is odd to find him so dismissive of visions here. I wonder what he would have made of all the computer-generated visions to which we have now become so accustomed on our television screens. We can re-create Solomon's Temple or the Courts of the Pharoahs - even Jacob's Ladder or the Transfiguration would not present to our technicians any insuperable problems. Visions generated in heaven might, by comparison, fail to impress.

But the important question, it seems to me, is what are they for?

If the purpose of some mind-blowing angelic vision were simply to amaze me - to anaesthetise my powers of reason, then I can do without that kind of ecstatic experience.

We must look for meanings. What we see with our eyes is evidently no longer reliable. What we see with our minds is what really matters.

49c   Try to remember all the things you have said and done, and everything the eyes have seen in a day. You will find it interesting for a little while, but the very act of trying to remember will bring fatigue, for you will find that you have absorbed more than you would have supposed possible, even in that few minutes of looking back. But the unconscious mind is *never fatigued* ; never tires of storing up all the material that comes to it. It began doing this when you were a baby, and it has been keeping it up ever since.

The unconscious mind has what might be called two sides; the bright side and the dark side. The bright side is close to the censor, and wakes you up exactly at seven o'clock in time to get breakfast and catch the eight-fifteen train to the city, and to remind you of all the things you wish to remember that come up in a busy life.

The dark side conceals those things you wish to forget. It is only the conscious mind that can recall, but if you have been sufficiently forceful in your forgetting, the unconscious mind will attempt to make you remember, in dreams.

This does not mean that the unconscious mind is always concealing something unpleasant. The reverse is really true; the unconscious mind is only trying to fulfil unfulfilled wishes - wishes, very often, that are hang-overs from childhood. Everyone has these unfulfilled wishes, and the unconscious mind, which has no power of itself to judge between your past and your present, between right and wrong, is quite as likely to bring up an old wish as a new one. Then the censor, or safety valve, changes the message into fairy tale, adventure or fantasy, and the night's rest is a peaceful one.

Mary Stewart Cutting, *What Dreaming Means to You*

49d It is amazing what profound ignorance prevails even among fairly
well-informed persons regarding the blind and their feelings, desires
and capabilities. The seeing are apt to conclude that the world of the
blind - and especially the deaf-blind person - is quite unlike the
sunlit, blooming world they know, that a handicapped person's
feelings and sensations are essentially different from their own, and
that mental consciousness is fundamentally affected by infirmity.
Sighted people blunder still further and imagine that the blind are
shut out from all beauty of colour, music, and shape. They need to
be told over and over that the elements of beauty, order, form, and
proportion are tangible to the blind, and that beauty and rhythm are
the result of a spiritual law deeper than sense. Yet how many people
with eyes take this truth to heart? How many of them take the
trouble to ascertain for themselves the fact that the deaf-blind inherit
their brain from a seeing and hearing race fitted for five senses and
that the spirit fills the silent darkness with its own sunshine and
harmony?

Helen Keller / Ray Silverman, *Light in my Darkness*

49e Another instance of the archetype is that of the 'wise old man', the
teacher, the sage who is the embodiment of the wisdom of the ages...
When bewildered with the problems of life, we look for some such
authority for a teacher and guide. Indeed we may venture that Jung
himself embodies this archetype to some of his followers; and very
worthily he fulfils that rôle! But there is an 'ancient wisdom' in us
all which, in the ordinary affairs of life, goes beyond what we call
'common sense', and acts as a guide to us in the more fateful
problems of our lives, and which in our dreams may appear as the
old wise man, the patriarch, the father. We do well to heed what he
says, for intuition, so often represented as a wise old man, is often a
better guide than reason.

These archetypes, relating as they do to deep-seated ideas and
feelings in the collective unconscious, cannot adequately be
expressed in the language of reason and therefore take form in fairy
stories, in myths of the race, and in dreams, and also find expression
in music and the primitive as well as in modern art.

There would be no function for the artist and musician to
perform if all that we experience could be expressed in words, for
art and music can give expression to feelings which cannot be
otherwise expressed, nor otherwise appreciated. So these archetypal
images can sometimes be best expressed in symbolic art forms,
which are pictorial representations of what is going on in the
personality and especially in the unconscious.

J. A. Hadfield, *Dreams and Nightmares*

9f   It is that death by which we may be literally said to die daily; a
death which Adam died before his mortality; a death whereby we
live a middle and moderating point between life and death - In fine,
so like death, I dare not trust it without my prayers, and an half
adieu unto the world, and take my farewell in a colloquy with God:-

> The night is come, like to the day;
> Depart not thou, great God, away.
> Let not my sins, black as the night,
> Eclipse the lustre of thy light:
> Keep still in my Horizon; for to me
> The Sun makes not the day, but Thee.
> Thou, whose nature cannot sleep,
> On my temples sentry keep;
> Guard me 'gainst those watchful foes,
> Whose eyes are open while mine close.
> Let no dreams my head infest,
> But such as Jacob's temples blest.
> While I do rest, my Soul advance;
> Make my sleep a holy trance;
> That I may, my rest being wrought,
> Awake into some holy thought;
> And with as active vigour run
> My course, as doth the nimble Sun.
> Sleep is a death; O make me try,
> By sleeping, what it is to die;
> And as gently lay my head
> On my grave, as now my bed.
> Howe'er I rest, great God, let me

Awake again at last with thee;
And thus assur'd, behold I lie
Securely, or to awake or die.
These are my drowsie days; in vain
I do wake now to sleep again:
O come that hour, when I shall never
Sleep again, but wake for ever.

Sir Thomas Browne, *The Night is Come*

49g   ...Over Lamb, at this period of his life, there passed regularly, after
taking wine, a brief eclipse of sleep. It descended upon him softly as
a shadow. In a gross person, laden with superfluous flesh, and
sleeping heavily, this would have been disagreeable; but in Lamb,
thin even to meagreness, spare and wiry as an Arab of the desert, or
as Thomas Aquinas, wasted by scholastic vigils, the affection of
sleep seemed rather a network of aerial gossamer than of earthly
cobweb - more like a golden haze falling upon him gently from the
heavens than a cloud exhaling upwards from the flesh. Motionless in
his chair as a bust, breathing so gently as scarcely to seem certainly
alive, he presented the image of repose midway between life and
death, like the repose of sculpture; and, to one who knew his history,
a repose affectingly contrasting with the calamities and internal
storms of his life. I have heard more persons than I can now
distinctly recall observe of Lamb, when sleeping, that his
countenance in that state assumed an expression almost seraphic,
from its intellectual beauty of outline, its child-like simplicity, and
its benignity. It could not be called a transfiguration that sleep had
worked in his face; for the features wore essentially the same
expression when waking; but sleep spiritualised that expression,
exalted it, and almost harmonised it.

Thomas de Quincey, *Literary Reminiscences / Charles Lamb*

**Appearances can be deceptive. If my dreams are trying to tell
me something, let them not speak in riddles.**

50   HEAVENLY BODIES
- Sun, Moon and Stars

50a   Everything we read in Matthew's gospel about the sea roaring, the sun and moon being almost snuffed out, and the stars tumbling out of the sky refers to the final state of the universal 'Church' when doctrinal disputes rage (the sea roars), when love towards God fails (the sun is eclipsed), when kindness and common decency decline (the moon grows dim), and when people have no notion of what faith is all about (the stars disappear). There are similar 'last judgement' prophecies elsewhere with much the same meaning.

The 'last judgement' of an individual happens when he dies. After several days, the body grows cold and he is received into the next life, welcomed first by the *'celestial'* angels. If he cannot get along with them, then the *'spiritual'* angels take over, and if that doesn't work out, then *'good spirits'* do what they can to make him feel at home. He gravitates toward the company that shares the lifestyle to which he has been accustomed, and then he feels as though he has got his body back: 'judgement' begins: the evil eventually go to hell, and the good to heaven.

Arcana Caelestia, 2119, 2120

50b   Swedenborg can be very heavy, and, if you take it all literally, this is just about as heavy as it comes. Warnings of cosmic disaster on such a scale, if we took them seriously, would no doubt cause global panic, especially since Swedenborg went on to say that these events were imminent - and that was in the 18th.century!

I take some comfort from the assurance that no threat to planet Earth was ever intended, but the spiritual meanings are pretty grim even so. It often seems, these days, that we are more terrified of impact from bits of space debris than we are of a decline in moral standards, although from his grandstand in the spiritual world Swedenborg clearly sees the latter as the greater danger.

I have never quite understood how it is that the imminent prospect of either judgement or annihilation doesn't cause widespread panic among the elderly. It obviously doesn't - quite the reverse in fact. Can we, I wonder, detect the hand of 'providence' in this?

At least, in the hereafter, we can now look forward to a gentle reception. I am glad to know that new arrivals in the next world are allowed to find their own level, and are neither straightway pitch-forked into hell, nor catapulted into heaven.

50c   Death is the fundamental mystery of life. It is certain for all and yet we do not know what it means.

The mystery can be reduced to simple dilemmas. When we die does everything end for us, or is there some way that we go on? Is there nothing more to us than the sum of our material parts, or does the soul exist? Is the notion of the soul a figment of human psychology, or perhaps an invention of religion? Or could it be something wonderfully real?

Science, which can weigh, measure and assess the corpse of a dead person, is powerless to tell us whether anything spiritual occurs after death. A widely held assumption of science, though it is by no means unanimous, tends to be that there is no soul, and that 'dead means dead'. Some scientists promote such views as though they are facts that have been empirically tested. Yet there are no facts here, only assumptions that cannot be proved. Indeed, the scientific case in this area is religious in nature since it expresses a passionate *belief* in the non-existence of the soul, but has no evidence to support that claim.

Religion presents the opposite case, equally passionately, on equally flimsy grounds. There is no scientific proof of the existence of the various religious heavens and hells and afterlife realms. Nevertheless, the religious or spiritual point of view strongly asserts that the soul does exist, and will undergo a judgement after death, and can transmigrate through many forms, and can be reborn.

Graham Hancock / Santha Faiia, *Heaven's Mirror*

0d   The sunlight falls on us in a stream that in our eyes resembles the colour of our ordinary fires. It may look white on the ground, but like all small children who love to show the sun's beaming face in their pictures, we think of it as yellow and symbolise it as golden. Yet for a long time we have known that sunlight can be divided up into 'all the colours of the rainbow', and indeed many more than we can detect in the rainbow. As a child I used to visit a neighbour's house where glass prisms, probably saved from some old chandelier, were left lying on the window bars. On fine days they threw a dozen or more little coloured patches, running from blue through green and yellow to red, on walls and ceiling, on furniture and sometimes on to one's own clothes and skin. As we played, or worked at our sewing class, all these delicious patches wheeled steadily round the room. One which was full on a clock face when it said three o'clock would be sliding off its edge by a quarter past. Already before this I had been told that a rainbow was caused by the splitting of sunlight by water drops; belonging to a scientific family that information came my way as soon as I was capable of recognising these lovely arcs. But they were so enchanting, so obviously magical, that I never really accepted this explanation in my heart. But with the coloured patches in my friend's nursery, I did. Nothing I have seen since, not even the elaborate spectrohelioscopes displayed at Conversaziones of the Royal Society, has made me so absolutely aware of the spectrum of sunlight and the wheeling of the sun in the sky.

Jacquetta Hawkes, *Man and the Sun*

0e   Above all else, however, Cheops' Pyramid is intensely religious, with the main cultic purpose of assisting the dead king in his ascent to the sky. In brief, therefore, the monument is a sepulchre with a potent function which, for lack of appropriate terminology, can be said to be astrological. This is a widely accepted consensus and is confirmed by the liturgy of the Pyramid Texts. The religion and rituals of the Pyramid Age were a sky religion, whereby the king became a star and his star soul became established or transferred to the southern stars of Orion and Sirius and to the northern stars, which included the three circumpolar constellations of Ursa Major, Ursa Minor and Draco. The supreme task of the ancient architect was to express these vital elements of the sky religion in the design of the monument. When all is said and done, the pyramid structure was primarily an instrument of rebirth for the departed king.

Robert G. Bauval, *The Orion Mystery*

50f   Similarly, the stars had their importance in the measuring of time, and two or three of the major constellations were deities of some weight; but only one group of stars achieved lasting importance in the Egyptian scene. Again, this importance had to do with triumph over death. In the clear Egyptian air the stars stand out with brilliance. Most of the stars swing across the sky with a scythe-like sweep and disappear below the horizon. But one section of the skies employs a smaller orbit, and there the stars may dip toward the horizon but never disappear. Those are the circumpolar stars swinging around the North Star, stars which the Egyptians called 'those that know no destruction' or 'those that know no weariness'. These undying stars they took as the symbol of the dead who triumphed over death and went on into eternal life. That north section of heaven was in early times an important part of the universe. Visibly there was no death there; therefore, it must be the place of eternal blessedness for which Egyptians longed. In the early mortuary texts, which we moderns call the Pyramid Texts, the goal of the deceased was the region of Dat in the northern part of heaven, where he would join the circumpolar stars 'which know no destruction' and thus live for ever himself. There were located their Elysian Fields, the 'Field of Reeds' and the 'Field of Offerings', in which the dead would live as an *akh*, an 'effective' spirit.

Henri Frankfort et al, *Before Philosophy*

50g   Gardeners used to say that fruit trees planted under the radiance of the full moon would always provide an abundant crop. They supposed that the fullness of the moon's light created a warming effect and consequently orchard trees like peaches which came into blossom at night would never be damaged by frosts. This particular belief has its origin in a more ancient age, for Varro, writing on the subject around 36 BC, wrote: "Trees which are planted in a row are warmed by the sun and the moon equally on all sides, with the result that more grapes and olives form, and that they ripen earlier".

All seeds of plants that bear foodstuff above ground - fruit and nut bearers, salads and herbs - should be planted in the first and second quarters of the moon. All seeds of plants that bear foodstuffs below ground - root vegetables, tubers, ground nuts - should be planted in the third and fourth quarters of the moon.

Just like those gardeners who sowed by moonlight, other Old-World gardeners sowed and planted by starlight; the light here coming principally from the brilliance of the Pole Star. They planted in rows running from north to south, partly to align with the radiation from the Pole Star, but also to ensure, quite practically, that plants acquired an equal amount of sun on either side.

Bernard Schofield, *A Miscellany of Garden Wisdom*

The ancients were greatly moved by the mysteries of space. As we probe the stellar depths may we never lose that sense of primitive wonder.

---

51   BRANCH LINES
- The Language of Trees

51a   **When the Bible talks about a garden, a grove, a wood, or about separate trees - olive, vine, cedar, poplar or oak, one could easily think that was the end of the matter. But, in fact, garden, grove and wood mean wisdom, intelligence and knowledge. Olive, vine, cedar, poplar and oak mean various aspects of religious goodness and truth - celestial, spiritual, rational, natural and sensual respectively. All the literal forestry is just so much scaffolding: it's the spiritual sense that matters.**

Now a description from one of Swedenborg's spiritual world adventures -
The trees were planted in a perfect spiral, each variety following on from another in order of importance. Between the tree in the middle and the beginning of the spiral was an area of sparkling brilliance, so that the trees shone with ever-diminishing degrees of light. The innermost, called trees of paradise, bore the finest fruits quite unlike anything on earth. After them were trees rich in oil, then those producing wine, then those with a glorious aroma, and finally those useful for all kinds of woodwork. Here and there were garden seats woven from living saplings with their several fruits. There were also gates leading to lawns and flower beds.

The angel explained, "Everything in our garden represents some heavenly principle or 'use'. People who like to be useful themselves instinctively see that this is the case: to anyone else it looks just like any ordinary stretch of woodland."

The True Christian Religion, 200 [2]*, 741* [2]

51b   So the Bible has plenty of heavenly silviculture, but the ordinary reader could be forgiven for not seeing the wood for the trees. I'm not entirely comfortable with Swedenborg's other-worldly experiences either; they seem a bit over-theatrical to me, probably because they stretch earthly language to the limits. Even so, I think I prefer woods to look like woods.

Trees *are* wonderfully expressive though - especially big ones, making patterns against the sky. Most convincing for me, however, are the *meanings* of the various sorts of timber: they are so apt. Olive trees live for ages; they give oil with all its soothing properties, and the grain is very beautiful when carved and polished - a patient, loving tree. The vine, of course, is not massive, but lively and productive of wine - the sort of tree to make life worth living. The wonderfully scented cedar grows straight; it knows where it's going, and can easily be sawn into manageable pieces - an intellectual sort of tree. The poplar likewise, fairly fast-growing, a no-nonsense tree; and the oak, strong, very serviceable and reassuring to the touch. I think Swedenborg got it about right.

1c   Season of mists and mellow fruitfulness,
Close bosom-friend of the maturing sun;
Conspiring with him how to load and bless
With fruit the vines that round the thatch-eaves run;
To bend with apples the moss'd cottage trees,
And fill all fruit with ripeness to the core;
To swell the gourd and plump the hazel shells
With a sweet kernel, to set budding more,
And still more, later flowers for the bees,
Until they think warm days will never cease,
The summer has o'er-brimmed their clammy cells -

John Keats, *Ode to Autumn*

1d   Below Canal Bridge, on the right bank, grew twelve great trees, with roots awash. Thirteen had stood there - eleven oaks and two ash trees - but the oak nearest the North Star had never thriven, since first a pale green hook had pushed out of a swelled black acorn left by floods on the bank more than three centuries before. In its second year a bullock's hoof had crushed the seedling, breaking its two ruddy leaves, and the sapling grew up crooked. The cleft of its fork held the rains of two hundred years, until frost made a wedge of ice that split the trunk; another century's weather wore it hollow, while every flood took more earth and stones from under it. And one rainy night, when salmon and peal from the sea were swimming against the brown rushing water, the tree had suddenly groaned. Every root carried the groans of the moving trunk, and the voles ran in fear from their tunnels. It rocked until dawn; and when the wind left the land it gave a loud cry, scaring the white owl from its roost, and fell into the river as the sun was rising.

Henry Williamson, *Tarka the Otter*

51e   Most of us love trees. They are our friends in many ways. Some give us fruit and blossom, others wood with which to make a variety of things, but the aspect that appeals to most of us is their beauty all the year round. The countryside is enriched by them and the bareness of the streets is softened by their restful greens.

When a tree is in full leaf, the skeleton, so to speak, that is, the trunk and branches, is still there underneath. The successful drawing of trees depends very much on bearing in mind all the time that the shape of the foliage is relative to the branching. It is rather like drawing a human being fully dressed. If you do not take into account the body inside the clothes, your drawing will not look right.

We have the Beech tall, aloof and austere, the Ash more graceful with an air of good-breeding and poise. Then the Horse Chestnut portly and smug, whilst the Silver Birch is a sort of fairy of the forest. The Oak stands amongst them all, bound up with our traditions, unassailable in the majesty of its strength.

Life is apt to bring many disappointments and if we are inclined to feel all else has failed us, the trees and grass and flowers of the field always offer refreshment and remind us that the world of nature has still much beauty with which to gladden our hearts.

Gregory Brown, *How to Draw Trees*

51f   The tree (Beech) has been termed 'Mother of the Forest' and has been used as a nurse for other trees by all foresters for many generations, but in course of time she becomes less maternal and a mixed forest of oak, ash, and elm, with beech, eventually becomes a pure beech woodland. Under the dense foliage of the glade, or even a single tree, sheltered from the burning rays of the sun, weary travellers have found cool and refreshing rest. Its shade has been gratefully accepted by all people for more than two thousand years and is recorded by the early Greeks and Romans. Pliny says:

"There is a little hill named Carne within the territorie of Tusculum not far from Roman Citie side, clad and beautiful with a goodly grove and tuft of beech trees, so even and round in the head as if they were curiously kept cut and shorne artificially with garden sheares...In it there was one especiall faire tree above the rest, which Pabienus Crispus; a man in our daies of great authoritie...cast a fancie and extra ordinarie liking unto; insomuch as he was wont not onely to take his repose and lie under it, to sprinkle and cast wine plentifully upon it, but also to clip, embrace and kisse it other whiles."

The tree, its leaves, and fruits were far more highly valued in early times. Pliny refers in eloquent terms to the value of its nuts, or mast, and the leaves which were used for cattle fodder, and bedding. Evelyn wrote, "With it the turner makes dishes, trays, rims for buckets, trenchers, dresser boards and other utensils. It serves the wheeler and joiner for large screws, etc., the upholsterer uses it for sellies, chairs, bed-steads, etc. It makes shovels and spade graffs for the husbandman, and is useful to the bellows-maker. Floats for fisher nets, instead of corks, are made of its bark. It is good for fuel, billet, bavin, and coals, though one of the least lasting; and its very shavings are good for fining of wine. Its very leaves afford the best and easiest mattresses in the world to lay under our quilts instead of straw. I have sometimes lain on them to my great refreshment."

Alexander L. Howard, *Trees in Britain*

1g   At Upsala, the old religious capital of Sweden, there was a sacred grove in which every tree was regarded as divine. The heathen Slavs worshipped trees and groves. The Lithuanians were not converted to Christianity till towards the close of the fourteenth century, and amongst them at the date of their conversion the worship of trees was prominent. Some of them revered remarkable oaks and other great shady trees, from which they received oracular responses. Some maintained holy groves about their villages or houses, where even to break a twig would have been a sin. They thought that he who cut a bough in such a grove either died suddenly or was crippled in one of his limbs. Proofs of the prevalence of tree-worship in ancient Greece and Italy are abundant. In the sanctuary of Aesculapius at Cos, for example, it was forbidden to cut down the cypress-trees under a penalty of a thousand drachms. But nowhere, perhaps, in the ancient world was this antique form of religion better preserved than in the heart of the great metropolis itself. In the Forum, the busy centre of Roman life, the sacred fig-tree of Romulus was worshipped down to the days of the empire, and the withering of its trunk was enough to spread consternation through the city. Again, on the slope of the Palatine Hill grew a cornel-tree which was esteemed one of the most sacred objects in Rome. Whenever the tree appeared to a passer-by to be drooping, he set up a hue and cry which was echoed by the people in the street, and soon a crowd might be seen running helter-skelter from all sides with buckets of water, as if (says Plutarch) they were hastening to put out a fire.

Sir James George Frazer, *The Golden Bough*

A busy life, like a great tree, needs strong roots. Please keep mine well-watered, but don't overdo it.

52   A NOBLE VINTAGE
- Wine that maketh glad the heart of man

2a   **'Plenty of grain' means natural goodness, and 'plenty of wine' means the truth that comes from caring behaviour. They work on a natural level because these qualities are honest and down-to-earth. If we are talking about something rather more intellectual, then the appropriate symbols might be simply 'bread and wine' where bread refers to what is 'celestial' and wine to what is 'spiritual'.**

   In the Bible, the 'Church' is sometimes called a vineyard, and the fruit of the vine means heavenly truth, so anyone reared in a Christian environment soon gets the picture - natural refreshment serves the body, but spiritual refreshment serves the soul.

   Arcana Caelestia 3580, The True Christian Religion 708, 709

2b   *In vino veritas* (in wine is truth). Under the influence of a good wine, many a truth has been uttered that might have been best left unsaid. Swedenborg, however, is clearly concerned with something rather more profound, and, as most wine-lovers like myself know only too well, the happiness that comes out of a bottle is, alas, short-lived compared to the contentment of a purposeful life.

   Even so, wine is perhaps the most cheerful of earth's comforts, and certainly one of the most potent of all Biblical symbols - a foretaste of heaven. Swedenborg explores literally *thousands* of permutations of goodness and truth found in the pages of the Old and New Testaments. You need a clear head to follow him, but there is no better metaphor than the subtlety and variety of a well-stocked cellar.

2c   There never was such a goose. Bob said he didn't believe there ever was such a goose cooked. Its tenderness and flavour, size and cheapness, were the themes of universal admiration...

Mrs.Cratchit entered - flushed, but smiling proudly - with the pudding, like a speckled cannon-ball, so hard and firm, blazing in half of half-a-quartern of ignited brandy, and bedight with Christmas holly stuck into the top...

At last the dinner was all done, the cloth was cleared, the hearth swept, and the fire made up. The compound in the jug being tasted, and considered perfect, apples and oranges were put upon the table, and a shovel full of chestnuts on the fire. Then all the Cratchit family drew round the hearth, in what Bob Cratchit called a circle, meaning half a one; and at Bob Cratchit's elbow stood the family display of glass. Two tumblers and a custard-cup without a handle.

These held the hot stuff from the jug, however, as well as golden goblets would have done; and Bob served it out with beaming looks, while the chestnuts on the fire sputtered and cracked noisily. Then Bob proposed:
"A merry Christmas to us all, my dears. God bless us!"
Which all the family re-echoed.
"God bless us every one!" said Tiny Tim.

Charles Dickens, *A Christmas Carol*

52d   Another jug, Anton. Not that you should fetch me one now, but that a jug has once more spilled into our text. It is ever thus. When men come together to do business, when they join for pleasure, when they work, when they worship, when they woo, when they eat, when they brood alone - always there must be wine there. It is ink to the spirit, helping words flow out. It is excitation to the flesh. It is a taper lighting the mind. You remember the wine-press in Erfurt, and the notion it stamped on me for a like invention. You have seen my cellar. You know how wine sits *at the bottom* of all I do. Do not then punish me with such looks for quaffing it. It is a balm and joy. What else would you have me drink? Rhine water? Had I supped at that, my veins would be cankered by now, and I not alive to tell my tale.

Wine also goes well with writing. I do not mean your writing, Anton, since a scribe must look hard at what he pens, and keep his mind clear, and to such labour wine is a distraction. But for myself, giving out the writing, wine is a useful heat. Many a day begins with my brain frozen like a millpond. But then wine at breakfast comes up like the sun and melts me, so that when later you climb the stairs - the noise of your footstep gladdening me, even before I see your handsome face - my memories are unlocked and I am ready to gabble at you like a goose. And you can trust what I pour forth as faithful recollection. Even when dusk has drawn near, and I am the better by a jug or three, what I dictate to you has true substance - not a phantasm conjured by drunkenness but the lees in the bottom of life's jug. Why then condemn me? Why such frowning? Is it from envy? If I ration you by day, keeping you to swigs for refreshment, it is only so your hand be correct. Any dusk when we have done our work, you know you can stay and we two empty more jugs together. I cannot go with you to the tavern, since I walk too slow there and besides dislike the general company. But we can make a kind of tavern of it here. Bring that girl of yours, Anton. Let the three of us carouse. Though I am jealous of your person, I would not hog you all night.

In the meantime let this book be the jug we share. I think a book, when it reads well, can indeed seem like a jug of wine, making a glow through all the body. Better than a jug, a book is never finished. You can reach the end and it is all still there and always will be, forever replenished like the wine at Cana. To think of men years ahead taking sustenance from this little jug of ours - that is a pleasing notion, and determines me, while my brain is still fermenting, to squeeze a vintage out, full and candid to the palate.

In my cups you shall know me and all that I have done.

Blake Morrison, *The Justification of Johann Gutenberg*

Being almost famished with hunger, having not eaten a morsel for some hours before I left the ship, I found the demands of nature so strong upon me that I could not forbear showing my impatience (perhaps against the strict rules of decency) by putting my finger frequently on my mouth, to signify that I wanted food. The Hurgo (for so they call a great lord, as I afterwards learnt) understood me very well. He descended from the stage and commanded that several

ladders should be applied to my sides, on which above one hundred
of the inhabitants mounted and walked towards my mouth, laden
with baskets full of meat, which had been provided and sent thither
by the King's orders upon the first intelligence he received of me. I
observed there was the flesh of several animals, but could not
distinguish them by taste. There were shoulders, legs, and loins
shaped like those of mutton, and very well dressed, but smaller than
the wings of a lark. I ate them by two or three at a mouthful, and
took three loaves at a time, about the bigness of musket bullets.
They supplied me as they could, showing a thousand marks of
wonder and astonishment at my bulk and appetite. I then made
another sign that I wanted drink. They found by my eating that a
small quantity would not suffice me, and, being a most ingenious
people, they slung up with great dexterity one of their largest
hogsheads, then rolled it towards my hand and beat out the top. I
drank it off at a draught, which I might well do, for it did not hold
half a pint, and tasted like a small wine of Burgundy, but much more
delicious. They brought me a second hogshead, which I drank in the
same manner, and made signs for more, but they had none to give
me. When I had performed these wonders they shouted for joy and
danced upon my breast, repeating several times as they did at first,
'Hekinah Degul.'

Jonathan Swift, *Gulliver's Travels*

52f   And the third day there was a marriage in Cana of Galilee; and the
mother of Jesus was there: And both Jesus was called, and his
disciples, to the marriage. And when they wanted wine, the mother
of Jesus saith unto him, They have no wine. Jesus saith unto her,
Woman, what have I to do with thee? mine hour is not yet come. His
mother saith unto the servants, Whatsoever he saith unto you, do it.
And there were set there six water pots of stone, after the manner of
the purifying of the Jews, containing two or three firkins apiece.
Jesus saith unto them, Fill the water pots with water. And they filled
them up to the brim. And he saith unto them, Draw out now, and
bear unto the governor of the feast. And they bare it. When the ruler
of the feast had tasted the water that was made wine, and knew not
whence it was: (but the servants which drew the water knew:) the
governor of the feast called the bridegroom, And saith unto him,

Every man at the beginning doth set forth good wine; and when men have well drunk, then that which is worse: but thou hast kept the good wine until now.

John 2, 1-10

2g The wine of Love is music,
   And the feast of Love is song;
And when Love sits down to the banquet,
   Love sits long:

Sits long and arises drunken,
   But not with the feast and the wine;
He reeleth with his own heart,
   That great, rich Vine.

James Thomson, *The Vine*

We mortals are good at asking unanswerable questions. Some, no doubt, would improve with keeping. Help me not to worry about the others.

Index of Biblical Quotations

(AV) - Authorised Version (NIV) - New International Version

(GCNC) - General Conference of the New Church - Pentateuch

(JB) - Jerusalem Bible (RSV) - Revised Standard Version

Index of Authors and Sources

The works listed are those where I found the passages used in this collection.
They are not necessarily the places where those passages first appeared.

BARNITZ Harry W.
Existentialism and the New Christianity pp265-266,
Philosophical Library, New York 1969   **43g**

BAUVAL Robert G.
The Orion Mystery pp266-267, BCA
William Heinemann 1994   **50e**

BELL Clive
Civilisation p104, Penguin 1938   **17e**

BENSUSAN S.L.
Gardener's Path in *Fireside Papers pp140,145,*
Epworth Press 1946   **33d**

Garden End in *Fireside Papers p21,* Epworth Press 1946 **21g**

BENTINE Michael
The Door Marked Summer p158, Granada 1982   **14d**

BERNE Eric
Games People Play p145, Penguin 1968   **1f**

BLAKEMORE Colin
The Mind Machine p248, BBC Books 1988   **13e**

BOGARDE Dirk
A Short Walk from Harrods (Front Flap) BCA Penguin 1993 **2f**

BOWEN Gwen (Knight)
Journey into Dawn Unpublished 2001   **13c**

BRONOWSKI Jacob
The Ascent of Man p176, Futura (Macdonald) 1981   **46f**

BROWNE K.R.G.
Foreword *to Heath Robinson Devices p7,* Duckworth 1977 **26g**

BROWNE Sir Thomas
The Night Is Come in *Poems of Sleep and Dream*
Ed.Carol Stewart *p58,* Frederick Muller 1947   **49f**

BROWN Gregory
How to Draw Trees pp4,6, Studio Publications 1943   **51e**

BULLEY Margaret
Art and Understanding pp28-29, Batsford 1937   **8e**

BURNFORD Sheila
The Incredible Journey pp80-81, Hodder 1963   **16f**

BURNHAM Rod
The Hate that Plagues Mankind
in *Mensa Magazine* February 2001, Mensa 2001   **36f**

BUTLER Samuel
The Notebooks in *Memorials* Ed.June Benn *p305,*
Ravette 1986 **44c**

CALDER Nigel
Spaceship Earth p203, Viking (Penguin) 1991 **45c**

CAMILLE Michael
Gothic Art pp41-42, Weidenfeld & Nicolson 1996 **23d**

CHRISTIE Walter R.
The Icon of Sophia in *Seeing Through Symbols*
Ed.Carol & Robert Lawson *p102,* Chrysalis Books 1998 **30g**

CLARIDGE Amanda and WARD-PERKINS John
Pompeii AD79, Exhibition Catalogue - Royal Academy
pp36-37, Imperial Tobacco 1976 **46g**

COHEN Jack and STEWART Ian
The Collapse of Chaos p285, Penguin 1995 **39g**

COUCHE Edith
Lighting Chinese Lanterns,
Church of Zenana Missionary Society n.d.
in *The Lion Christian Meditation Collection*
Ed.Ward and Wild, *p340,* Lion Publishing 1998 **20g**

CRANMER Thomas et al
The Book of Common Prayer pp53,60, C.Knight 1860 **46d**

The Collect for the Third Sunday before Lent
in *The Book of Common Prayer* **39e**

CUPITT Don
Only Human p69, SCM Press 1985 **20e**

CUTTING Mary Stewart
What Dreaming Means to You pp35-37, Rider 194? **49c**

DAVIES Tom
Stained Glass Hours p25, New English Library 1985 **10g**

DA VINCI Leonardo
Trattato della Pittura in *Notebooks of Leonardo da Vinci*
p182, Oxford University Press 1953 **26f**

Trattato della Pittura ms 2038 in the Bibliothèque Nationale
in *Notebooks of Leonardo da Vinci pp180-181*
Oxford University Press 1953 **43f**

DRUMMOND Henry Gordon
Degrees pp8-9, New Church College 1908   **27c**

ECKERSLEY Glennyce S.
An Angel at my Shoulder pp8-9, Rider (Ebury Press) 1996   **46c**

ELIOT T.S.
Choruses from *The Rock* (Extract)
in *Selected Poems p115*, Faber & Faber 1963   **21f**

From *The Rock* in *An Anthology of Religious Verse*
pp103-104, Penguin 1942   **23e**

EWING Elizabeth
Dress and Undress pp11-12, Bibliophile (Batsford) 1981   **48d**

FAIIA Santha & HANCOCK Graham
Heaven's Mirror p ix, Michael Joseph 1998   **50c**

FEYNMAN Richard P.
The Uncertainty of Values in *The Meaning of It All*
p39, Penguin 1999   **34e**

FITZHERBERT John
Wife and Husband (1523) in *Country Life in England*
Ed.E.W.Martin, *p27*, The Country Book Club 1967   **12c**

FLETCHER Martin
Sundry Thoughts on Problems of Parenting
in *Mensa Magazine, June 2001, p17*, Mensa 2001   **42g**

FOSTER Richard
Freedom of Simplicity (Harper & Row 1981)
in *The Lion Christian Meditation Collection pp361-362*
Lion Publishing 1998   **48f**

FRANCIS St.of Assisi
Prayer in *A Year of Grace* Ed.Gollancz, *p335*,
Penguin 1955   **44f**

FRANKFORT Henri et al
Before Philosophy pp56-57, Penguin 1949   **50f**

FRAZER Sir James George
The Golden Bough pp110-111 (Abridged), Macmillan 1959   **51g**

FRIEDMAN Richard Elliott
The Disappearance of God p242, Little, Brown & Co,
The Softback Preview 1997   **13f**

GRIFFITHS Bryn
Cerrig Y Gof in *The Stones Remember pp22-23,*
J.M.Dent 1967   **37f**

GRIMM The Brothers
The Golden Key in *Grimms' Household Tales p303,*
Eyre and Spottiswoode 1946   **36g**

The Peasant in Heaven in *Grimms' Household Tales,*
pp281-282, Eyre and Spottiswoode 1946   **47e**

GROSE David F.
The Origins and Early History of Glass
in *The History of Glass* Ed.Klein & Lloyd, *p13,*
Little, Brown & Co 1993   **37c**

GUTHRIE Douglas
Lord Lister, His Life and Doctrine pp63-64,
E & S Livingstone 1949   **40c**

HADFIELD J.A.
Dreams and Nightmares p125, Penguin 1954   **19e**

Dreams and Nightmares pp45-46, Penguin 1954   **49e**

HADHAM John
Good God p85, Penguin 1940   **21d**

Good God p81, Penguin 1940   **26d**

HANCOCK Graham & FAIIA Santha
Heaven's Mirror p ix, Michael Joseph 1998   **50c**

HARDY Thomas
The Return of the Native p250, Folio Society 1971   **11g**

The Return of the Native pp260-261, Folio Society 1971   **12g**

The Man He Killed
(*The Collected Poems of Thomas Hardy,* Macmillan)
in *Soldiers' Verse* Ed.Patrick Dickinson, *pp46-47,*
Frederick Muller 1945   **32f**

An Indiscretion in the Life of an Heiress p29,
Hutchinson 1985   **35f**

HARLEY Clifford
Spirit and Life Within the Genesis Story pp12-13,
The Swedenborg Society 1963   **4d**

HAWKES Jacquetta
A Land p15, Penguin 1959   **11c**

Man and the Sun pp22-23, Cresset Press 1962   **50d**

HIGGINS Kathleen M. and SOLOMON Robert C.
A Short History of Philosophy p125,
Oxford University Press 1996   **24g**

HILTON James
Goodbye Mr.Chips pp115-116, Hodder Paperbacks 1969   **19d**

HODGKINSON Liz
Getting to Know Yourself in *The Personal Growth Handbook*
pp34-35, Judy Piatkus 1993   **25g**

HODGSON Leonard
Essays in Christian Philosophy in *A Diary of Readings*
Ed.John Baillie, *Day 43*, Oxford University Press 1981   **14g**

HOGGART Richard
The Uses of Literacy pp88-89, Penguin 1958   **7d**

HOLBECHE Soozi
The Power of Gems and Crystals p92, Judy Piatkus 1990   **23f**

The Power of Gems and Crystals pp175,177,
Judy Piatkus 1990   **37e**

HOWARD Alexander L.
Trees in Britain pp18-20 in *Britain in Pictures* Series
Collins 1946   **51f**

HOWITT William
The Rural Life of England Vol.II (1838)
in *Country Life in England* Ed.Martin *p195,*
Country Book Club 1967   **32d**

HUXLEY Aldous
The Doors of Perception pp12-13, Grafton Books /
Collins 1977   **8d**

ISHERWOOD Margaret
Faith Without Dogma pp49-50, George Allen & Unwin 1964   **24e**

Faith Without Dogma pp98-99, George Allen & Unwin 1964   **27f**

JOHNS Beth
Heads, Hearts, and Hands p48
The General Church of the New Jerusalem 1989   **22f**

JOHNSON Samuel
The Rambler No.184 (1751) in *A Diary of Readings Day291*
Ed.Baillie, Oxford University Press 1981   **20d**

LAWRENCE D.H. *continued*
Sons and Lovers pp50-51, Penguin 1951   **22c**
England, my England pp8-9, Penguin 1962   **41f**

LEE Laurie
A Rose for Winter p11, Penguin 1971   **11f**

LEWIS C.S.
The Problem of Pain p134, Fontana 1957   **2g**
The Last Battle pp164-165, Penguin 1967   **40f**

LEWIS I.M.
Ecstatic Religion p18, Penguin 1978   **34f**

LIVELY Penelope
An Ancient Place in *My England p92*, Heinemann 1973   **11d**

LUCRETIUS
The Nature of the Universe Tr.Ronald Latham *pp145-146*,
Penguin 1955   **31f**

MADELEY Edward
The Science of Correspondences Elucidated p190
New Church Missionary & Tract Society 1883   **4c**

MADSEN Truman G.
The Radiant Life p98, Bookcraft 1994   **44d**

'MAN The Unknown'
My Religion in *My Religion p87*, Hutchinson 1925   **44e**

MARTIN Friar of Cochem (1634-1712)
Das grosse Leben Christi in *Heaven – a History*
Colleen McDannell & Bernhard Lang *p196*,
Yale University Press 1988   **9f**

MAWER Simon
Mendel's Dwarf p163, Anchor / Transworld Publishers 1998   **35c**

MICHELL John
The Dimensions of Paradise pp11-12,
Thames & Hudson 1988   **6e**

MONTEFIORE Hugh
The Probability of God p173, SCM Press 1985   **5e**
The Probability of God pp28,39, SCM Press 1985   **29e**

MOODY Raymond
Reunions pp11-12, Little, Brown & Co 1994   **8g**
Reunions p30, Little, Brown & Co 1994   **30e**

MOORE Doris Langley
Fashion through Fashion Plates p9, Ward Lock 1971   **48e**

MOORMAN John R.H.
The New Fioretti in *A Diary of Readings* Ed.Baillie *Day 274*
Oxford University Press 1981   **16e**

MORRIS William
Quoted in *Country Life in England* Ed.Martin *p158,*
Country Book Club 1967   **1g**

MORRISON Blake
The Justification of Johann Gutenberg pp194-195,
Chatto & Windus 2000   **52d**

MUMFORD Lewis
The Condition of Man p413, Martin Secker & Warburg 1944   **45d**

NILSSON Lennart
Behold Man p30, Little, Brown & Co 1974   **6g**

NORTON Dianne
Adding Spice to Life in Ageing: An Adventure in Living
Ed.Sally Greengross, *p32*, Souvenir Press 1985   **43d**

NUNN Percy
Education, Its Data and First Principles pp184-185
Edward Arnold 1960   **47f**

PASCAL Blaise
Pensées in *Memorials* Ed.June Benn *p187*, Ravette Ltd 1986   **18f**

PASTERNAK Boris
Doctor Zhivago Tr.Hayward / Harari *p19,*
Collins and Harvill 1959   **32c**

PAYNE John Howard
There's no place like Home in *Parlour Poetry*
Ed.Michael R.Turner *p175*, Pan Books 1974   **9e**

PITCHFORD Denys Watkins ('BB')
The Little Grey Men pp174-175, Penguin 1965   **44g**

POPE Alexander
Happy the Man in *The Good Life* Ed.Warren *p93,*
Eyre & Spottiswoode 1946   **47d**

POWERS Margaret Fishback
Footprints in *The Lion Christian Meditation Collection*
Ed.Ward & Wild *p394*, Lion Publishing 1998   **14f**

PRIESTLAND Gerald
The Tragedy of Life in *Gerald Priestland at Large p154*
Collins / Fount Paperbacks 1983   **13g**

Enjoy, Enjoy! in *Priestland Right and Wrong p129,*
Collins 1983   **38g**

PULS Joan
Every Bush is Burning pp74-75
(World Council of Churches 1985)
in *The Lion Christian Meditation Collection p229,*
Lion Publishing 1998   **3d**

PURCE Jill
The Mystic Spiral p7, Thames and Hudson 1985   **4g**

The Mystic Spiral p15, Thames and Hudson 1985   **27d**

READ Herbert
The Meaning of Art p32, Penguin (Faber & Faber) 1950   **45g**

'READ Miss'
A Fortunate Grandchild pp13-14, Penguin 1985   **42f**

REES-MOGG William
An Humbler Heaven p80, Hamish Hamilton 1977   **3g**

REID Louis Arnaud
Philosophy and Education p27, Heinemann 1962   **3c**

RHODES L.Wemyss
On the Top of the Pillars p73, C.W.Daniel 1926   **29f**

RHINE J.B.
The Reach of the Mind pp178-179, Penguin 1954   **46e**

RICHARDS Ian
Abbeys of Europe p14, Paul Hamlyn 1968   **12f**

Abbeys of Europe pp12-15, Paul Hamlyn 1968   **39d**

ROBINSON Andrew
The Story of Writing p8, BCA / Thames & Hudson 1995   **10f**

ROBINSON R.Hayes
in *Hymns Ancient and Modern No.22,*
Wm.Clowes & Sons 1916   **43e**

ROLT L.T.C.
Winterstoke p208, Constable 1954   **41d**

ROUSSEAU Jean Jacques
Emile Tr.Barbara Foxley *p5,* J.M.Dent 1955   **42e**

ROWLAND Kurt
Pattern and Shape pp78-84
in *Series: Looking & Seeing No.1*, Ginn 1964   **6c**

RUSSELL Bertrand
'Useless' Knowledge in *In Praise of Idleness pp41-42*,
George Allen and Unwin 1948   **45f**

SACKVILLE-WEST Vita
English Country Houses p47, Collins 1945   **9c**

SAYERS Dorothy L.
Introduction to Dante's *Divine Comedy pp11-12*,
Penguin 1949   **4f**

The Zeal of Thy House in *Four Sacred Plays pp67-68*,
Victor Gollancz 1948   **26c**

SCHOFIELD Bernard
A Miscellany of Garden Wisdom pp82-83,
Harper Collins 1993   **50g**

SCHWARZ Oswald
The Psychology of Sex pp170-171, Penguin 1949   **15f**

SCOTT Robert Falcon
Last Notes in *Edward Wilson of the Antarctic pp290-291*,
John Murray 1935   **32g**

SEGAL Erich
Acts of Faith pp383-384, BCA / Hutchinson 1992   **25e**

SENIOR Elizabeth and **KITZINGER Ernst**
Portraits of Christ (King Penguin) *pp3-4*, Penguin 1940   **30c**

SHAKESPEARE William
Sonnet 116 in *The Penguin Book of Marriage*
Ed.Bel Mooney *p30*, Penguin 1991   **15c**
As You Like It Act II Scene vii 139   **18c**

SHAW Bernard
Preface to *The Black Girl in Search of God pp7-8*,
Penguin c1945   **48g**

SILVERMAN Ray / Keller Helen
Light in my Darkness p102, Chrysalis Books 2000   **49d**

SIMONS David R.
Unity in the Universe p11, Simons 1962   **39f**

SOLOMON Robert C. and HIGGINS Kathleen M.
A Short History of Philosophy p125,
Oxford University Press 1996   **24g**

STANLEY Michael
Eve, the Bone of Contention pp39-40, Seminar Books 1992   **33g**

STATHAM H.Heathcote
Architecture for General Readers p7, Chapman & Hall 1895   **9g**

STEVENSON Robert Louis
El Dorado in *The Bedside Book* Ed.Arthur Stanley *p198*,
Victor Gollancz 1947   **21c**

STEWART Ian and COHEN Jack
The Collapse of Chaos p285, Penguin 1995   **39g**

STUART Muriel
The Seed Shop in *The Bedside Book* Ed.Arthur Stanley
pp238-239, Victor Gollancz 1947   **33e**

SUTTON Eric A.
The Happy Isles pp155-156, J.M.Dent & Sons 1938   **33c**

SWIFT Jonathan
Gulliver's Travels pp9-10, Oxford University Press 1963   **52e**

TAYLOR Eugene
A Psychology of Spiritual Healing p5, Chrysalis Books 1997   **36d**

TEMPLE William
Personal Religion and the Life of Fellowship
in *A Diary of Readings* Ed.Baillie *Day 51*,
Oxford University Press 1981   **28f**

THOMAS Edward
Adlestrop in *The Oxford Book of Twentieth Century
English Verse p132*, Oxford University Press 1978   **19g**

THOMAS Lewis
The Medusa and the Snail pp100-101, Bantam Books 1980   **7f**

The Medusa and the Snail pp41-42, Bantam Books 1980   **35g**

THOMSON James
The Vine in *The Bedside Book* Ed.Arthur Stanley *p235*
Victor Gollancz 1947   **52g**

TILBY Angela
Soul pp39-40, BBC Education 1992   **25f**

TODOROV Tzvetan
Facing the Extreme p84, Weidenfeld and Nicolson 1999   **1e**

TOMLINSON R.R.
Children as Artists (King Penguin) *p5*, Penguin 1947 **22e**

TOURNIER Paul
The Strong and the Weak p231, SCM Press 1963 **1c**

The Strong and the Weak p206, SCM Press 1963 **2c**

TYRRELL G.N.M.
The Personality of Man p30, Penguin 1946 **28e**

VALLINS G.H.
Better English p84, Pan Books 1953 **10c**

VAN DIJK Kay
Can I Let You Go My Love? pp157-158, Acorn Editions 1997 **15g**

VAN DUSEN Wilson
The Country of Spirit in *The Presence of Other Worlds p65*,
J.Appleseed 1992 **6d**

Emanuel Swedenborg's Journal of Dreams p64,
The Swedenborg Foundation 1986 **31g**

VAN LOON Hendrik
The Arts of Mankind p252, George G. Harrap 1955 **30d**

VOLTAIRE
Candide Tr.John Butt *p20*, Penguin 1947 **14e**

On the Pensées of Pascal in *Letters on England*
Tr.Leonard Tancock *p139*, Penguin 1980 **39c**

WALSH Jill Paton
Knowledge of Angels p72, BCA / Colt Books 1995 **5f**

The Serpentine Cave pp181-182, Doubleday 1997 **30f**

WARD-PERKINS John and **CLARIDGE Amanda**
Pompeii AD79, Exhibition Catalogue - Royal Academy,
pp36-37, Imperial Tobacco 1976 **46g**

WATSON Lyall
Lifetide pp100,131,
Hodder & Stoughton / Coronet Books 1980 **7e**

Gifts of Unknown Things pp35-36,
Hodder & Stoughton / Coronet Books 1980 **26e**

Lifetide p51, Hodder & Stoughton / Coronet Books 1980 **27e**

Gifts of Unknown Things pp82-83,
Hodder & Stoughton / Coronet Books 1980 **31d**

WATTS A.F.
The Language and Mental Development of Children p36,
George G.Harrap 1944   **10e**

WAUGH Evelyn
Brideshead Revisited pp19-20, Penguin 1951   **19f**

WHITEHEAD A.N.
Adventures of Ideas p313, Penguin 1942   **17f**

WILDE Oscar
The Ballad of Reading Gaol
in *The Works of Oscar Wilde p827,* Collins 1949   **28d**

WILLIAMSON Henry
Tarka the Otter in *Trees p24,* Lennard Publishing 1988   **51d**

WILSON Colin
Mysteries p229, Granada / Panther Books 1979   **5g**

Mysteries p349, Granada / Panther Books 1979   **41c**

WINNICOTT D.W.
The Child, the Family, and the Outside World p86,
Penguin 1964   **22g**

WINTER David
Hereafter p80, Hodder & Stoughton /
Christian Book Promotion Trust 1972   **28g**

WOLFE W.Beran
How to be Happy though Human pp160-161, Penguin 1957   **27g**

Adaptations from Swedenborg

Index of Books and Paragraphs

Numbers refer to paragraphs, not pages, and any number after a stop
refers to sub-sections which are marked in the margin of most editions.

Apocalypse Explained

64   week **48**

Arcana Caelestia

6-13	**26**	6388	**47**
425	**37**	8002	**47**
561	**2**	8443	**43**
854	**23**	8478	**20**
978	**5**	8603	**27**
1488.3	**41**	8941	**37**
1496	**17**	8945	**27**
1588	**33**	9103	**23**
1919	**14**	9846	**37**
2053	**25**	9905	**23**
2119-2120	**50**	9927	**18**
2625	**13**	10023	**31**
2694	**14**	10042	**16**
2996	**6**	10057	**43**
3528	**31**	10199	**31**
3580	**52**	10500	**21**
3686	**21**		
3858.9	**37**	**Charity**	
4390	**41**	137,138,142	
4814	**13**	146,158	**12**

Conjugial Love

92,218.2	**15**
176,329	**42**
393	**31**
395,398	**42**

Divine Providence

34.2	**44**
37	**38**
56-59	**14**
71	**28**
129-132	**40**
134,134a	**49**
148	**14**
227	**19**
338.4	**41**
398-399	**22**
405	**22**

God, Providence, Creation

112	**45**

Heaven and Hell

178-9,181	**34**
183	**9**
185	**34**
228-230	**46**
234-238	**10**
248-9,271	**7**
347	**34**
445	**18**
456,462a	**8**
464	**17**
464	**33**
488,489	**11**
541,593-4	**29**

Last Judgment

33-34	**29**

New Jerusalem and its Heavenly Doctrine

5	**21**
100-105	**1**
133-135	**25**
140	**36**

Rational Psychology

201	**38**

True Christian Religion

43-44	**32**
65	**6**
200.2	**51**
201-202	**4**
205.1	**16**
282	**24**
304	**44**
326,329	**24**
395	**36**
469	**35**
523,531	**24**
603	**36**
708-709	**52**
741.2	**51**

Worlds in Space

52	**30**

Published by and available from

The Swedenborg Society
20-21 Bloomsbury Way
London. WC1A 2TH Telephone 020 7405 7986
E-mail: swed.soc@netmatters.co.uk

The Swedenborg Foundation Inc.
320 North Church Street
West Chester, Pennsylvania 19380. USA.
Telephone 00 1 610 430 3222
E-mail: customerservice@swedenborg.com